CLAIMS TO FAME
THE
B-17 FLYING FORTRESS

CLAIMS TO FAME
THE
B-17 FLYING FORTRESS

STEVE BIRDSALL AND ROGER FREEMAN

ARMS AND
ARMOUR

Arms and Armour Press
A Cassell Imprint
Wellington House, 125 Strand, London WC2R 0BB

Distributed in the United States by Sterling Publishing Co., Inc.
387 Park Avenue South, New York, NY 10016-8810

First published 1994
This paperback edition 1997

British Library Cataloguing-in-Publication Data:
a catalogue record for this title is available
from the British Library

ISBN 1-85409-424-6

Designed and edited by DAG Publications Ltd.
Designed by David Gibbons; edited by Philip Jarrett;
Printed and bound in Great Britain by
Hartnolls Limited, Bodmin, Cornwall

Contents

INTRODUCTION

The Flying Fortress, more formally known as the Boeing B-17, is generally acknowledged to be the most famous United States military aircraft of all time. Fame does not necessarily stem from extraordinary achievement or some distinctive excellence, but more commonly from continual prominence in communications to the public. Indeed, it was a journalist who coined the description 'flying fortress', when describing the prototype bomber following its presentation to the press at Seattle in 1935. The manufacturers were quick to register the name and emblazon the centre motif on the control columns of production aircraft with 'Flying Fortress'. The name caught the imagination of the public, particularly those in what had come to be called the news media, who championed this warplane above all others in the United States arsenal.

As the airmen who eventually took the B-17 to war were aware, it was no more a fortress than any other bomber of its time. An aluminium shell offers little protection against steel and high explosive. Nevertheless, because of the aircraft's sound construction and inherent stability in flight, it proved to be remarkably durable in the face of enemy endeavours to shoot it out of the sky. As the main vehicle for conducting the USAAF's campaign of high-altitude daylight precision bombing over Europe in 1942 and 1943, the B-17 became involved in some of the most vicious and protracted aerial battles of history, accounts of which helped to reinforce its standing in the public eye. In effect the Flying Fortresses, and the young men who took them to war, became legendary despite the fact that other contemporary warplanes contributed more to victory.

The common practice among USAAF personnel of giving names to individual aircraft added further glamour to the B-17's fame. Thus endowed, a particular aircraft that had an exceptional or unusual combat record was acclaimed in its own right. There were many Fortresses distinguished in this way that, through the exploits in which they were involved, became better known than the crews who flew them, often to the point of fame within their operating unit and sometimes far beyond. This book sets out to tell the stories of a selection of these distinguished B-17s and their crews. The main arena of the aircraft's combat use was Europe, and thus coverage of this theatre predominates. However, the B-17s that were in action on the Pacific war fronts are not neglected, and neither is the type's combat debut with the RAF.

A man-made inanimate thing cannot have a personality, but it may well have distinctive traits. As the following accounts will show, the uses to which the aircraft were put and the events that befell them while in human hands could bestow upon them some intangible air akin to personality. While this could be no more than human feeling towards a machine based on its past associations, sentiments of pride, awe, fear and the like directed at an individual aircraft could give it a special status, setting it apart from near-identical types from the same production line. Many of the men who flew and serviced these bombers saw them as beings, and regarded them just as a knight of old regarded his charger.

ACKNOWLEDGEMENTS

Establishing the assignments and operational employment of an individual aircraft half a century after its existence is difficult in the case of those that served with the United States Army Air Forces during the Second World War. A central record of assignments was kept while the aircraft remained in the so-called Zone of the Interior, the United States, but once it was transferred overseas this documentation ceased. There appears to have been no requirement for a central register of individual aircraft in combat theatres, so to trace a particular machine it is often necessary to search many documents in the hope of finding a reference to it by serial number. To assemble an aircraft's complete history in this way is difficult, for it may not be possible to locate relevant material in American archives. Many wartime records were apparently not taken back to the USA at the end of hostilities.

Therefore, in piecing together the aircraft histories in this book, the authors have had to approach many veterans who were associated with the aircraft concerned, and other persons who, for various reasons, have knowledge of the subject. They are: Gene Aenchbacher (97 BG), Dave Aiken, Harry Alsaker (97 BG), Alvin Anderson (379 BG), Edwin O. Anderson (97 BG), Virgil E. Annala (301 BG), John W. Archer, Bernard Bains, Gordon F. Bavor (43 BG), A. J. Beck (5 AF), Dana Bell, Robert O. Berger (43 BG), Fred Blair (43 BG), Quentin Bland, Serge Blandin, Paul Blasewitz (43 BG), C.D. Boggs (99 BG), Victor Bonomo (94 BG), Lloyd H. Boren (11 BG), John Bosko (92 BG), Peter M. Bowers, Frank Brady (5 BG), Ralph H. Brant (94 BG), Robert K. Braungart (99 BG), Graham Bratley, Roy Brockman (96 BG), Ralph Burbridge (97 BG), Wallace Bush (99 BG), Robert H. Butler (43 BG), John W. Carpenter (19 BG), James G. Carroll (5 BG), Ken Cassens (379 BG), Carol Cathcart, Byron B. Clark (379 BG), Thomas J. Classen (5 BG), Wathen F. Cody (19 & 43 BGs), George Coen (99 BG), Albert Cole (43 BG), Charles R. Cole (43 BG), Hank Cordes (91 BG), O. K. Coulter (43 BG), Marbury Councell (96 BG), George Cracraft (401 BG), David Crow, Ted Darcy, Tony DeAngelis (43 BG), Ralph K. De Loach (43 BG), Dommonick DeSalvo (379 BG), James Dieffenderfer (19 & 43 BGs), Abel Dolim (94 BG), Rene Donnat, Charles B. Downer (43 BG), Richard E. Drain (99 & 390 BGs), James V. Edmundson (11 BG), Robert D. Elliott (92 BG), S. C. Ellis (379 BG), Erwin H. Eckert (301 BG), Andy Esler (19 & 43 BGs), Jeff Ethell, Ken Everett, Jean Faivre, Al Fischer (43 BG), Arthur A. Fletcher (19 & 43 BGs), Thomas Ford (2 BG), Eric Foster, Max J. Friermood (11 BG), Danny P. Galatro (483 BG), Edward L. Gammill (43 BG), Wayne Gillespie (2 BG), Kevin Ginnane, William H. Greenhalgh, Werner Girbig, Jake Grimm (483 BG), Phil Gudenschwager, Clifford Hall, Mitchell

Hall (381 BG), Ken Harbour, Harvey Harris (379 BG), David W. Hassemer (19 & 43 BG), Hugo Havet (379 BG), Don Hayes (97 BG), Henry Heckman (384 BG), Theo J. Heller (99 BG), Albert Henke (99 BG), Stephen Hennrich (379 BG), Berchie Hettinga, Ed Hicks (97 BG), Dale R. Hish (483 BG), C. David Hoffmann (97 BG), C.F. Hollenberg (2 BG), Jack D. Hoover (317 TCG), Bruce Hoy, Jack Ilfrey (20 FG), Harold James (97 BG), Lloyd E. Kane (97 BG), Joseph Kellerman (99 BG), Chester C. Kennedy (19 & 43 BGs), Walter Klukas (99 BG), Dan Knight (401 BG), Rudolph C. Koller (2 BG), Leonard J. Lawson (43 BG), Alfred R. Lea (452 BG), Richard Leahy, Glen Lewis (19 & 43 BGs), John Littleton, Al Lloyd, John Lowdermilk (91 BG), Neil MacNeil (379 BG), John Marshall, Reese Martin (96 BG), Conrad Marvel (19 BG), Robert E. May (11 BG), Lex McAulay, Paul McDuffee (91 BG), John Mills, Bruce E. Mills (379 BG), John Mitchell, Roy Morgan (11 BG), John M. Nushy (381 BG), Carey O'Bryan (19 BG), Thomas J. O'Connor (2 BG), Janice Olson, Dave Osborne, Allen Ostrom (398 BG), George W. Parks (91 BG), Bill Parsons (2 BG), Rod Pearce, Herbert C. Penner (381 BG), David Pennefather, Col. Henri Perrin, Jim Peterson (43 BG), Marilyn Phipps, George Prezioso (43 BG), James N. Price (11 BG), Boardman C. Reed (388 BG), Charles W. Reseigh (381 BG), John Rice (2 BG), Charles W. Richards (2 BG), Leon H. Rockwell (5 BG), Gerald Rose (384 BG), Morley L. Russell (97 BG), Irving Sagor (43 BG), Ellinor Sallingboe, Waldo Schauweker (43 BG), James Shoesmith (91 BG), Chris Shores, Francis G. Sickinger (19 BG), J. R. Simonson (91 BG), Ron Sismey, Delbert Smith (43 BG), Jack B. Smith (379 BG), Glen Spieth, Philip C. Sprawls (11 BG), Harry A. Staley (43 BG), E.P. Stevens (43 BG), Donald L. Stillman (2 BG), Freddie Stokes (90 Sqn, RAF), Lewis Sutton (19 & 43 BGs), Ewald A. Swanson (483 BG), Anne Tatler, William D. Tatler (2 BG), Albert N. Thom (11 BG), Robert W. Toombs (483 BG), Helen Trentadue, Ernest J. Vandel (43 BG), George Walker (11 BG), Edward C. Ware (301 BG), Geoffrey Ward, Robert Watkins (379 BG), Pamela Watson, William T. White (97 BG), James Whitney (379 BG), Robert A. Wilde (99 BG), J. C. Wilfret (43 BG), William Wilson (43 BG), Keith Windrum (99 BG), Walter Wolcott (379 BG), George Wyatt, Edward O. Yelton (96 BG), Harold W. Yeomans (19 & 43 BGs).

We are indebted to all for their time and trouble in contributing to this project, and tender our sincere thanks.

The authors also wish to thank Bruce Robertson for his editorial guidance, Patricia Keen for conducting interviews, Ian Mactaggart and George Pennick for photographic services and Jean Freeman and Alice Apricot for producing the copy. We are both mindful that a work of this nature could not be produced without the kindness and support of the many who have contributed, and we apologise to any who we might have inadvertently overlooked.

Steve Birdsall, Mona Vale, Australia.
Roger A. Freeman, Dedham, England.

The Very First of the Very Many

In tradition, the Flying Fortress bomber has become synonymous with the vast, bloody air battles fought by the US air forces during their onslaught on Hitler's war industry. While this may fairly be the aircraft's main claim to fame during the Second World War, the B-17 also served with other forces and in other guises. Moreover, although it was used principally by the United States Army Air Forces it was, in fact, the Royal Air Force that first took this most famous of all American warplanes into battle.

Late in 1940, when Britain was still in dire peril, the US government agreed to supply twenty of these bombers for use by the RAF. This was largely a political decision; Churchill wanted this highly publicized American warplane to endorse US support for Britain. Roosevelt was likewise in favour, particularly as his government was in the process of placing huge orders for warplane production, and British use of this hardware would help justify the investment.

On the other hand, senior USAAF officers deplored the move. For all the media hype, these commanders knew that the then current model B-17 was seriously deficient in several respects. Committing the aircraft to combat in that state could produce adverse comment that might seriously affect the funding of their own development plans for this strategic bomber. The RAF, although it was desperately short of aircraft, was not happy about using the B-17 in a form of daylight operations it did not believe viable.

Nevertheless, the twenty Fortresses were sent and, after some consideration, RAF Bomber Command proposed to take advantage of the type's very-high-altitude capabilities. If it could operate above 35,000ft it would probably be immune from anti-aircraft fire and fighters would have great difficulty in intercepting it. Number 90 Squadron was formed to operate the Fortress, its aircrew being specially selected and trained. During nine weeks of operations in the summer of 1941 it was found that the B-17C, or Fortress I in British Service terminology, had difficulty in maintaining altitude above 30,000ft with combat loadings. Several shortcomings were highlighted and much was learned about the use of the Fortress and sub-stratospheric operations, although little harm was dealt the enemy in 48 bombing sorties.

When mankind wishes to distinguish between similar inanimate objects produced in large numbers, individual numerical identities are usually bestowed upon them. The manufacturer of a military aircraft gave it a serial number, which is generally known as a constructor's number. The recipient service added its own serial number and, if the aircraft passed to another nation, that air force substituted its serial number for the previous one. Thus the first of the twenty Fortress Is allotted to the RAF received the British serial AN518. It had hitherto been B-17C serial 40-2066 of the US Army Air Corps, the '40' signifying 1940, the fiscal year of the funds for its purchase. Boeing, which made the bomber, labelled it 2067 for its own purposes, although the USAAC reference was dominant to Boeing in the Company's transactions.

Although AN518 may have been the first British Fortress numberwise, it was not the first to reach the UK. It arrived in May 1941 and, after being painted in the required camouflage colours, reached No. 90 Sqn at its Polebrook, Northamptonshire, base on 9 August that year. In No. 90 Sqn it had yet another identity as B-Beer, the individual aircraft-in-squadron letter used in vocal and Morse transmissions. Beer, later changed to Baker, might have been the official phonetic term for transmissions but, as was their will, RAF airmen often referred to AN518 as B-Bertie.

B-Beer first went to war on the last day of August, flying a lone sortie to Bremen. The pilot found he could not attain the desired altitude, and the target area was partly obscured by cloud. Even so, four 1,000lb bombs were deposited from 31,000ft. Two days later the aircraft was sent out to bomb Duisburg, only to be turned back when the crew discovered that the intercom was not working properly. It was essential to have communication with all gunners on operations, so that they were in constant touch with the fire controller in his astrodome 'bubble' behind the flight deck. An attempt to cure the problem was apparently unsuccessful because the intercom failed again, on 4 September, after 'B' had climbed to 15,000ft en route to Germany. Despite this problem it was considered one of the best of all the Fortresses on the station, as there were never more than a dozen at one time, and half of these were often unserviceable. Most noticeably, AN518's engines did not seem to be beset by excessive oil-throwing at high altitude, then a persistent trouble with some of the aircraft.

Pilot Officer Frank Sturmey and crew used B-Beer for the last successful attacks made by No. 90 Sqn Fortresses flying from Britain when, on 25 September, four 1,100lb GP HE American bombs were dropped on Emden from 32,000ft. By this date, with only nine of the original twenty Fortresses left and no additional aircraft forthcoming from the USA, plus little bombing success and significant losses to fighter interception, Bomber Command decided to withhold No. 90 Sqn from operations.

Training flights continued, but in mid-October it was decided to send five serviceable Fortresses to the Middle East, where it was felt they could probably be used with greater effect and would be less vulnerable to enemy defences. One of the five was AN518. During the air movement from Polebrook to Portreath on 27 October, the force was reduced to four when one of the aircraft suffered a blown cylinder head and had to be left behind. This Fortress had been in the hands of Pilot Officer Freddie Stokes and his five-man crew, who then took over AN518 for the overseas flight.

There were some misgivings about the chosen point of departure from the UK, as AN518's pilot relates:

> Portreath aerodrome was situated on the top of very high cliffs that line the coast in that part of north Cornwall. After we had landed there was a certain amount of apprehension about getting off again, the runway seemed short and also slightly uphill. Especially as we were so heavily laden with spares, extra fuel tanks and additional personnel. I had on board the squadron crew chief; Flt Sgt Murray, and the squadron Engineering Officer, a Texan, Flt Lt O'Camb, and so much equipment it must have been a most uncomfortable flight for them. That night we put the problem out of our minds. The dawn soon came – time to go. After a bit of "After you – No, after you", I was the first off. Three-quarters of the way down the runway my earlier fears seemed about to be justified. We were still labouring along like an albatross trying to get airborne. A flop into the sea looking a distinct possibility. The end of the runway loomed up with our wheels still on the ground, the edge of the cliffs ahead. A sharp hauling back on the control column and we hopped over, only to sink 100ft towards the sea. We levelled out without getting wet and climbed gently away towards the Scilly Isles on our course for Malta. Looking back we could see each of the other three planes sink over the cliff's edge as they left England, exactly as we'd done.

The circuitous route, planned to avoid fighter interception, involved a wide sweep out over the Atlantic to keep well away from occupied France, then flying in across the Pyrenees, down to Tunisia and into Malta from the south. The flight time was 6¾ hours. The following morning Freddie Stokes flew AN518 on the next stage of the journey, a flight of nearly five hours to El Fayoum in Egypt, where lack of a windsock caused him to land inadvertently downwind. The following afternoon the Stokes crew set off for their ultimate destination, Shallufa, near Suez, only to be caught out by the rapid descent of the sun. Runway lights appearing in the darkness were a welcome sight, but after a safe landing it was discovered that they were on Shandur airfield, not Shallufa, which was finally reached next day.

The first operation set up for the Fortresses in the Middle East was a raid on the important port of Benghazi. The CO of the No. 90 Sqn detachment, Squadron Leader MacLaren, on the advice of his technical personnel, protested that this would be beyond the range capabilities of the Fortress with the desired loadings and other factors, notably the climatic conditions of the Middle East. Theoretically the B-17C had a 2,000-mile range, but many in the contingent believed it imprudent to attempt an attack on such a distant target as Benghazi on the first raid. High authority held sway, however, and the operation was given the go-ahead. Two Fortresses were despatched; AN529 with Flying Officer 'Steve'

Stevenson and, an hour later, AN518 piloted by Stokes, delayed by an instrument fault.

The penetration flight was without incident, but the hot weather reduced the rate of climb and increased engine temperature. Eight 500lb bombs were dropped on the target by AN518 from 36,000ft. By now it was apparent that fuel consumption was excessive, and the concern about range appeared to have been justified. The captain of B–Baker recalled what happened as follows:

Soon after we had set course for base, our radio operator, Sgt McGregor, passed me a note saying that he had picked up an SOS from Steve. He had run out of fuel and was forced-landed in the desert, well inside enemy lines. We were about an hour behind him so it was obvious that by the end of that time we too could be experiencing the same problem, and also over hostile territory.

We were then at 20,000ft so to stretch our petrol as far as possible eased off the power, losing height slowly all the way. Rather than risk coming down many miles from anywhere, I headed for the coast and the road that ran alongside. There would be a better chance of being picked up in that area, even if it meant by the Germans. Fortunately we crossed into friendly territory but only as one of the engines ran out of fuel. Ahead we could see a very small landing ground and I put down there very hurriedly. It was really there for a flight of Hurricanes, no runways, no buildings, only underground bunkers and an odd tent or two. Putting down was tight. Only by prompt and violent application of the brakes did I avoid burying the nose in a sand dune at the far end of the strip. We were not at all welcome. It was already 3 o'clock in the afternoon, we had been seven hours in the air but were told that we couldn't stay and had to get airborne again. Apparently the German lines were not very far away and their bombers came over regularly at night and did the place over. Accordingly, they gave me some fuel and very insistently ordered us to leave without any further delay. But where to? We couldn't get back to Shallufa before nightfall, so I was told to do what the others were doing – disperse myself. The resident Hurricanes simply took off and put down for the night on a flat area of the desert a mile or two away. The petrol bowser too didn't hang about. It just headed for the sunset and hid in the sand dunes, to return next morning.

Just a short distance along the coast was an emergency landing ground, nothing more than another piece of firm sand, and that was where I was advised to go. I found it just before nightfall. There were no facilities whatsoever. The half dozen men there lived underground in bunkers with no buildings or tents on the surface. Not even a wind direction indicator. They gave us a meal of bully beef, sweet potatoes and tomatoes, all washed down with Australian beer. There was no sleeping accommodation so we kipped down in the aircraft, I spent the whole night in my driver's seat. As predicted, the Luftwaffe did attack the place back along the coast and dropped a number of flares which not only lit up the target area, but our Fortress too. The reflected light from its fuselage was so bright that the wonder was we were not spotted. Next day, after waiting for a sandstorm to subside, we were able to make the trip back to Shallufa.

The problems highlighted on the Benghazi raid, and the loss of a Fortress (although the crew were rescued), led to the detachment being taken off operations while its employment was reassessed. A lower maximum operational ceiling of 28,000ft was desirable to obtain long range, but this would then expose the Fortresses to fighter interception. The fine desert sand whipped up by winds and other aircraft played havoc with filters and contributed to engine wear and unreliability. Engine failure during a fuel consumption test in January 1942 claimed one of the remaining three Fortresses, two men being killed while trying to bale out.

It was finally decided that the detachment would be used chiefly in attacks on enemy shipping, and on 3 February 1942 it was re-labelled as a detachment of No. 220 Sqn, a Coastal Command unit with headquarters in the UK. The usual method of operation was for one of the Fortresses to be sent out to bomb when low-level-reconnaissance Martin Marylands had spotted suitable targets. The first such sortie involving AN518 occurred on 23 January, when Flying Officer Taylor's crew attempted to locate an Italian warship without success.

On St Valentine's Day Freddie Stokes and crew took B-Baker on a shipping strike:

> The target this time was a tanker heading south off the Greek coast for Navarino Bay. It was escorted by a destroyer and we were hoping that with a bit of luck we could get both of them. It was to be another long trip and meant using the advanced landing strip, LG05, in the wilderness of the Libyan desert. Accommodation here was primitive, for our overnight stay we slept in a tent erected some three feet below ground level. This was to afford some protection in the event of an air raid. Take-off time was early next morning and, unusually for me, I didn't sleep a wink that night. Probably a combination of the strange environment and a mind over-occupied with the raid next day. As this was against a naval target we had with us a supernumerary crew member, a naval observer ex-*Ark Royal*, name of "Digger" Spademan – obviously an Australian. Digger came with us to help in the identification of the targets.
>
> About an hour after take-off the thin cloud we were in became thicker and blacker and our ride decidedly bumpier. We carried on

15

climbing, hoping to break clear, but conditions worsened and our fears were soon confirmed. We were in one of those frightening cumulonimbus clouds. And we knew that over the Med' they were inclined to be more powerful than those we encountered in the UK. Soon hailstones the size of golf balls were hitting us and we bounced about so violently there was a real danger of complete loss of control. Normal flying became impossible and we knew we had to get out, and quickly. There was no way of knowing how high this cloud was, the only sure way out was down. This wasn't easy either. With some of the crew sick from all of the buffeting, I throttled well back and let the 'plane sink as quickly as I dared. Eventually, at about 500ft, we broke through and could see the sea beneath and all around us, no land in sight. We should have been over Greece but that didn't really matter as long as we were out of that weather.

A radio fix didn't give us too much comfort. We had been blown so far off-course we could get back, but only by being careful with the fuel we had left. Our track took us slap over the island of Crete, then in the hands of the enemy. There was no question of flying round it, we just hadn't got the fuel, it had to be "keep straight on" and hope that no one down below tried taking a shot at us. After being in the air over seven hours we did get back to our base in the desert at about 2.00 p.m. There was little or no fuel left in the tanks, and the leading edges of the wings were a bright silver where the hailstones had stripped off the paint.

A week later AN518 was back at LG05, and on 22 February it set off to find a convoy escorted by the Italian fleet. As Freddie Stokes relates:

Again we had Digger Spademan on board to act as adviser and help in ship identification as we left our desert landing ground at 11.00 a.m. The weather that February day was fairly clear, with a certain amount of broken cloud at 4,000ft; occasionally hiding the sea. Steadily we climbed to our operating height of 17,000ft, our load was eight 500lb bombs. Not enough to unduly worry the heavily plated battleships and cruisers, but enough to sink the merchantmen or any of the destroyers. Then, quite suddenly, without really searching, through a hole in the thin cloud the whole of the convoy was right ahead of us. In the centre was the pride of Mussolini's navy, the *Vittorio Veneto*, a battleship with its escort of destroyers and cruisers... an impressive sight, each ship trailing its straight white wake which broke into sharp curves as soon as we were spotted and evasive action began. Simultaneously substantial anti-aircraft fire started, and soon we were surrounded by countless balls of black smoke from bursting shells. The track we were on was almost due west and the bomb aimer locked his sight on to the battleship. But then he and Digger started to argue whether they should go for it or whether the merchantmen would be a better target.

I was hoping for a straight run with a successful outcome and an easy return to base. It was not to be. By the time they had made up their minds it was too late, we had overflown the target area. All the time the barrage of shells was going on around us. So it had to be straight on, turn round and have a go from the opposite direction – west to east. Lo and behold, this run had to abandoned too. Apparently the Sperry bomb-sight could not operate over a certain ground speed and on this approach we had a very strong tailwind that rendered it inoperative. A few sharp words passed between myself and Mike Nisbet (bomb aimer) leaving no doubts that the battleship was the target and next time had got to be "it". The automatic pilot was again disconnected and we ploughed on which didn't please me a bit. I had never seen any virtue in hanging about over a target longer than necessary, especially when being shot at. We therefore had to press on over the target and turn around to come in on our original course from the east. This time there should have been no problems, apart from the very persistent and accurate shell fire. The bomb doors were open, the navigator operating his sight was in control of the 'plane as it slithered about the sky in response to his adjustments. Any second we would hear the cry "Bombs gone" and we could go home. Instead we heard a far less welcome cry from Hollingsworth in the astrodome, "Fighters. Port side."

I looked back over my shoulder through the bulge in the Perspex window panel expecting to see an undefined speck in the distance. But no, no speck, a real big twin-engined Messerschmitt 110 less than 200 yards away and blasting away for all he was worth. Almost simultaneously the bombs were released and I was able to disconnect the automatic pilot to resume normal manual control for what turned out to be a 20-minute dogfight. Our chances weren't very good; past experience had proved that the Fortress was no match for one Messerschmitt, let alone two. In my previous squadron in the UK I had learned with the co-operation of a Spitfire squadron and practised in action tactics that could be of help when attacked by fighters. They were based on the fact that the enemy would not open fire outside a range of about 200 yards. To do so would be too inaccurate and ineffective, so we did not react too soon. When we did, any evasive action we took would be just before he fired and would be a slight dipping of the nose and a not too violent turn into him. This would be sufficient to take us out of his sights and he would have to have another go. It could be fatal to go into a dive, keep him high and burning fuel, and this we did too. After every pass at us, on full power we climbed, and in fact when it was all over we had reached 23,000ft, some 5,000ft higher than when the scrap started.

With two of them having a go it meant throwing the Fortress about in a fashion it certainly wasn't designed for. At one time only too aware of the limitations to the stresses that it would stand I had real doubts about it holding together. However, the end came quite dramatically. The gunners in the back claimed a hit on one of our adversaries and saw him heading for the sea in a vertical dive. Then it was quiet. "Holly" on the lookout couldn't see anything of the other and rather unbelievingly we set a steady course for home with no injury to any of the crew.

All of these goings-on had been observed at sea level by a Maryland reconnaissance 'plane shadowing the Italian fleet. They reported that we had either hit or achieved a near-miss on the battle-ship, not doing considerable damage because the bombs we had dropped were not armour piercing, but enough to frighten the life out of the admiral commanding the fleet. He immediately ordered the whole of the supporting naval vessels to turn round and head back to Taranto and safety. This, of course, left the six merchantmen alone and exposed and I learned later that our submarines disposed of them shortly afterwards.

Our troubles were not quite over however. We knew we had been hit but to what extent we did not know. As an insurance we made for the North African coast at 2,000ft, keeping near to it all the way back. Rounding one headland after all we had been through we again came under fire. This time it was so-called "friendly" fire from one of our own destroyers escorting a supply ship into Tobruk, then completely surrounded by the enemy. I suppose we did look very much like a German Focke-Wulf Condor in outline. We survived this and made base, where we had a chance to survey the damage. The two survival dinghies stowed behind my head had been hit and blown away, so it was as well we didn't have to ditch, we should have had quite a swim. There were several holes all over the fuselage, even one through one of the propellers, but amazingly all vital parts had been missed. I had an unusual and rewarding experience when we climbed out of the 'plane. As usual I was last out and there was the crew all lined up and each one of this usually most undemonstrative lot shook my hand.

Fortress AN518 was classified as having Category B damage, requiring a specialist team of repairers and taking several days' work. The detachment to the Middle East had originally been advised for two months. Already four had passed, and a fifth went by before, at last, the remaining aircraft and personnel were to return to the UK on 9 April, joining No. 220 Sqn at Nutts Corner, which was already operating the four Fortress Is that did not go to the Middle East.

At this juncture the Japanese advances in Burma had produced another critical situation. Instead of heading home, on 26 April the two Fortresses, AN518 and AN532, set off for Habbaniya, Iraq, en route to India. After arriving in northern India on May Day, the Fortresses eventually moved across the sub-continent to east Bengal, Pandaveshwar airfield being the assigned operational base. However, no operations were forthcoming and AN518 only took to the air for the occasional air test.

Keeping both Fortresses airworthy was an increasingly difficult task for the mechanics for, if anything, the climatic conditions were more injurious to the aircraft than those in the desert, the high humidity playing havoc with many components. Some grand plans for committing the Fortresses to combat were mooted, but they came to naught and in June the RAF decided to turn the two survivors over to the USAAF, who were by then operating a few later-model Fortresses in India. On 28 June Pilot Officer Stokes flew AN518, carrying the CO and ground staff, to Allahabad, en route to Karachi where the detachment had been relocated. Although officially returned to the USAAF on 1 December 1942, AN518 was actually relinquished by the No. 220 Sqn detachment on 25 August, at which time it was the only survivor, AN532 having been destroyed in a crash.

In USAAF hands AN518 reverted to its previous identity, 40-2066, and was re-engined for use as a transport by the US 10th Air Force. Eventually age told, and the aircraft ended its days as a cannibalized wreck parked in a corner of an airfield near New Delhi.

Perhaps the last words on this most venerable of the first twenty Fortress combatants belongs to her most frequent pilot, Freddie Stokes: '... a lady and a graceful and elegant one at that'.

The Legend of Suzy-Q

During 1941, as a war in the east became increasingly inevitable, efforts were made to strengthen America's Pacific garrisons, and the Boeing B-17 Flying Fortress played a major part in that planning. At the time of the Japanese attack on Pearl Harbor, Major Stanley Robinson's 7th Bomb Group had already begun its movement to the Philippines, where it was to be based at Del Monte, on the southern island of Mindanao. In fact, en route, the advance element of its air echelon had arrived over Oahu, Hawaii, during the initial Japanese air strike on 7 December 1941.

In the six weeks before the Japanese attacks, 7th Bomb Group air crews had been collecting brand-new B-17Es virtually as they were rolled out of Boeing's Seattle factory, and flying them to the Sacramento Air Depot, where they were made 'combat ready'.

The Japanese attack decimated the aircraft of the 5th and 11th Bomb Groups at Hickam Field in Hawaii, destroying five of their precious B-17s and damaging three more. In the Philippines, news of the attack on Pearl Harbor was first heard on commercial radio, with official word arriving about an hour later. There, the 35 B-17s of the 19th Bomb Group, pride of the Far East Air Force, were based at Clark Field, about 60 miles north of Manila, and down at Del Monte. Hitting Clark just after midday, the Japanese bombers destroyed all but seven of the 19 B-17s based there, and only two or three were left undamaged. So, by nightfall on 8 December, the enemy had already destroyed or crippled half the American bomber strength in the Philippines.

The Philippines soon became untenable for the bombers, which were flown back 1,500 miles to the south, to Batchelor Field near Darwin, Australia. While the aircraft were now relatively safe from enemy attack, the use of Australia as a rear base for operations against the Philippines proved impractical because of the distance involved. So the B-17s in Australia were patched up, overhauled, and then, at the end of December, sent to a new base at Singosari airfield, five miles north-west of Malang, in the Timur region of Java. This sod field, about 5,000ft long, had no radar or anti-aircraft defences.

Meanwhile, the 7th Bomb Group was still gathering strength. On Christmas Eve Captain Felix Hardison took delivery of 41-2476, and exactly one week later he was back in Seattle, signing for another brand-new B-17E, serial number 41-2489. This aircraft would for ever be associated with Hardison and his wife, Priscilla. In less than a year it would no longer be just 41-2489, it would become *Suzy-Q*, the 'fightingest Flying Fortress in the world'.

Hopes in Java were raised by the arrival of the first 7th Bomb Group B-17Es in the middle of January, and particularly when, by the end of the month, 21 had arrived. They were quickly put into action. Early in the morning of 16 January two B-17Es and three Liberators flew from Malang to Kendari, the advanced base on Celebes, where they took on fuel and bombs. The two Fortresses, piloted by Major Conrad Necrason and Captain John 'Duke' DuFrane, bombed enemy transports in Menado Bay. As they were completing a second bomb run they were jumped by fifteen Japanese fighters, who received an unpleasant surprise from the new B-17Es. Following their usual routine, the fighters attacked from the rear, expecting little return fire. Thanks to the relatively slow closure speed and little need for deflection aiming, the B-17 tail gunners had a field day. Six enemy fighters were claimed shot down and both B-17s returned safely to Kendari, but Japanese fighters caught them on the ground. Necrason was able to get his aeroplane into the air and return to Java, but DuFrane's B-17, 41-2459, was strafed, and he and his crew were forced to hitch a ride home in a Liberator.

The use of forward airfields became impossible as the Japanese advance rolled southward. They took over Kendari on 23 January, and soon Japanese bombers were appearing over Java. On 29 January Major Stanley Robinson, leading his fifth mission within a week, was shot down. He was flying with Captain Walter Sparks and his crew in 41-2476 when 30 Japanese fighters attacked and overwhelmed the formation of five B-17s. Robinson's aeroplane dived steeply into the sea and no parachutes were observed.

Despite the critical situation, eighteen more new B-17Es arrived in Java during February, and one of these carried Captain Felix Hardison and his crew. They had flown 41-2489 to Java by the south-eastern route, taking off from MacDill Field in Florida and coming by way of the South Atlantic, Africa, the Middle East and India, arriving at Singosari on 7 February 1942.

Even in these desperate times a new crew was not sent out right away. This was probably fortunate for Hardison and his men, because on 8 February there was a bloody mission against the airfield at Kendari, now in Japanese hands. The nine American bombers encountered a similar number of fighters at 14,000ft, after breaking through the clouds and still climbing. The Japanese, in co-ordinated frontal attacks, hit Captain 'Duke' DuFrane's lead aircraft, 41-2456, causing flames to erupt from the bomb-bay. The bomb-bay fuel tank was jettisoned, but the fire had already taken hold. As many as six parachutes were seen before the aircraft exploded in mid-air, but there were no survivors. Lieutenant William Prichard's 41-2492 swung wildly and nearly crashed into a Zero. Riddled by gunfire, the Fortress disappeared into the clouds, trailing flame.

Lieutenant Paul Lindsey in 41-2483 also sought refuge in the clouds as the fighters gained the upper hand. His damaged aircraft fell into a tailspin and Lindsey and his copilot fought to regain control. At 9,000ft, with the aircraft still spinning, the copilot and navigator baled out through the bomb bay and the tail gunner also abandoned the B-17. The rest of the crew were about to jump when Lindsey finally recovered from the spin and brought the nose up. Without a copilot or navigator, and with his compass and other instruments shot away, Lindsey made his way back.

The first combat mission in 41-2489, a fruitless search for a Japanese aircraft carrier reported south of Java, was flown by Lieutenant Charles Hillhouse on 9 February. Felix Hardison's first mission in the aircraft was a pre-dawn strike by eleven aeroplanes led by Captain Donald Strother on 12 February 1942. Ten of the B-17s bombed a convoy in the Makassar Strait, but in terrible weather the results went unobserved. Hardison led a three-aircraft mission to attack ships off Bali on 20 February, when a large transport was claimed sunk. The number of his B-17 that day was not recorded.

With the Java bases on continuous air raid alert, time was running out, and the evacuation to Australia began. By 26 February 1942 there were only four flyable B-17s left at Madioen, and four crews. These combat crews carried out their own maintenance, fuelled the aircraft and loaded the bombs. There was little food and no rest.

Felix Hardison's hand-written notes cover those last desperate days.

Subject to air raid alarms all day the 28th of February, the crew did maintenance work on the ship until midnight, then serviced with fuel and eight 300-kilogram bombs for bombing the Japanese landing target areas off Rembang, Java. Took off at 0245, March 1st 1942; arriving over the target area found it obscured by large thunder heads. We let down through the clouds to an altitude of 3,000 feet over the target area, and opened our bomb bay doors. The moon had set earlier and due to pitch dark under the clouds we were unable to pick up a target except occasional flashes of pocket torches. We flew back and forth over the target two times inviting search lights, but finally decided to wait for dawn rather than waste our bombs. Circled a point of land near Rembang to keep from getting lost until first light. Took us longer to arrive back over the target than we anticipated; the sun was rising while on our run at 3,800 feet indicated. Found the enemy lying about one half mile off the coast – transports in two parallel rows with warships forming a protective screen. Fifty-seven transports and warships were counted twice by the copilot-pilot. Troops and equipment were going ashore in self-propelled barges which the gunners engaged throughout the run and withdrawal, inflicting some casualties and damage. The bombardier picked one of the largest transports to bomb, getting several near misses and one direct hit. Some difficulty was experienced in following the PDI [Pilot's Directional Indicator] because of the near misses from heavy anti-aircraft fire, several tracers penetrated the ship but no material damage was sustained by either men or 'plane. The bombed vessel was last seen listing badly to starboard believed to be sinking.

It was all over in Java. At Madioen the exhausted Hardison crew was denied rest by six air raid alarms during the day. In the early morning of 2 March they flew to Broome in north-western Australia, with 25 men on board, then continued on down the continent to Melbourne.

Captain Felix Hardison flew on the last mission from Java and down to Australia in 41-2464, which survived to fly with the 64th Squadron of the 43rd Bomb Group, where she was named *Queenie*. Sergeant E. P. 'Lucky' Stevens, Lieutenant Roger Kettleson's ball turret gunner, carefully painted the name on her nose in neat yellow letters. Long retired from combat, *Queenie* was flying with 5th Air Force Service Command at the time of her loss on 8 July 1944. The B-17 went down somewhere between Nadzab and Biak, but no trace of the aircraft or the 19 people aboard has ever been found.

There is no record of who flew 41-2489 out of Java, or exactly when, but she survived.

The veterans of the Philippines and Java were reorganized in Australia as the 19th Bomb Group, under the command of Lieutenant Colonel Kenneth Hobson, senior surviving officer of the 7th Bomb Group. This 'new' group included 14 survivors of the Java disaster and nine of a flight of twelve B-17Es that had been brought to Australia by Major Richard Carmichael's 40th Reconnaissance Squadron.

In May Captain Felix Hardison became commander of the 19th's 93rd Bomb Squadron, based at Longreach in Queensland. Records from that period are incomplete, but there is no mention of 41-2489 until the middle of May 1942, when the 19th resumed operations. Hardison flew four missions in 41-2489 before the end of the month. On 18 May, flying out of Batchelor Field, they attacked shipping targets in Koepang Bay on Timor, then flew a similar mission on 20 May. Five days later they flew a mission against Vunakanau, the largest of the enemy airfields near Rabaul on New Britain, staging through Port Moresby in New Guinea and returning there to reload fuel and bombs for a second mission. Three B-17s, 41-2489, 41-2664 and 41-2668, took off from Port Moresby at 1310 on 27 May, again heading for Rabaul.

According to Sergeant Durward Fesmire, who had become Hardison's bombardier:

> After bombing Hardison came down to the deck so that Johnny Geckeler in the top turret could shoot up anti-aircraft emplacements firing at higher aircraft. Back over Port Moresby we ran into bad weather and they radioed that we couldn't land there because they were socked in all the way to 25,000 feet, and to go on to Horn Island. When we finally saw land we were so short of gas that Hardison had her running on two engines and throttled back and losing altitude. We had missed Horn Island, for the land turned out to be the tip of the Cape York Peninsula of Queensland. The Old Man saw a clear spot in the trees and said he was going to set her down.

They were down in an area known as Piccaninny Plains, north-west of the town of Coen. Radio operator Sergeant Orville Kiger was able to get a message out which reached Allied Combined Headquarters at Townsville via Horn Island. It asked them to 'send 200 gallons fuel, shovels and water'. A further message advised that they were all safe.

Cryptic messages continued to be relayed across the north of Australia. At 0130 in the morning of 29 May, Townsville received an SOS, and sent the following to Coen; 'You drop picks, lime and gasoline Capt Hardison'. At 2240 on the night of 31 May, Hardison sent a message to Townsville via Coen that they were 'out of food for a day and a half, send to 12489 now'. At 2250 that message was relayed to RAAF Operations at Townsville, and at 0307 on 1 June Coen advised Townsville 'land party will reach at 2359Z/31'. In other words, they were already there.

The party was led by Maurie Shephard, owner of a trucking business in Coen. The aircrew and the Australians set about stripping the B-17 of guns, ammunition and anything else to reduce weight, and then cleared and levelled a makeshift runway. Fesmire remembered:

> Hardison had only a skeleton crew. He held her on the brakes and gave her full power until the tail pulled up then let her roll. About a third of the way down he gave her one-third flaps and when they reached the end of the strip and pulled her off she was only doing 80, but they made it.

Hardison landed safely at Coen 25 minutes later, and a message was flashed from Coen to the 19th Bomb Group at Longreach; 'Bl7 12489 landed here 071OZ'.

By the middle of 1942 early B-17Es such as 41-2489 were obsolete. This B-17 had left the factory with a twin-gun belly turret which was remotely sighted through a clear blister toward the rear of the fuselage, using a periscope. Such turrets had restricted vision at best, and on the sod fields of Java the sighting blisters became caked with mud on take-off, rendering them useless. The turrets had been removed from 41-2489 and her sister ships to be replaced by hand-held guns. Newer B-17Es had the vastly superior manned Sperry ball turret.

On 4 July 1942 a war correspondent named Howell Walker, working for *National Geographic Magazine*, went along on a 93rd Squadron attack on the Japanese airstrip at Lae. His story provides some interesting insights into Felix Hardison's outfit. Walker's original version was subject to the rigorous censorship of the time, so Felix Hardison became 'Captain H.' and the mission was stated to be mounted from 'the operational base of an American heavy-bombardment unit'.

Walker's story begins:

> 'Captain H. was the commanding officer at whose invitation I was present. He would lead the mission in his Flying Fortress, honorably christened *Tojo's Physic*.'

This was a six-aeroplane mission. Hardison led 'A' Flight, and Captain Dean 'Pinky' Hoevet led 'B' Flight. Walker wrote:

Six Flying Fortresses in two flights of three, both in V formation, approached the Japanese-held base of Lae in New Guinea.

"Open your bomb bays," Captain H. ordered calmly over the interplane phone.

Through a side window I watched the bomb bay doors open on the ship off our right wing. At the same time those on the Fortress off our left opened. I could not see the three 'planes in B flight, for they followed directly behind us ...

Antiaircraft guns began firing as we flew in at 28,000 feet. Their shells burst below us. A few seconds before Captain H.'s bombardier released his load, the Japanese gunners fled for shelter.

Looking out of the side window, I saw bombs fall away from the Fortress off our right wing. They seemed to float through the air as in a slow-motion picture.

Walker reported that 'a tremendous fire' blazed on the edge of the aerodrome, and there were two other fires nearby. 'For almost ten minutes after dropping bombs we sailed on our way, unmolested by ground gunfire or enemy pursuit 'planes.'

Then the fighters caught up with them, and Walker described their attack vividly:

Their tracer shots poured past our windows like a horizontal hail of red-hot rivets ... The pursuit 'planes harried us for 25 minutes; yet only one of their thousands of shots hit *Tojo's Physic*, and damage was negligible. Our Fortresses definitely bagged one of the Zeros, possibly two.

The Zero surely shot down could not be credited to any one bomber. Virtually every ship in the two flights had guns on this Jap. Tracers converged on the enemy craft in a beautiful display of marksmanship.

After the Japanese fighters had disappeared altogether, we continued on our course still at 28,000 feet above sea level. Through openings in the clouds we could see the sharply folded mountains, deep valleys, and winding rivers of southeastern New Guinea.

The sun sank behind cumulus banks between the sea and our ships; darkness slowly climbed up to us; and the last few peeks through rifts showed that we had left New Guinea and were now out over the Coral Sea, heading back to our advanced base.

Hardison brought *Tojo's Physic* down on Horn Island, off the northern tip of Australia, in darkness. Behind him his right wingman, Lieutenant Richard Smith in

41-2633, hit a runway light, blowing the left tyre. The landing gear collapsed and the two left propellers were damaged, but nobody was injured. The crews stayed overnight at Horn, and the next day *Tojo's Physic* led the four serviceable B-17s back to attack Lae, but the weather turned bad and they were forced to bomb by dead reckoning.

There was an unfortunate aftermath to the incident involving Smith's B-17. On 27 July Captain Carey O'Bryan flew *Tojo's Physic* up to Horn Island, carrying an extra crew to fly the patched-up 41-2633 back to Australia. Shortly after their arrival the last aircraft landing from a returning mission veered off the runway and neatly sheared the nose off *Tojo's Physic*, cruelly ending her career.

After the untimely decapitation of *Tojo's Physic*, Hardison flew 41-2665 on 30 July, then 41-2643 on the 7 August 1942 mission to Rabaul, when Captain Harl Pease was lost. Two days later Lieutenant Hugh Grundman and his crew were all killed when 41-2643 was shot down by fighters over the same target and crashed in Rondahl's Plantation on New Britain island.

In New Guinea, the Japanese were advancing overland toward Port Moresby after a successful landing at Buna on 21 July. The Australian forces were retreating and it was only at Milne Bay, on the southeastern tip of New Guinea, that the Allies held the initiative. It seemed certain that the Japanese would also attempt to land there, and on 25 August reconnaissance aircraft were able to shadow a convoy long enough to conclude that its destination was Milne Bay.

The situation was critical. At Mareeba, nine B-17s were made ready to go out against the convoy, and all available medium bombers were ordered to Port Moresby for attacks on the following day. The official history of the Army Air Forces in the Second World War states; 'The weather, which had been bad for two weeks, if anything worsened, with the result that the B-17s could not find the enemy and, as so often before, turned back without dropping their bombs.' There is more to the story than that.

A week earlier, Captain Dave Hassemer had brought a brand-new B-17F to Australia to join the 19th Bomb Group, then based at Mareeba, Queensland. Named *Hoomalimali*, it was the first of the new model Flying Fortresses cleared into Mareeba, and was given quite a reception. Felix Hardison chose to lead the nine-aircraft mission to Milne Bay in *Hoomalimali*.

Hardison wrote in his report that the nine aircraft should have got off from Mareeba two hours earlier. As it was, they left at 1400 on 25 August, making it impossible for them to have sighted any targets in Milne Bay by daylight, and they landed at Port Moresby at 2000 that night. The mission had begun poorly, and things got worse. Another of the recently-arrived B-17Fs, *Georgia Peach*, piloted by Captain Harry Hawthorne, landed with a flat left tyre. While the aircraft was being towed from the runway it collided with a Cletrac, killing the driver and damaging the right inboard engine and propeller of the B-17. After emergency repairs the B-17 and crew returned to Mareeba the next day. So eight B-17s, led by Hardison in *Hoomalimali*, took off from Port Moresby an hour before dawn, at 0400 on 26 August.

Lieutenant Lewis Sutton, the navigator on 41-2663 with Lieutenant Bruce Gibson, said:

> Weather was horrible, ceiling approximately 2,000 feet, sometimes less. Anti-aircraft accurate. My notes indicate that we sighted two cruisers, two destroyers and two transports. Every 'plane but two were hit. Captain Webb's crew down in flames. Our 'plane had a hole a foot wide in the right wing section, barely missing a wing tank. The hole was flowered up in a mushroom pattern on top of the wing. We felt that a naval shell had gone through the wing, obviously not exploding. Corporal Robert Swan, our waist gunner, was nicked in four places fortunately none serious.

The bombardier in Captain John Chiles' aircraft was killed, and the navigator was badly wounded. In *Hoomalimali*, Hardison made a bombing run over one of the warships but the bombs hung up, so he turned to make another run. The bombs still refused to drop, and the aircraft took hits as Hardison made a third, and then a fourth run. After several more runs Hardison finally agreed to let his bombardier salvo the load, and four bombs reportedly struck close to the stern of a destroyer. On the final run the rest of the bombs went down, but missed by 100ft or more. The RAAF's hand-written Central War Room Daily Operations Diary records cryptic details of the mission. Against 4391, *Hoomalimali*, it notes 'bomb racks failed, salvoed after twelve runs'.

Tugboat Annie dropped five bombs which landed parallel to a cruiser, about 10ft away, and the ship was reportedly listing. Lieutenant Percy Hinton in 41-2668 claimed a hit on a transport which was 'observed sinking', but overall the operation was a costly failure.

The B-17s headed for home, and the mission ended as it began – bleakly. Captain Kenneth Casper brought in *The Daylight Ltd.* and groundlooped the badly damaged B-17 into a tree. There was a terrific crash and the aircraft was a write-off, but the crew was safe. Hardison noted later that the officers of the 93rd Squadron did some purposeful drinking that night.

On 29 August Hardison was flying another of the new B-17Fs, 41-24384, against Vunakanau near Rabaul. During September he flew a couple of missions in 41-24458, an aircraft later lost with General Kenneth N. Walker.

When it was time for the 19th to go home and hand over the best of their aeroplanes to the 43rd Bomb Group, Felix Hardison was reunited with an old friend, 41-2489, which had been flown up to Mareeba around the end of September 1942. The orders sending the 19th Group home were dated 23 October 1942. For the flight home Major Felix Hardison shared the cockpit of 41-2489 with Colonel Richard Carmichael, the group commander. Of the original crew of eight which had flown together in Java, six were back aboard 41-2489 – Hardison; Lieutenant Ellsworth McRoberts, the original copilot; navigator Lieutenant Albert Nice; engineer Technical Sergeant William Bostwick; radio operator S/Sergeant Orville Kiger and tail gunner Sergeant John Irons.

In Hawaii the B-17 was spruced up for the final leg of the return journey. The 93rd's bold Indian head insignia was painted on the nose below the name *Suzy-Q*, along with a list of the places the veteran aircraft had been to on her epic journey.

Suzy-Q spent the remainder of 1942 at Hamilton Field and then, in the middle of February 1943, she was flown to Boeing Field. Hardison, en route to Spokane to take up an operations officer post in the Second Air Force at Fort George Wright, was reunited with the aircraft for the last time.

A legend was building. In February 1943 a *Life Magazine* story by Caroline Iverson began:

> *Suzy-Q* is the fightingest Flying Fortress in the world. There's just one thing she wants to do and that's to kill Japs. She knows her big job is to lay a string of bombs on an enemy ship or airdrome and knock equipment and men to hell in a thunderous boom. But she also likes to snuggle in low over a target and, with machine guns blazing, pick off every damn Jap in sight. Then she sticks her blunt glass nose up toward the sky once more and hightails for home hundreds of miles away.

The story asserted that each gunner could claim ten or more Japanese aeroplanes shot down, 'more than any other gun crew in the Pacific', that *Suzy-Q* had 'run more long range bombing missions against the Japs than any other 'plane' and was 'credited with killing more Japs, directly or indirectly, than any other 'plane in the US Army Air Forces'.

Suzy-Q was reduced to salvage in July 1946.

Mission To Rabaul

On 29 November 1941 Lieutenant John Dougherty of the 7th Bomb Group accepted Boeing B-17 Flying Fortress No.41-2429 on behalf of the Army Air Forces and flew it to Fort Douglas, Utah, where it was assigned to the 88th Reconnaissance Squadron. One week later 41-2429 was the lead aeroplane of a flight of six B-17Es from the 88th which took off from Hamilton Field, California, in the evening of 6 December 1941, bound for the Philippines via Hawaii. In the cockpit were Major Richard H. Carmichael and Captain James Twaddell.

As the tired B-17 crews approached Hickam Field at the end of their 14hr initial flight, a bizarre scene unfolded before their eyes. Scores of aircraft were darting through the air and clouds of smoke were billowing into the sky.

Carmichael wanted nothing to do with Hickam Field at that moment. It appeared that while they had been flying between California and Hawaii a full-scale war had erupted. He changed course and headed towards Bellows Field, to the northeast. His wingman, Lieutenant Harold Chaffin in 41-2430, decided to stick with the 'old man', but three of the other four aircraft were critically low on fuel and pressed on to land safely at Hickam, while the fourth was landed on a golf course. Carmichael's and Chaffin's B-17Es were totally defenceless, and all the crews could do was hope that the enemy aeroplanes would ignore them. As Bellows came into view, Carmichael's heart sank. It, too, was under attack, and so was nearby Kaneohe Field.

Carmichael turned to the northwest and raced across the centre of Oahu to Wheeler Field. Their luck was holding, as no Japanese fighters had bothered them, but time was running out. At Wheeler the situation was similar; dense clouds of smoke rose from rows of Curtiss P-40 fighters burning on the ground. The situation became even more desperate for the B-17s because the American defenders, responding at last to the surprise attack, were putting up a thickening barrage of anti-aircraft fire and shooting at anything in the sky.

Not far from Wheeler there was an emergency fighter field, shown on their maps as Haleiwa. This was a short strip, even for fighters, being only 1,200ft long, but the two B-17s, low on fuel, had to get down. Carmichael turned 41-2429 into the wind, lowered the landing gear and flaps, and 'dragged' the Flying Fortress on to the runway in a near stall. Chaffin emulated his actions in 41-2430, and both B-17s survived. These two aircraft had been together since their construction at Seattle, when Lieutenant David Rawls had taken delivery of 41-2430 on 29 November. Ironically, both are still together today, as scattered wreckage not far from Rabaul on the island of New Britain.

Carmichael's B-17, quickly daubed with camouflage paint, spent the next couple of months flying long search patrols out of Hawaii. Then, on 8 February 1942, Carmichael in 41-2429 led twelve B-17Es from Hickam Field on a special mission to assist in protecting the line of supply in the South Pacific. Designated the 40th Reconnaissance Squadron, these B-17s were drawn from the 22nd and 88th Squadrons of the 7th Bomb Group. They flew to the Fijis by way of Christmas and Canton Islands. After completing a dozen missions they proceeded to New Caledonia and then on to Townsville, Australia, making their unexpected arrival there on 19 February.

The twelve bombers, then under US Navy control, were ordered to prepare immediately for an early morning strike against Simpson Harbour at Rabaul. The plan was to take off from Townsville a little after midnight on 23 February, arrive over Rabaul six hours later, and return to Australia after a refuelling stop at Port Moresby.

Nine B-17s were loaded for the mission, but the force was reduced by a third before it left the ground. One aircraft was unable to start engines owing to water in the fuel system, and two more were damaged in a taxying accident in the darkness. The other six Fortresses, led by Carmichael, pressed on. Bad weather on the way to the target broke up the two flights of three B-17s, cloud protected the harbour and the mission was a valiant failure. Lieutenant Fred Eaton's B-17, 41-2446, was forced to crash-land in a swamp south of Buna on the way back, but the crew was safe.

Between that first Rabaul mission and 1 April, Carmichael's B-17s flew perhaps eleven more bombing missions, including five more to Rabaul, one to Koepang in Timor, and four against Japanese installations in the Lae and Salamaua areas of New Guinea. All six Rabaul strikes combined had put only fifteen B-17s over the target – an average of fewer than three aircraft per mission.

On 25 March 1942 three 40th Reconnaissance Squadron aeroplanes were sent on a special mission. They were to rescue General Douglas MacArthur and his family and key staff, who were coming down to Del Monte from Corregidor by Navy PT boat, and bring them to safety in Australia. Captain Frank Bostrom took 41-2447, Lieutenant Harold Chaffin was in 41-2408 and Captain William Lewis flew 41-2429. The copilots – Ed Teats, Jack Adams and Bill Railing – were all from the original 19th and familiar with Del Monte field.

Chaffin's aircraft had only one bomb bay fuel tank, so he stood by at Batchelor Field while 41-2447 and 41-2429 flew on to Del Monte. General MacArthur, along with his wife, son and some of his key staff, boarded 41-2429, but the pilots had problems starting the engines. So everyone moved to Bostrom's B-17E and after a 'hair-raising' take-off made a long but uneventful trip to Australia.

Lewis and Railing finally got 41-2429 started and the remainder of MacArthur's staff scrambled aboard. When Bostrom's aircraft landed at Batchelor Field, Chaffin and Adams then took one of the bomb bay tanks from 41-2447 and flew to Del Monte the following evening to collect the MacArthur party's baggage.

By the middle of 1942 older Flying Fortresses such as 41-2429 were obsolete and their places had been taken by newer B-17Es with manned ball turrets, while brand-new B-17Fs were being rolled out of Boeing's Seattle plant. The old aeroplanes had fought long and hard since the first days of the war, and were showing signs of wear. The war could well have been over for 41-2429, but a young pilot named Harl Pease came along. Born in Plymouth, New Hampshire, on 10 August 1917, Pease enlisted in the Air Corps Flying Cadet Training Program shortly after war broke out in Europe in 1939. He was commissioned a Second Lieutenant on 21 June 1940 after graduating from the Air Corps Training Center at Kelly Field, Texas.

Pease's first assignment was as a B-17 pilot with the 19th Bombardment Group at March Field in California. When the 19th moved to Clark Field in the Philippines in October 1941 it had more pilots than aircraft, so Pease flew as navigator for Captain Cecil Combs, commanding the 93rd Squadron. His first combat mission, on 10 December 1941, was an attack on invading enemy forces at Aparri on Luzon, but the results were not determined. He was evacuated to Java by submarine on 7 February 1942, and then to Australia in March.

On 12 March Pease was piloting 41-2452, one of three B-17s ordered to Del Monte on the abortive first attempt to evacuate General Douglas MacArthur. Pease and his copilot, Lieutenant Carey O'Bryan, landed after dark with only one brake and supercharger problems. There was no sign of the MacArthur party, and it was suicidal to be caught on the ground during daylight, so Pease and O'Bryan loaded their aeroplane with stranded 19th Bomb Group personnel and took off for Australia. The stories that MacArthur refused to fly with the youthful pilot in his battered aircraft are totally untrue.

When the 19th Bomb Group was rebuilt, Pease became Operations Officer in Hardison's 93rd Squadron, and on 10 July 1942 he was promoted to Captain.

On 6 August 1942 six aircraft from the 93rd Squadron took part in a mission against Lae, returning to Horn Island, off the northern tip of Australia. After refuelling they took off in mid-afternoon for Seven Mile Strip at Port Moresby, because a major mission to Rabaul was planned for the following day. It was a maximum effort to divert Japanese attention from Guadalcanal in the Solomons, where the 1st Marine Division was going ashore in the morning of 7 August.

Captain Harl Pease's 41-2668 blew an engine on take off, forcing him to change course for Mareeba. Lieutenant Vincent Snyder, Engineering Officer of the 93rd Squadron, shepherded Pease and his crippled B-17 to Australia. Pease was determined to go on the Rabaul mission, but the only B-17 still available was old 41-2429. It was war weary, with electrical problems and 'weak' engines which had caused it to abort several missions before it was finally taken out of combat service. Pease thought it would make it through the mission; Snyder disagreed.

Sergeant Alavar Liimatainen, Pease's regular radio operator, had gone to the hospital, and Private Edward Troccia had been assigned to replace the sick airman. But on the way to the aeroplane Liimatainen flagged down the truck carrying his crew and convinced Pease that he was able to go on the mission. Troccia later joined Snyder's crew as left waist gunner.

Pease and his crew landed at Seven Mile in the very early morning of 7 August, a few hours behind Snyder, who 'raised hell in no uncertain terms' when Pease arrived with 41-2429. But Pease talked Major Felix Hardison into letting him go along, and the crew was able to snatch a few hours' precious sleep. The rest of the 19th had been there since the evening of 6 August.

The B-17s began taking off around 0730, and the mission began badly when a runaway supercharger on 41-2617, piloted by Lieutenant Charles Hillhouse, caused it to rear into the gravel bank beside the runway. Another aircraft, 41-2657, suffered engine failure soon after take off and aborted the mission, and 41-9015 turned back with electrical problems.

In the end it was a thirteen-aeroplane mission, led by Colonel Richard Carmichael, flying with Captain John Dougherty in 41-2536. Climbing to 20,000ft, the B-17s crossed New Guinea south of Salamaua and flew direct to the centre of New Britain, where they turned east to Rabaul. As they passed through a weather front along the south coast of New Britain they encountered scattered cloud, but there was unlimited visibility in the target area.

Swinging south toward Vunakanau at 22,500ft, the B-17s began their 15-minute run to the target. However, their bomb bay doors were barely open before they came under attack by approximately twenty Zeros. Hardison was leading the six 93rd Squadron aircraft in 41-2643. His report, typically succinct, states:

> Attacked at 11:40 before reaching target at 22,000 feet. Enemy A/C Zero type (Grey) approximately 20 strong. No formation. Direction of attack was from rear, front, sides, above and below. Continuous attack lasting 20 minutes. First attack was on rear 'planes in formation, subsequent attacks made on every 'plane. E/A attack individually using no peculiar method. Estimated 7 E/A destroyed by group. One B-17E failing to return.

The one B-17E lost was 41-2429, Pease's aircraft.

The second element of three aeroplanes from the 93rd was a little above and behind Hardison, with Captain Edward Jacquet in *Tojo's Jinx* leading and Pease flying off his right wing. After bombs away, Hardison began a diving left turn to escape the fighters and to cover Carmichael in the lead ship, who had one gunner dead, another wounded and his oxygen system shot out. The speed of the leading B-17s increased rapidly, spreading the formation as they raced toward the protection of broken cloud at 15,000ft. Hardison's left wingman, Snyder in 41-2464, was also in trouble; 'Our No.1 engine was already very rough and throwing oil out the breather. On the first pass by the Zeros our oxygen system was shot away. We continued in formation, though the lack of oxygen became noticeable to all the crew...'

Major John Bridges, in 41-2665 off Jacquet's left wing, was the first to notice that something was wrong. He called his top turret gunner, Sergeant Elvin Moncrief, asking 'Where's Pease? What happened to Pease?'. Moncrief, busy shooting at the Japanese fighters, did not reply, but Bridges soon saw for himself what was happening. Pease was having engine problems and was already falling behind, and under persistent fighter attack. Bridges was one of the last to see Pease's B-17, and he reported that he saw it fall about 1,000ft with the left inboard engine out. A blazing 400gal bomb bay fuel tank was jettisoned, but it seemed that the entire aircraft was afire.

In Snyder's B-17 Edward Troccia, cursing a jammed machine gun, saw 41-2429 falling back and thought that both inboard engines were burning. There were some reports of two parachutes from the doomed B-17, but the final report to 19th Bomb Group Headquarters stated that the aircraft had crashed in flames and that the crew was killed.

The Medal of Honor was posthumously awarded to Captain Harl Pease and presented to his parents by President Franklin D. Roosevelt in a ceremony at the White House on 4 November 1942. All eight members of Pease's crew were awarded the Distinguished Service Cross.

The war continued, and the assumptions about the loss of 41-2429 became accepted as fact. Officially, Harl Pease and his crew were presumed dead, as several months after the war there was still no trace of any of them.

Then, in 1948, a document dated 16 February 1943 came to light. This included a translation of a monitored Tokyo broadcast which indicated that a 'Captain Peace', an American bomber pilot, had been shot down and taken prisoner. The Army no longer believed that the evidence was strong enough to justify the finding of his presumed death, and the American Graves Registration Service convened a board of review on 10 October 1949.

Their subsequent report revealed that, on 25 June 1946, a search party had located the wreckage of a crashed warplane along the Powell River on New Britain, some 40 miles south of Rabaul. The wreckage was widely scattered, most of the fuselage lying in the river. Natives guiding the search party stated that when they had first found the wreckage there were three bodies beside it, but that the river had washed them away. In another section of the aeroplane, away from the river, the party recovered two complete sets of human remains, along with several coins and a diamond ring. The aircraft was mistakenly identified as a North American B-25 Mitchell.

The remains recovered from the wreck were ultimately identified as those of Pease's Australian copilot, Flight Sergeant Fred Earp, and Sergeant Alavar Liimatainen. Earp was interred in the war cemetery at Rabaul, and Liimatainen was buried in Marquette, Michigan, his home town.

Another visit was made to the site on 9 March 1947, and the wreckage was finally identified as a B-17 by Technical Sergeant Robert Smith. The serial number was confirmed as 41-2429.

The 604th Quartermaster Graves Registration Company undertook yet another investigation of the crash area on 9 December 1948. A local native insisted that he had seen the aeroplane go down and that he had seen an airman parachute from it before it exploded. The man was dead when they reached him, and his body was buried by a Catholic missionary. The native took the Americans to the spot where the man had been buried, and they found scattered human remains, a billfold and two shoes, but no identification could be made.

Father George W. Lepping, a Catholic priest, was one of the civilians interned by the Japanese when they occupied New Britain. His memories leave no doubt that Captain Harl Pease and Sergeant Chester Czechowski successfully abandoned their blazing B-17 only to be captured by the Japanese. He stated:

I arrived at the prison camp at Rabaul on 7 September 1942. Captain Pease and Sergeant Czechowski had been brought to the camp about 10 August after their 'plane had been shot down on 7 August. There were two more American airmen prisoners, Lieutenants Massey and King who had been shot down some months earlier, and two Australian coast watchers. The military prisoners were held in much tighter security than the missionaries and other civilians, being handcuffed and roped to their beds at night.

I remember Captain Pease had been wounded, the Japanese pilots who shot down his B-17 had machine gunned the crew as they were parachuting down and Captain Pease had taken a bullet through the calf of his left leg. He asked for medical attention but the Japanese laughed and said, "We don't treat American airmen!". One of the civilian prisoners had some medical supplies and treated the wound daily until Captain Pease was able to walk again.

I have never been able to keep Harl Pease out of my mind ... Harl would show us the stars and how the pilots steered their 'planes by them, and he related the pleasant time he had with the Dutch civilians while flying missions from Java. He told how the crews would put the warm beer in the 'planes when they went on a mission so they would have cold beer when they returned from the high altitude ...

The Japanese looked up to Pease ... The Fortresses were semi-gods to them, and to have a Captain of a "Boeing", as they called them, was something to be remembered ...

About 8 a.m. on 8 October 1942, Captain Pease, Sergeant Czechowski, the other two American airmen and the two Australian coast watchers were given some picks and shovels we had in camp and told they were going to a camp in the Kokopo area to work on a new airfield that was being constructed ... we gave the six men some spare articles of clothing we had ... in the early afternoon the digging tools and the extra pieces of clothing were returned to the camp. We never saw the six men again. The other prisoners who had been there from the beginning of imprisonment in January knew the routine. The six men had been forced to dig their own graves and then they were executed by the sword.

Over the years four of the nine men aboard 41-2429 have been accounted for. Pease and Czechowski were executed as prisoners, Earp and Liimatainen's remains were identified. The other five will almost certainly never be found.

What of 41-2430, the aircraft which followed Carmichael and 41-2429 through the chaos over Oahu on 7 December 1941? Lieutenant Harold Chaffin flew it to Australia with Carmichael's 40th Reconnaissance Squadron in February 1942, and it served with the 19th Bomb Group before being assigned to the 65th Bomb Squadron of the 43rd Bomb Group. By then 41-2430 was named *Naughty But Nice*. On the night of 25 June 1943 it was on a mission to Vunakanau with Lieutenant Charles Trimingham and his crew. Over the target they were caught in the searchlights and an anti-aircraft hit started a fire in the No.3 engine. From out of the darkness, a Japanese Irving night fighter closed in to finish the job. Only Lieutenant Jose Holguin, the navigator, survived, as a prisoner of the Japanese.

Bound For Glory

America was in the war, and War Bond drives were raising money for all manner of causes. The *Seattle Post-Intelligencer* was helping to sell Defence Bonds to the people of Seattle and the Pacific Northwest to raise the cost of a Flying Fortress, then set at $280,535 for a brand-new B-17E. The goal was achieved in March 1942, when the contributors 'bought' B-17E 41-2656, which had been accepted by the Army Air Forces an 3 March. The special aeroplane needed to have a name, and a suitably imposing one was chosen: *'Chief Seattle' from the Pacific Northwest*. One of Boeing's painters added the words to both sides of the B-17's nose.

A formal presentation ceremony, held at Boeing Field on 5 March, was broadcast live on CBS radio, with Boeing's president, Philip G. Johnson, and Earl Millikin, the mayor of Seattle, officiating. Florence Teats, chosen to smash a bottle of champagne against a metal rod protruding from one of the swivel mounts in the aircraft's nose, was the wife of Lieutenant Edward Teats, one of the B-17 pilots of the 14th Squadron in the Philippines who had been flying against the Japanese since their initial attack.

The aircraft was accepted by Major General Frederick L. Martin, who had commanded the Hawaiian Air Force at the time of the Pearl Harbor attack and was then commanding the Second Air Force, based to the east at Spokane. When the festivities were completed, *Chief Seattle* was flown to Lowry Field near Denver in Colorado, where it remained until May. The following month it was at Hamilton Field and Sacramento Air Depot, being equipped for the flight to Hawaii. Assigned on 8 July to Project 'X' – the movement of heavy bombers to the Far East – the aircraft was in the Southwest Pacific Theatre by August.

Lieutenant Morris Friedman and his crew collected *Chief Seattle* from the Charleville Depot in Queensland. On 6 August 1942 orders assigned the crew and aircraft to the 435th Squadron of the 19th Bomb Group, which was flying critical reconnaissance missions. Two days later Friedman and his aircraft were at Port Moresby, ready for their first combat mission.

In the early morning of 9 August *Chief Seattle* headed out on a reconnaissance of the Japanese bases of Rabaul on New Britain and Kavieng on New Ireland, a flight of a little under nine hours which turned out to be a routine mission. *Chief Seattle*'s crew reported the number of vessels in and around Rabaul's Simpson Harbour, and the number of aircraft at the Vunakanau airstrip.

On 11 August *Chief Seattle* took off on its second mission, a reconnaissance flight over the Madang area of New Guinea. Bad weather and problems with the left inboard engine terminated the flight after three hours. A United Press correspondent, Frank Hewlett, who was in Port Moresby, interviewed the crew of the celebrated aeroplane for stories which later appeared in their hometown newspapers.

A mission was scheduled to take off at 0600 on 14 August, the briefing being carried out the previous evening at Seven Mile Strip. This, yet another surveillance of enemy activities, was to cover Buna, Gasmata, Rabaul and the sea lanes linking them, the aircraft then flying on to Kavieng and back home to Port Moresby. This time, however, *Chief Seattle* was to be flown by a different crew. The pilot, Lieutenant Wilson L. Cook from Bradley, Oklahoma, was a veteran who had already flown more than 40 missions. He had been copilot on Lieutenant Frank Bostrom's 41-2416, which had arrived over Hawaii on 7 December 1941 during the initial Japanese attack. Bostrom's unarmed aeroplane had been chased almost right around Oahu by Japanese fighters before he successfully landed the shot-up B-17E on a fairway of the golf course near Kahuku.

Chief Seattle lifted off from Seven Mile Strip at 0602 on 14 August 1942 and was never heard of again. She simply disappeared.

The combat report of the Japanese *Tainan Kokutai* for 14 August may hold the answer. This states that nine Zeros in three flights, led by Lieutenant Jojii Yamashita, took off from Lae at 0520 to patrol over a convoy which was coming in to Buna from the northwest. At 0635 they sighted a lone B-17 going north, and after a 'prolonged' air battle the bomber was shot down. All nine fighters made attacks, and the leader of the second flight, Lieutenant Takeyoshi Ono, suffered heavy damage to the wing of his fighter. He was forced to land at Buna with his number two man, PO2/c Sahei Yamashita. His number three, PO3/c Masami Arai, was shot down and killed by gunfire from the Flying Fortress.

The remains of *Chief Seattle* and Wilson Cook's crew have never been found.

Tales of the South Pacific

The Battle of Guadalcanal was one of the critical campaigns in the Pacific War. It began on 7 August 1942 with an amphibious assault by US Marines on the Japanese-held islands of Guadalcanal, Tulagi and Gavutu, and months of fierce fighting followed before the islands were secured. There was only one heavy bomber unit in the theatre, the 11th Bomb Group, under the command of Colonel Laverne G. 'Blondie' Saunders.

General Millard F. Harmon, commander of US Army ground and air forces in the South Pacific Theatre, had been given authority to divert aircraft on their way to General George Kenney's 5th Air Force in Australia to support the Guadalcanal operations. This was only to be done in extreme emergency, but what constituted an 'emergency' was always a matter of opinion, and Kenney felt that Harmon was 'sandbagging' him. However, there was little he could do when his replacements had to pass through the neighbouring theatre.

There were some intriguing situations, such as the occasion when Captain Edward Steedman and his crew were flying a brand-new B-17F named *Jezabel* from Hawaii to Australia via Christmas Island, Canton and Fiji. They left Fiji at 0200 on 15 August 1942 for the eleven-hour flight to Brisbane, but halfway between New Caledonia and Australia they received a message instructing them to land in New Caledonia. Steedman banked *Jezabel* into a 180° turn and landed at Plaines des Gaiacs, to learn that the crew and their new aircraft were being taken into the 11th Bomb Group. *Jezabel* was one of a total of just nine new B-17Fs assigned to the South Pacific Theatre.

Other crews found that assignments could be changed en route. *Omar Khayyam* was one of three B-17Fs and two B-25s ordered from Hamilton Field to Australia on 5 September 1942. Its pilot was Lieutenant Edwin C. McAnelly. Lieutenant Joel Kleiman, the copilot, was originally from New York, and had come up with the aircraft's name, which was painted on at Hickam Field. The artwork showed a drunk in a turban clinging to a street sign indicating the intersection of 42nd Street and Broadway. Beneath the name *Omar Khayyam*, in smaller letters, was the legend *The Plastered Bastard*.

The McAnelly crew and *Omar Khayyam* were held in New Caledonia for the 11th Bomb Group 'by order of the commanding general'. Unhappy with this change of plans, the crew took off the next day under the pretence of checking out the compass, and managed to end up in Brisbane on 14 September 1942. A day later they flew on to Torrens Creek, but they were soon ordered back to New Caledonia. *Omar*

Khayyam and her crew had been assigned to the 403rd Squadron of the 43rd Bomb Group on 17 September and they were 'unassigned' on 20 September! The McAnelly crew arrived on Espiritu Santo the next day.

Omar Khayyam was immediately assigned to the 98th Bomb Squadron and flew its first mission on 4 October 1942 with another crew. Its short career ended spectacularly over New Georgia on 1 December when it was being flown by Captain Willis Jacobs of the 431st Squadron. A Zero slammed head-on into the top of the fuselage just behind the radio compartment, cutting the B-17 in two. The tail gunner, Corporal Joseph Hartman, managed to get out of the rear section. He was the sole survivor.

In the afternoon of 21 September 1942, Lieutenant John Livingston brought 41-24531 to Efate Island from New Caledonia. Before beginning operations with the 26th Bomb Squadron the new B-17 had a leakproof radio room fuel tank installed, and the aircraft's original radio tank and nose tank were removed.

The following day Livingston flew the aircraft to Espiritu Santo, and that afternoon took it up for a compass swing. There were also a few teething problems. On 23 September 41-24531 had to go back to Efate for replacement of a defective feeder tank, and on the following day it was 'out' for bomb-rack repairs.

Livingston took 41-24531 on an eleven-hour search mission on 25 September, looking over Gizo Harbour and checking Rendova Island for any trace of Captain Robert Richards and the crew of 41-9071, which had gone down on 8 September. Next day the aircraft was again sidelined with bomb-rack problems, and on 27 September Livingston flew it back to Efate, returning late in the afternoon with a load of spare parts. On 28 September, when scheduled for another search mission, 41-24531 blew her tailwheel tyre as she taxied out for take-off.

Finally, on 29 September, 41-24531 flew her first tactical mission, as part of an eleven-aeroplane raid on Tonolei Harbour on Bougainville. As they descended through towering pillars of cloud to the target the B-17s ran into a dozen Zeros, and the bomber gunners ultimately claimed eight fighters destroyed. Tonolei being completely closed in, the B-17s searched the west coast of Bougainville and found an enemy light cruiser. Bombs failed to release in two aeroplanes, so Lieutenant Bill Kinney in *The Aztec's Curse* and Lieutenant Frank Waskowitz in the aircraft known as the 'Blue Goose' made a second run. Putting up a deadly barrage, the Japanese warship blew a wing off the 'Blue Goose' and sent it spinning into the sea, burning and exploding. Altogether the bombers had unloaded 22 tons of bombs from 5,500ft, but all had missed. They landed at Guadalcanal in mid-afternoon, low on fuel after more than nine hours in the air.

Captain Walter Chambers piloted 41-24531 on a search mission on 1 October 1942, and two days later Livingston flew it up to Guadalcanal with a full load of 100lb demolition bombs for a tactical mission on 4 October to bomb Buka airstrip. The B-17s took off at 0300 and battled bad weather most of the way, only to find the target hidden by cloud. As it was impossible to bomb they turned back and chanced upon an estimated ten surface vessels, escorted by six Zeros and six floatplanes, off the coast of New Georgia. Four Japanese aircraft were claimed destroyed, but one Zero crashed into 41-9118, piloted by Lieutenant Donald Everitt of the 72nd Bomb Squadron, knocking off the B-17's tail. Livingston's aircraft had its right inboard engine shot out, but he was able to get safely to Espiritu Santo.

Livingston completed a couple of search missions from Santo in 41-24531, then made the four-hour flight to Guadalcanal on 11 October. The next day a further mission to Buka airstrip was begun, but weather again forced the B-17s to return with their bombs. On 13 October the mission was successfully completed and the aircraft landed on Guadalcanal to spend 'a miserable night', as the 26th Bomb Squadron historian aptly described it.

Japanese naval units were trying to knock out Henderson Field, and during the night of 13 October heavy shelling by the battleships *Kongo* and *Haruna* helped put the airfield out of action for a month. Two B-17s were damaged beyond repair, including 41-24528, the new B-17F which Lieutenant James Price had delivered just a month before. Riddled by shrapnel fragments, it was simply abandoned. In the early morning of 14 October Livingston took off from the 'bomb torn' runway and returned to Espiritu Santo.

On 11 November reconnaissance flights from Guadalcanal reported more than 60 Japanese ships in the Buin and Tonolei areas of Bougainville. The next day eleven transports carrying more than 13,000 troops and supported by the battleship *Hiei* and a force of cruisers and destroyers left the Shortland Island area and steamed toward Guadalcanal. In the early morning hours of 13 November they fought their way through a force of American cruisers. In retaliation, every available aircraft was ranged against the convoy during the day. Livingston and the crew of 41-24531 had been on alert as part of the 11th Bomb Group's 'Striking Force' for several days. With the other B-17s they found and bombed a Japanese cruiser at the northwest tip of Florida Island. The bombers claimed 'near misses' and Chambers' *The Aztec's Curse* took a 5in shell through the tail but returned home safely.

Henderson Field was hit hard that night but *Hiei*, crippled during the earlier battle, finally sank in the morning of 14 November, and seven of the transports were sunk or left burning. Livingston took 41-24531 on her fifth tactical mission, bombing a large transport northwest of the Russell Islands. During the night a smaller American naval force sank the battle cruiser *Kirishima*, forcing the Japanese to retreat.

The B-17s went out again on 15 November, to attack transports unloading between Cape Esperance and Russell Island. Livingston in 41-24531 led his flight up to 16,000ft, where they started a bombing run on a transport. The three B-17s laid their bombs across the ship, scoring an unknown number of hits. On the way home Livingston's crew reported sighting survivors clinging to pieces of wreckage or on rafts. They proved to be from the USS *Juneau*, a casualty of the wild naval battle off Savo Island two days earlier. By then the battle was practically over. Guadalcanal was saved, and was never again threatened with invasion.

On Wednesday 18 November a mission was launched to destroy the enemy shipping which had escaped during the naval battle and was now reported to be in Tonolei Harbour. The lead aircraft was 41-24531, piloted by Major Al Sewart, commander of the 26th Bomb Squadron, and Colonel 'Blondie' Saunders went along to assign targets. The other four aircraft in Sewart's flight comprised Captain Jack Thornhill in 41-2524, Major Ernest Manierre in 41-9213, Captain Philip Sprawls in *Alley-Oop* and Captain Donald Hyland in *Yokohama Express*. For the first time, Lockheed P-38 Lightnings were escorting the bombers.

Sewart led his five B-17s over the harbour at 12,000ft and bombardier Lieutenant Nelson Levi lined up on a large tanker. But the bombs in 41-24531 hung up, and when the lead ship failed to drop, so did the others. Saunders decided to go around again.

The second flight was composed of two aeroplanes from the 72nd Bomb Squadron, piloted by Major Narce Whitaker and Lieutenant Tom Classen, with three others from the 98th Bomb Squadron: Captain Walter Lucas in *Buzz King*, Lieutenant Cecil Durbin in *Omar Khayyam* and Lieutenant Roy Morgan in *Galloping Gus*. They arrived over the target, scored some hits on a large transport and set course for home. The escort fighters, 4,000ft above, saw both bomber formations turn from the target and were unaware of Saunders' decision to turn again for a second bombing run. Japanese fighters from Kahili, which had not even taken off until the bombers were nearing the target, were by then reaching their altitude, so the P-38s dropped their wing tanks and attacked the enemy fighters, chasing them off. The Lightnings then headed home, unaware that they were leaving Sewart's flight to make its second attack without fighter cover.

Alley-Oop's pilot, Captain Philip Sprawls, later recorded it all in his diary. 'We made a long sweeping turn to the right. The AA seemed to diminish some in our turn, but picked up again as we approached the target. Then, just before we dropped the bombs, the Zeros hit us!!! and I do mean hit!!! They were all over the sky!'

The five B-17s turned and made their second run, but again the lead ship's bombs refused to release. This time the rest of the flight dropped when they saw the bombs tumble from Major Manierre's B-17. It was a good run, and hits were claimed on a ship.

Sprawls continues:

Miraculously, we all dropped and made a slight left turn on our way home. At this time came the concentrated attack! The enemy fighters were coming from both sides, front and back, and bottom and top!!! Just like a big bee hive turned loose! They had land-based Zeros, float Zeros and float biplanes. Evidently they sent at us everything they had. Once, I was so scared, I tried to duck behind the instrument panel!

One Zero came up on the right side, did a chandelle, and fired six machine guns and two cannon thru our formation! I could see the smoke following the fire from his cannons; man, I didn't like that. His fire raked all the way from the lead airplane thru me! He even came between Hyland and Thornhill, cutting Hyland off from the formation. Hyland says it about scared him to death!

Colonel Saunders told this story; 'We'd made our second run across the target about 8:30 a.m. when about twenty Zeros got on us ... The Zeros made head-on attacks and they were plenty good – better than any I'd seen before. They came at us in a string.'

A burst of gunfire spattered the cockpit. Sewart's arm was nicked and copilot Lieutenant Jack Lee was hit in the right ankle. Lee grabbed for his leg then pitched forward, hit again in the stomach.

Saunders said:

> I unharnessed him and started to pull him out of the copilot's seat in order to take his place. Sewart was slapping his controls around, trying to outmanoeuvre the storming Japs. At last I got Lee on the floor and climbed into his seat.
>
> Then Sewart got it. A bullet went through his heart, killing him instantly. I grabbed the controls and jockeyed the 'plane into flying position.
>
> First one, then the second engine in the left wing was shot out ... The 'plane was beginning to lose altitude rapidly ... I was flying by the seat of my pants, as there wasn't an instrument left working in the 'plane except the clock.

Other pilots said that Saunders' aircraft, with one engine feathered and a wing tank ablaze, was 'flopping around' so crazily that they could not see how he continued to fly it. Saunders continued:

> I decided to make for some overcast and so we dived down. The left wing was red hot. The bank and turn indicator showed we were in a spin. I was afraid to open the bomb bay doors and jettison the bombs that remained for fear that we would lose flying speed and stall. I levelled the 'plane as best I could and tried to get Sewart's body out of the pilot's seat where the trim tabs were located, but Sewart was jammed in and the shifting weight as I moved caused the 'plane to lurch. I jumped back in the copilot's seat and levelled the ship again.
>
> We came out of the overcast at about five hundred feet and I saw I'd have to put her down. This was about 20 minutes after the pilot and co-pilot had been hit. Other 'planes stayed around to protect us but the Zeros didn't follow us that far. I told the other 'planes to take

our position and then I headed for a little island in order to come down as close to land as possible.

We were about a mile and a half out. The navigator, Lieutenant Donald O'Brien, was up with me and the rest of the crew was in the radio compartment, all set for the water landing. I brought her down dragging the tail on the water at 95 miles an hour. The wings hit and there was really a sudden stop.

The navigator and I went, sliding through the window in the cockpit – the smallest hole I ever went through in my life. The tail broke off and the rest of the crew went out through the break.

We thought Jack Lee was dead but he said, "Hey, get me out" and we did. The nose went down and the fuselage flipped over and crowned me. We got two rubber boats inflated and put Lee into one of them and started paddling for shore.

When we reached the island not knowing whether Japs were around, we pulled everything back into the jungle and made a bed for Levi, the bombardier, on one of the boats and made him as comfortable as we could.

Saunders had put the B-17 down off Baga Island, near Vella Lavella. Lee died as they took him out of the raft to lay him on the beach. Levi was in agony with a machine gun bullet through his knee. Saunders had banged his head hard on the windshield when 41-24531 hit the water, and had a cut on his left hand. The rest were unhurt except for grazes and bruises. Captain Jack Thornhill circled overhead for an hour, dropping blankets, food, pistols and a chart to the nine men they could see on the beach.

Soon friendly natives took them to their village and provided shelter until the following afternoon, when they were picked up by a US Navy Catalina and flown to Tulagi.

Lieutenant Thomas J. Classen had come to the South Pacific Theatre with the original 72nd Bomb Squadron in a B-17E named *Spook!*, one of twelve aircraft and crews sent down from Hawaii in late September 1942 to support the 11th Bomb Group. Commanded by Major Don Ridings, the 72nd operated essentially as a fifth squadron under Saunders.

On 6 February 1943 Tom Classen and his crew had flown up to Guadalcanal in their new aircraft, the 5th Bomb Group's one and only B-17F. This had belonged to General Millard F. Harmon, but he had turned it over to the 5th Group because they were so desperately short of aircraft. On its nose had been painted a pair of puckered lips beneath arched eyebrows, along with the name *My Lovin' Dove*. When Classen got it 'everything was all still nice and new ... man I did like that airplane, I can still feel it under me'. He flew this aircraft on six missions, and then it was lost. Classen said, 'she had less than two hundred hours and was the only new airplane we had. Broke my heart.' He tells what happened on 9 February 1943:

43

The take-off was at approximately 0300 after eight short hours ground time since our last landing at Henderson Field. This had left little time to brief, eat, sleep, and check the aircraft before departure. The operation at Henderson was not predicated on convenience. To get something to eat was a major operation. Our failure to thoroughly check our B-17, especially the guns which had been serviced by armament personnel, later proved to be a grave mistake.

The search sector we had drawn for this mission had within it the small coral island of Nauru ... Jap Zeros had been observed on it two days before and the following day it had been photographed. As I recall, the photographs revealed about a dozen Zeros parked in dispersals adjacent to a single strip. Large quantities of phosphorous were being produced on the island, which explained the protection for such a remote spot.

Our flight from the "Canal" was uneventful and shortly after sunrise the white streak of coral which encircled the island came into view. We immediately turned with the idea of passing about ten miles off shore, hoping to get by without being observed and still get a look at the harbour for possible naval activity. This was shortly accomplished and the island was now behind us – we thought we had it made. As we were comparing notes and talking over the interphone, I glanced out the side window down at the ocean and there paralleling our course at a lower altitude and rapidly overtaking us were two Zeros. I knew we were in for it and immediately alerted the crew to prepare for action.

I was not immediately concerned with the situation ... the crew was well trained and capable of holding their own with the best of them. The two Zeros, however, were quickly joined by six more ...

The air battle began about 0830, twenty miles northwest of Nauru, and lasted about 45 minutes. Top turret gunner Technical Sergeant Donald Martin later said, 'The way Captain Classen handled the ship in that fight was beautiful – I stood there and watched those babies come at us head on. You could see one of them kick his tail around to line up his guns on us. Then, when he'd almost get set, the Captain would stand us on our ear.'

Seven of the B-17's guns jammed during the fight, but the crew kept firing the remaining guns and claimed two Zeros. A cannon shell burst in the nose, wounding Lieutenants Robert Dorwart and Balfour Gibson, the navigator and bombardier. Copilot Lieutenant Ernest Ruiz was wounded in the legs by shrapnel, and everybody was nicked.

When the Zeros finally broke away to return to Nauru, *My Lovin' Dove* was about 800 miles northeast of Guadalcanal and in bad shape, with seven guns out of commission, two dead engines and three crew members wounded, although no one was seriously hurt. *My Lovin' Dove* was at 4,000ft but dropping fast, so the crew started to strip the aeroplane.

'To add to our immediate troubles, one of the two bomb bay tanks refused to salvo,' Classen remembers. 'The tank, which was still full of gas, hung half in the bomb bay and half out. The added drag of the open bomb doors was not helping any in maintaining altitude, but every effort to release this tank failed. We finally got rid of the weight by cutting the connecting hose with a knife, allowing the gas to drain out.'

The engineer, Martin, had to climb up on to the top of the right bomb-bay tank and push and kick it out. When it finally gave way he almost followed it out of the aircraft, only saving himself by clutching at fuel lines in the bomb bay and hauling himself back to safety. Classen continues:

> By this time the airplane had settled to about fifty feet and the white caps began to look mighty rough. However, the back end of the airplane had been stripped, the crew had moved forward into the radio compartment, and we began to hold our own against the force of gravity. As gasoline was consumed during the next two-hour period, decreasing our gross weight, we were successful in climbing to a more comfortable 800 feet ... we knew a ditching was inevitable due to an insufficient supply of gasoline. Before the fuel supply was exhausted, another engine decided that it could carry the burden no further and this ended our worries regarding the gas supply.
>
> The crew, having had two hours to prepare for this memorable event, were all ready when I rang the alarm bell alerting them for ditching. I had been growing more apprehensive as time went on and the window through which I planned to exit grew increasingly smaller. The airplane was turned into the wind and the final approach was begun.
>
> The crew, with the exception of Ruiz and myself, had assembled in the radio room ... the radio operator, Sergeant Jim Hunt, transmitted the final mission report, closed station, and assumed his position.
>
> Just before touchdown I noticed that the sea was running evenly spaced six-foot swells, which was better than I had hoped for. Holding the airplane off with what power I had available, I managed to time my approach and touched down on the top of one of these swells. Things must have been just right because we went in as graceful as could be expected. Upon contact, a great spray of water covered the windshield and I thought for a minute that we had gone straight down. I slammed open my window and made a hasty departure – head first – over the side. As I started to surface I contacted an obstruction which turned out to be the undersurface of the wing. After consuming about three quarts of sea water, I finally managed to swim out from under it and surfaced right behind the trailing edge.

The activity that was in progress on the top of the 'plane defies description. Emergency equipment, canteens, parachutes and people were coming out of the upper escape hatch simultaneously. The ball turret gunner, Cpl William Nichols, was running back and forth on the wing calling my name, believing that I was still in the cockpit. The raft release handles had been pulled after the forward movement of the 'plane had ceased and one raft was in the water fully inflated. The connecting cable on the other one had been shot in two and efforts were being made to open the compartment door from the outside. This was successfully accomplished; however, the CO_2 bottle was defective and failed to operate. By this time all crew members were in the water with the exception of those in the one serviceable raft. The airplane was sinking rapidly and only the tail remained visible above the surface of the water. As both rafts were tied to the airplane with a piece of parachute cord, we were becoming increasingly concerned about losing the collapsed one. Two of the crew had a hold of it and were trying desperately to break this connecting cord.

It was about this point that the airplane nosed down, the tail rising majestically out of the water in a final salute, and slid gently out of sight beneath the waves. The boys clinging to the deflated raft refused to let go and were pulled about twenty feet under water before the line finally broke. The saving of this raft, which we inflated immediately with a hand pump, undoubtedly saved the lives of at least half the crew because I hardly believe it possible that we could have all survived the next sixteen days without it.

Through this short, critical period the crew had performed in a commendable manner. The navigator, Captain Robert Dorwart, a calm and very unexcitable individual, had stepped off the wing of the airplane into the life raft, hardly getting his feet wet.

We were 600 miles from home base, afloat in a vast ocean, but safe for the moment ... I immediately became violently sick from the salt water I had swallowed and remained so for the rest of the day.

The Solomons are scattered over 600 miles, from Buka in the north to San Cristobal in the south, so the odds were in their favour if they could stay alive and afloat. Classen and his crew were at sea for 16 days before they finally sighted an island on the horizon. Classen continued:

The following morning about 0300 we crossed the reefs guarding the island and entered the quiet water of the lagoon. A few minutes later, weak and soaked to the skin, we were on the beach of an island which we later learned was one of the five islands of the Carteret group.

They found that another American, Delmar Wiley, a US Navy air gunner who had been shot down in a Grumman TBF Avenger, had been living for the past six months on another island in the group. Classen recalls:

> He had learned quite a bit of the native language. Wiley had not the slightest idea of our position, but pointed out a mountain peak visible on the distant horizon, which the natives called Buka. This clue was all we needed and we knew our position to be about fifty miles north of Bougainville, 400 miles inside Jap held territory.

Classen and his crew settled in for several weeks while he, Dorwart, Gibson and Wiley conceived and developed a plan to sail one of the native outrigger canoes the 150 miles to Choiseul. An initial attempt early in March was unsuccessful, and a second attempt also failed. On their third try they reached the northwest end of Choiseul in just three days. Continuing along the coast, they eventually made contact with Australian coastwatchers who arranged a PBY flying boat pick-up five days later. The rest of the crew was picked up from the Carterets a few days after that.

'Thus ended the 66-day mission, a period full of apprehension and of lessons learned the hard way,' concludes Classen.

My Lovin' Dove had hit the water at 1130 in the morning on 9 February. Classen rejoined his squadron on 13 April. There he could ponder the freshly painted Roll of Honour, listing those from the 72nd Squadron killed or missing in action. The name Captain Thomas J. Classen, in neat script, was right at the top.

What of the other B-17Fs in the South Pacific? *The Aztec's Curse* went on to fly with the 31st Bomb Squadron of the 5th Bomb Group. On 23 April 1943 Captain Leon Rockwell suffered brake failure on landing and ground-looped the aircraft. He says there was 'no damage until the tug knocked off the tail stinger'. The aircraft was destined for the boneyard. Exactly what happened to 41-24430 remains a mystery to this day. Assigned to the South Pacific in August 1942, it certainly got as far as New Zealand, but there the record ends. *Jezabel*, 41-24426 and 41-24535 all survived to return to the USA between July and November 1944.

The Ghost of Black Cat Pass

One of the most evocative relics in New Guinea is B-17E Flying Fortress 41-9234, lying on a hillside at the head of Black Cat Pass near Wau. For years this aircraft was a 'mystery' because it appeared to have Royal Air Force markings – roundels on her wings and fuselage, the British serial number FL461, and a camouflage scheme used by RAF maritime reconnaissance squadrons. But these markings were misleading, a trick of nature caused by the gradual effect of weathering over the years. The paint had been eroded in layers, and the B-17's wartime American markings had simply disappeared.

True enough, 41-9234 had originally been destined for Britain, and she was just one of 32 'Lend-Lease' B-17Es delivered to Cheyenne, Wyoming between the middle of May and very early June, 1942. These aircraft carried RAF markings and serial numbers, but retained their original Army Air Forces radio call numbers on their tails until they arrived in England, where these were simply painted over.

For reasons now clouded by time, three of these aircraft – 41-9196, 41-9234 and 41-9244 – did not leave for Britain, but instead were flown to Hamilton Field during the first week of August, then proceeded on to Hawaii and down to the Southwest Pacific, where they joined the 19th Bomb Group in Australia.

On 26 August 1942 41-9234 was one of the force of eight B-17s which made a low-level attack on a Japanese convoy at Milne Bay, on the southeastern tip of New Guinea. Lieutenant Jim Dieffenderfer, flying as copilot for Captain John Chiles on 41-9234 that day, recalls, 'We were supposed to assemble in an eight ship formation but due to darkness and weather never made it. When we got an airplane on each wing we headed for Milne Bay and got there in daylight ... Captain Clyde Webb was on our left wing ...'

Flying by dead reckoning, they let down through the gloom and found the convoy below them. With the ceiling down around 2,000ft the B-17s were given a murderous reception. Dieffenderfer says, 'Just before bomb drop we saw Webb get a direct hit in No.2 engine – he went over on his back and into the water, no sign of parachutes'. Webb's B-17, 41-24354, left a slick of orange fire which burned for ten minutes, and Chiles was also in trouble in 41-9234. Sergeant Wathen Cody, the flight engineer, recalled:

> We, the three of our B-17s got into firing range on our bomb run, all anti-aircraft guns on the shore and ships cut loose. The B-17 on our left got its left wing blown off and it went down, our 'plane was

getting hit. Our bombardier, Sergeant Earl Snyder, salvoed the bombs. Captain Chiles called the bombardier and no answer. So I went down to check. Lieutenant David Hirsch was bleeding badly all over, his face speckled with Plexiglas from the nose, big hole. His leg looked like it was blown off. Grabbed the first aid kit and Hirsch said take care of Snyder he's hurt worse than I am. Snyder was lying over the bomb sight with his hand on the bomb release handle, and when I got over him I could see a piece of jagged metal in his head, size about three inches around and about two inches deep in his head. So I went back to Hirsch and tied a tourniquet around his leg so he wouldn't bleed to death. Picked metal out of his face and arms. Then I pulled him up in the cockpit with us and laid him beside my turret.

About this time we were attacked by Zeros, we got in the clouds and got home, but our 'plane was all shot up.

Safely back at Mareeba, all of the crew except Snyder had survived what Cody calls, 'Our crew's first real bombing mission'. When they had arrived at Mareeba their original pilot had been assigned to Headquarters, and Jim Dieffenderfer says, 'Chiles woke me up in the middle of the night and told me to get the crew to the airplane, then he showed up to fly it ...'

As he walked away after returning, Cody remembers that the ground crews were counting the holes in 41-9234 and that 'This 'plane was painted white on the bottom and light blue on top ... blood ran out of the holes and the front of the 'plane was a terrible-looking mess'.

The blue B-17 was repaired and, assigned to the 28th Bomb Squadron, completed a reconnaissance mission on 5 September with Lieutenant Boris Zubko and his crew, and similar missions were flown on the following two days.

On 11 September 41-9234 was flown by Major Elbert Helton, the squadron commander, when he led five B-17s in an afternoon attack on two Japanese destroyers. Helton's bombs missed, but Lieutenant James Ellis in 41-2660 scored a direct hit on the stern of the destroyer *Yayoi*, which later sank.

Helton took 41-9234 on a mission against Buna airstrip on 12 September, and the aeroplane took part in a daylight Rabaul mission on 15 September. A week later Captain Jay Rousek flew 41-9234 to Seven Mile for a night mission against shipping in Rabaul Harbour, returning to Mareeba on 23 September.

On 5 October 41-9234, with eight other 28th Squadron B-17s, was airborne for a mission against Vunakanau and Lakunai, the Rabaul airstrips, but only three aircraft attacked. There are no records to show whether 41-9234 was one of them. Lieutenant Edward Habberstad failed to reach the target with 41-9234 on the big 9 October Rabaul mission, but Lieutenant Richard Hernlund took it over Rabaul in the early hours of 18 October.

On 23 October Lieutenant Walter Schmid and his crew were at Seven Mile to begin three days of armed reconnaissance missions, all in 41-9234 and all longer than ten hours, searching the sea lanes from morning until evening. The weary crew made the flight back from New Guinea to Mareeba in the morning of 26 October.

With Tonolei Harbour on Bougainville the target for 1 November, 41-9234's crew attacked a destroyer in the darkness, claiming a possible hit. Tonolei shipping was again the target on 13 November, when 41-9234 was part of a pre-dawn attack. That was the last mission of the 28th Bomb Squadron.

The battle-scarred B-17E was reassigned to the 43rd Bomb Group's 65th Bomb Squadron, and on 8 December 1942 she was in trouble again. The 65th attacked a force of Japanese destroyers, carrying troops to reinforce Buna and Gona, and 41-9234 was badly shot up. The official report stated that two of the crew were wounded and there were 75 holes through the aircraft, including hits in the main spar and hydraulic system. Turned over to the 61st Service Squadron on 12 December, 41-9234 was out of action until the second week of 1943.

During the first week of 1943 a Japanese convoy, heavily protected by fighters, had been sighted 50 miles east of Gasmata, heading for Lae. It was attacked repeatedly by Allied fighters and bombers, but on 8 January the harassed shipping reached New Guinea and unloaded about 4,000 troops. The B-17s were called upon to fly missions all day, and at 1000 the 63rd Squadron's Captain William Thompson, in *Panama Hattie*, took off from Port Moresby with Lieutenant Ray Dau, flying 41-9234, as his wing man. A third B-17 turned back shortly after take-off, but Thompson and Dau went on. It was the Dau crew's thirteenth mission.

The two aircraft reached the target around noon, fighting through a hornet's nest of Zeros. Lieutenant Albert Cole, Dau's bombardier, was hit in the cheek by a bullet which broke his jaw and ripped off the tip of his tongue. Dau offered to turn back, but Cole refused. On the bomb run anti-aircraft fire blew out the nose of the aircraft, and Cole was hit again, this time in the knees; the bomb sight protected the rest of his body. The bombs went away and Cole was trying to close the bomb-bay doors as Lieutenant Peter Hudec, the navigator, pulled him back out of the nose.

Flying through the heavy fire from guns on the ships and ashore, 41-9234 was hit by three bursts of anti-aircraft fire which knocked out the top turret, damaged controls and crippled both left engines. Sergeant Henry Bowen, the tail gunner, was hit by shrapnel and badly wounded. Then came a running battle with the Zeros that lasted about 30 minutes, Dau's gunners claiming three of the Japanese fighters.

With two engines out, Dau and his copilot, Lieutenant Donald Hoggan, were unable to climb or turn. Dau later said:

> We were headed up a small valley and couldn't get over the mountains. I knew it was just a matter of time, so I began looking for a soft place to set her down. We glided in on the side of a mountain at about 110 miles an hour, and as luck would have it, there were no trees – nothing but nice soft grass – so we slid along into a crash landing.

As the aircraft came to rest a fire broke out. When Cole heard someone shout 'Fire on board' he pulled himself to the nose and hurled himself out. The wounded flight engineer, Sergeant Lloyd Dumond, was tossed clear. Sergeant Bowen, already injured, was killed. Radio operator Sergeant Robert Albright was badly hurt. Lieutenant Hudec was able to extinguish the fire and luckily he and the rest of the crew were only cut and bruised.

A small party of Australians led by Corporal John Smith, with native carriers, made their way to the crash site and helped the Americans to Wau. The wounded were carried on litters and the party arrived about daybreak on 9 January. Cole was unconscious most of the time, and after his wounds were tended he was given Australian clothes. He was flown out of Wau in a Lockheed Hudson, and when he arrived at Port Moresby he was put into the Australian field hospital because of his borrowed uniform. Dumond had a similar experience.

Dau's radio operator, Albright, died six days later from his injuries. Albert Cole spent a couple of months in leg casts and completed his recovery in a hospital in Battle Creek, Michigan, his home state. Ray Dau completed his tour and returned to the United States in September 1943.

Blood and Sand

The enemy had reacted swiftly to the Torch landings on 8 November 1942, wasting no time in beginning the reinforcement of the twin cities of Tunis and Bizerte, on the North African coast. Bizerte in Northern Tunisia was strategically situated near the narrowest part of the Mediterranean. There the French had improved and fortified the outer harbour. Tunis, the Tunisian capital, was in the northeastern part of the country. Each city had an airfield protecting it; El Aouina for Tunis, Sidi Ahmed for Bizerte. Those two names, Tunis and Bizerte, dominated the bombers' target list for months to come, and the slugging match was long and bloody.

Lieutenant Colonel Paul Tibbets, flying *The Red Gremlin*, had led the first B-17 mission against Bizerte, when just six aeroplanes went in at 6,500ft on 16 November 1942. That had been a fairly informal little maximum effort. The B-17s had been fuelled using five-gallon cans of gasoline trucked to the aircraft and then passed up by hand to be emptied into the wing tanks. The bomb bays were loaded with British bombs. During November seven of the first eight missions flown by the B-17s of the 97th and 301st Bomb Groups were against these targets, and more than half of all the missions flown during the first three months. To the crews it quickly became known as the 'Milk Run'.

British ground forces had been in sight of Tunis on 28 November, but 15,000 reinforcements had enabled the enemy to counterattack successfully and force the Allies back. The ground war was temporarily deadlocked as both forces prepared for a decisive battle, but all plans were being stalled by the torrential rain.

Tunis and Bizerte got hot fast. By the second week of December Luftwaffe fighters were regularly rising up to defend the twin cities, and flak was intensifying to a point comparable with the tougher targets in Europe.

The B-17s had been flying from Tafaraoui, almost 600 miles from Bizerte and close to the limit of the tactical radius of the Flying Fortress. At Christmas 1942 the B-17s of the two groups moved up to a new field at Biskra, a palm-studded oasis shielded from the Saharan furnace by the Atlas mountains. The B-17s then came under the control of the newly-formed Fifth Bombardment Wing, commanded by Brigadier General Joseph Atkinson, a former 97th Group commander.

Biskra was a winter resort, where the officers occupied a tourist showplace which was reportedly where Charles Boyer and Marlene Dietrich, stars of the lurid early Technicolor romance 'Garden of Allah', had stayed during filming. Wing Headquarters was set up in the casino, where intelligence officers operated off the gaming tables.

The missions to Tunis and Bizerte became so regular that aircrew members have difficulty remembering which events occurred over which targets, and one B-17 pilot said that he 'never thought there was very much difference anyway'.

For the record, it was Tunis on February 1, 1943. Major Robert Coulter, commander of the 340th Bomb Squadron, was leading his unit and the rest of the 97th Group that day. Coulter decided to fly with Captain Jesse Wikle's crew, which meant that the regular copilot, Lieutenant John Balaban, was left at home. It was Balaban's lucky day.

Engine start was at 1110, and take-off 15 minutes later. One of Coulter's scheduled wing men had engine trouble before take-off, so Lieutenant Kendrick Bragg's *All American*, a spare from the 414th Bomb Squadron, filled the hole.

Delivered by Boeing on 28 June 1942, *All American* had been one of the original aircraft assigned to the 92nd Bomb Group at Bangor, Maine, and was flown to England by Lieutenant Frank Ward and his crew. Transferred to the 414th Bomb Squadron of the 97th Bomb Group on 24 August 1942, it was assigned to Lieutenant Kendrick R. Bragg and his crew. Bragg, from Savannah, Georgia, had been an outstanding full-back at Duke University and had played in the 1942 Rose Bowl game. The crew chose the name *All American*, and tail gunner Sergeant Sam Sarpolus personalized his section by stencilling 'It's more blessed to give than to receive' between his twin guns. Bragg flew *All American* on the early daylight missions from England, then on 20 November both aircraft and crew left Hurn, bound for Gibraltar and North Africa.

On 6 January 1943, in a letter to his family, Bragg summed up the situation this way; 'We bomb all day and get bombed most nights. I've been lucky with my ship in the air, but we park her for the night and Jerry fills her with holes before morning. This has really happened only twice, but twice too much.' The mission to Tunis on 1 February would prove just how lucky Bragg and his ship were.

Lieutenant Ralph Birk, navigator on Wikle's *Flaming Mayme*, recalled:

> We were briefed to join the 301st Group just north of the mountains and follow them – the target to be docks and shipping at Tunis and ... to make the bomb run from west to east. As we flew north, the 301st kept getting off to the left (according to our briefing) and I so advised Major Coulter ... it finally got to the point that it seemed as tho' they were heading for Bizerte, so the major told me to give him the word when we were directly west of our target, which I did – we then broke off from the 301st and proceeded as briefed – our fighter escort of course stayed with the 301st.
>
> Immediately after our bomb run, we passed underneath the 301st, who had apparently been briefed to make their run north to south – in short, someone must have fouled up. Anyway, we were unable to catch up with them and rejoin formation.
>
> Shortly thereafter, as we had taken up a southwesterly heading to return to base, Me 109s in line astern overtook us, flying out of range

and proceeded to get ahead and make a frontal attack. The leader fired, but missed us and as he was pulling out I was trying to get my right hand gun to bear on him – and so facing somewhat to the rear – the number two man was putting bullets into the nose – I heard them. The next thing I knew I was lying on the ceiling on my back held there by centrifugal pressure ...

It all happened too fast to tell, and nobody is sure exactly what happened. Lieutenant Tom White, navigator for Lieutenant Jack Gallup in *Superman*, says:

> My most vivid memory of all our missions to Bizerte or Tunis was seeing Wikle's 'plane go down. It appeared to be descending vertically, with the underside of the 'plane facing our 'plane. I saw smoke from all four engines, but it could have been normal exhaust ... most of the members of our crew had been with most of the members of Wikle's crew for many months, I think since training in Sarasota, Florida, and they were among our closest friends ... I remember I was suddenly praying for Wikle's crew which surprised me completely, since I was in no way a religious man.

Inside *Flaming Mayme*, Ralph Birk was forcing himself over on to his stomach so that he could get to the tunnel, when something hit him on the head. As he noted, 'That's all I knew until I woke up falling through the air all by myself. I did have presence of mind enough to look around to see if I was clear before pulling, but wasn't smart enough to make a delayed drop ... very shortly after I hit I was captured, only some five miles or so from our lines.'

Tail gunner Sergeant Robert Knight had been trapped. After the B–17 had broken apart the rear section spun, throwing him back by his guns every time he was nearly free. He finally got out just a few hundred feet from the ground. Lieutenant Alfred Blair, the bombardier, also survived, wounded by shrapnel from a cannon shell which had hit his bomb sight.

Another drama was unfolding in *All American*. Navigator Lieutenant Harry Nuessle had been jotting down cryptic notes in his log:

> I.F.F. set – 13:08 ... 13:11½ 1st flak bursts extremely accurate one four-gun flak battery definitely located about 2 mi S. of City ... Camera on – 13:12 ... Bombs Away 13:13 ... Camera off – 13:13:10 (turned to avoid flak) ... 13:18 ship 124477 fired at 190 – saw small piece fly from E/A, began to smoke as it pulled away
>
> About 13:25 ME 109 made head on attack – Passed within inches of ship doing ??? damage

Harry Nuessle expanded on this two days later, in a letter to his brother:

Long after we had left the target, and after having sustained two different attacks by ships coming out of the sun, we saw two unidentified 'planes climbing alongside of us about two miles to the right. They continued well in front of us and suddenly cut in to attack – one directly at the nose of the lead ship, one at us. Burbridge the bombardier covered the one coming at us with the nose gun; I took the other with the gun 45 degrees out the side of the nose. It was the first time we had ever experienced this sort of attack – an infrequent tactic due to the extremely high rate of closure between ships coming head-on. Between my own fire and fire from the lead ship, the Jerry going for the latter was last seen smoking off in the distance. Meanwhile I could see this other Joe coming at us, his wings looking as though they were afire from his flaming guns. About 300 yards out he began to roll over in order to be able to pull down and away after his attack – but somewhere about half way around, either Burbridge's fire or fire from the lead ship must have gotten the pilot or disabled the 'plane because he never completed his intended roll and rapid pass under our ship – for one horrible instant he was right there inches in front and above us – I ducked instinctively, though God knows had he hit us head on no amount of ducking would have saved any of us. But he passed over us with a distinctly audible swoosh followed by a tremendous jar and a whoomp! Our 'plane began to dive, and I reached for my 'chute ...

Bombardier Lieutenant Ralph Burbridge, up front with Nuessle, remembers:

Sitting in the nose at the 0.30 calibre gun, I could see him open up with his wing guns and cannon ... I was firing at it all the way ... it was a Messerschmitt 109, single engine. I figure one of us must have killed the pilot because the 'plane crashed right into us – we were a good target that close. He just disintegrated, the others told me later. When we hit, our 'plane almost stood up on its tail. Then we went down at a very sharp angle. I thought to myself, boy, this is it.

In the cockpit, Lieutenant Kendrick Bragg and co-pilot Lieutenant Godfrey Engel had been watching enemy fighters far to the north, streaking along in the same direction. They were out of range and harmless for the moment, but Bragg told his gunners to keep an eye on them. Then he noticed the top turret on Coulter's aeroplane swing around toward the nose of *Flaming Mayme*. Bragg then looked again at the enemy fighters. He recalled:

They had suddenly turned and were racing toward us. The two small specks increased rapidly in size as they came nearer ... on they came, one 'plane about thirty seconds behind the other, ready for a one-two punch ... we were in a tight formation now with Coulter. He began a slight dive to avoid the oncoming fighters and I followed. They patterned us, managing to stay about level with us. In a split second they were in shooting range and our forward gunners opened fire. Brilliant tracer bullets flew in both directions, as though a score of boys were fighting it out with Roman candles. The first attacker half-rolled onto our flight to make a quick getaway. As he did I saw Coulter's bomber burst into smoke and start earthward in an uncontrollable spiral.

The second enemy fighter was now our primary concern. As he half-rolled out in front of us and blazed away with all his guns our gunners found the mark ... he was at about 300 yards when his guns stopped, but he kept coming straight in ... all our forward guns opened up to turn him but evidently the pilot had been killed ...

I rammed the controls forward in a violent attempt to avoid collision. The rate of closure of the two 'planes was close to 600 miles an hour and my action seemed sluggish. I flinched as the fighter passed inches over my head and then I felt a slight thud like a coughing engine. I checked the engines and controls. The trim tabs were not working. I tried to level the *All American* but she insisted on climbing. It was only the pressure from knees and hands that I was able to hold her in anything like a straight line. Engel tried his controls. He got the same reaction, but we found that by throttling back the engines we could keep her on a fairly even keel. I tried to call the pilot of the lead 'plane which had gone down only a moment before, but there was no answer ...

The top turret gunner, Technical Sergeant Joe James, had broken in on the intercom with a masterpiece of understatement; 'Sir, we've received some damage in the tail section'. Someone else said something about a hole you could drive a jeep through, and the crew remember somebody repeating 'You could drive a jeep through that hole' all the way home. Turning the controls over to Engel, Bragg unbuckled his harness and went back to the rear of the aircraft.

Lieutenant Jack Davenport was the pilot of *Flying Flit Gun*, a B-17 which had been christened by *Life* photographer Margaret Bourke-White. He had been scheduled to fly on Coulter's left wing, but when they started the motors there had been an oil-pressure problem with the right inboard engine. Davenport shut the engines down and his crew chief, John Vlad, quickly found and fixed the fault. As Davenport recalled:

We scrambled off and caught up in about twenty minutes, but a standby spare from the 414th was in our spot, so we filled in the diamond as the seventh ship of the 340th. We had a nice view.

About five minutes after "bombs away" it was fighters at one o'clock. Just two Me 109s I believe, and they attacked in tandem from about 12:30 ... I can remember seeing a great deal of debris going by my window and pulling up slightly. Strangely, after this encounter, I don't remember seeing a single airplane but Bragg's, and we got on his left wing and came home ... Bragg was holding his speed at about 140; when he tried to increase it the sharp ragged point of the dorsal fin vibrated violently side to side and we prudently loosened our position and flew a little higher.

What had happened? German records reveal that the *Freya* radar at Tunis picked up the American formation, estimated to be twenty B-17s escorted by twenty Lightnings, at 1225, and between 1310 and 1320 33 German fighters rose to meet them. They comprised nineteen Messerschmitt Bf 109s from Jagdgeschwader 53, based at El Aouina, and fourteen Focke-Wulf Fw 190s. Although not proven, it seems likely that the pilot of the aircraft which hit *All American* was Feldwebel Erich Paczia of 6/JG 53, the only German pilot lost that day, who was merely listed as 'missing in the Pont-du-Fahs area'.

Oberleutnant Julius Meimberg, flying with 1/JG 53, was the only Bf 109 pilot to claim a B-17 kill, and may be the pilot who downed *Flaming Mayme*. Meimberg, a veteran of battles over France, was ultimately credited with more than 50 victories. His report is as inconclusive as other accounts. He made a head-on attack on a formation of about a dozen B-17s. Selecting the lead bomber as his target, he completed his attack, but return fire from the B-17s set his fighter on fire, making the cockpit a 'sea of flames'. Meimberg baled out near Pont-du-Fahs and landed safely with a badly burned hand and other injuries. All of the incidents occured in the vicinity of Pont-du-Fahs, between Tunis and Biskra. If it was Erich Paczia who flew into *All American*, he was probably dead or badly wounded, as he was a skilled and experienced pilot with sixteen victories to his credit.

In *All American*, Kendrick Bragg remembered:

As I opened the door of the radio compartment and looked back into the fuselage I was stunned. A torn mass of metal greeted my eyes. Wires were dangling and sheets of metal were flapping as the air rushed through the torn wreckage. Three-fourths of the 'plane had been cut completely through by the enemy fighter and a large piece of the wing of the Me 109 was still lodged in the tail of our 'plane ... It left our tail section hanging on by a few slender spars and a narrow strip of metallic skin.

Crawling along that narrow strip was Sam Sarpolus, the tail gunner, bringing with him four gun brushes, his parachute, and Bragg's jacket. He'd left four gas masks, remembering later 'I looked at them a minute and thought the hell with them'. Bragg continued:

> I climbed into the upper turret to see the damage from the outside. The tail section was swinging as much as a foot and a half out of line with the front of the 'plane. The horizontal stabilizer on the left was gone completely and the rear third of the 'plane seemed to be trying to hang on for dear life.
>
> We were now out of danger of enemy action so I called the crew to assemble in the radio compartment. I explained our situation to them as I saw it. Our 'plane was under limited control, beneath us was the African jungle, steep mountains and enemy territory. If we stayed with our 'plane our chances of survival depended upon how long the tail and fuselage could hold together. If she broke apart, the two tumbling parts might make it impossible for us to free ourselves from the falling 'plane. I was going to attempt to ride her down, but they could decide, each man for himself, what was best for him to do. They elected to stay ... ready to abandon ship upon signal from the pilot's cabin. Then I prayed I'd never have to ring the signal bell.

All American had lost about half of her horizontal stabilizer surface in the collision, and Bragg had no way of knowing at what air speed his partial tail might stall on approach and landing. He made several 'simulated landings' at altitude, but noted no difference.

> As we neared the field we fired three emergency flares, then we circled at 2,000 feet while the other 'planes in our formation made their landings and cleared the runways. We could see the alert crews, ambulances and crash trucks making ready for us. Without radio contact with the field we had to wait for the signal that all was clear and ready for us. When we got the signal, I lowered the landing gear and flaps to test the reaction of *All American*. They seemed to go reasonably well, considering.
>
> We now had two alternatives. We could attempt a landing or we could bale out over the field and let the 'plane fly alone until she crashed – always a dangerous thing to do. I had made up my mind to set her down. She had brought us safely through so far; I knew she would complete her mission. The crew decided to ride her down too. A green flare from the field signalled that all was clear for our attempt at a landing.
>
> I made a long careful approach to the strip with partial power until the front wheels touched the levelled earth and I could feel the grating as she dragged without a tail wheel along the desert sands. She came to a stop and I ordered the copilot to cut the engines. We were home.

The ambulance had raced after the landing B-17, but Bragg laconically said, 'No business, Doc'.

There was an unreal quality to those first minutes of realization that they had got through it in one piece. Sergeant Elton Conda was not a regular member of Bragg's crew, but had flown as ball turret gunner that day. When Bragg had asked him if he would fill in, Conda had flippantly asked, 'Can you fly?'.

The people at the 97th's field were duly impressed. Legend has it that when three sightseers crawled inside the fuselage it groaned and finally broke in two. But it was the photo taken by Lieutenant Charles Cutforth, navigator on *Flying Flit Gun*, which told the story to the world. With a keen sense of history, Harry Nuessle mailed his small print of the picture home with a plea to the censor: 'Should there be some law, rule, or regulation against sending the picture below to my wife, please seal the flap above and return – it is an unduplicatable shot and one I would hate to lose'.

The centre rear section of *All American* was removed and dumped unceremoniously in the desert. It was replaced by a matching section from another crippled Fortress in the Biskra boneyard, maybe *Little Eva*, *Special Delivery* or *Queen Bee-17*. This work took the 50th Service Squadron nearly three months, and the repaired aircraft was then assigned to the 353rd Squadron of the 301st Bomb Group. The lucky ground crew chief was M/Sergeant Virgil E. 'Hock' Annala. He said:

> For all intents and purposes the marriage of the forward section and the after section made her look like a B-17. The flight characteristics were something else. She had become loaded with desert sand in every nook and cranny and every opening or port. Initially on run-up we had to open the pilot and copilot sliding windows because the sand and grit sifted down out of the overhead so that it was difficult to see the instruments. By using a vacuum cleaner and doing repeated run-ups, the sand quit sifting out of the headliner, however the wings were a different story. We opened every opening and vacuumed as far as the hose would reach. We did this constantly. A terrific amount of sand was disposed of in this manner.

Ed Ware, Annala's assistant, only ever knew *All American* by the last three digits of her serial number, 41-24406. He adds:

> We thought we would never get 406 into flying shape as she had been cannibalized while being repaired ... But she was a lot of trouble due to scarcity of parts to get her combat ready. When we were first assigned 406 I recall the windshield was cracked and that held up combat status for some time, along with a strut which didn't want to stay up, then one of the superchargers gave us a lot of trouble.
>
> On the first flight we got 406 on, the interphone cut out at 11,000 feet, there was trouble with generators, brakes failed and rpm's acting

strangely ... We always felt the flight crews believed her to be jinxed.

Annala agrees; 'Her service with the 301st in a combat role was short-lived. She was extremely slow and plagued with problems.'

Official 301st Group records show that the aircraft attempted five missions, with an 'Early Return' on two, those of 14 and 17 April. Completed missions were to Palermo on 16 April and again two days later. The last combat mission was to Bo Rizzo on 10 May 1943. After that final mission Ed Ware drily noted in his diary the 'Historic event, #406 completed another mission on May 10th but tailguns and upper turret were out. Supercharger regulators #2 and #4 engines were erratic. These we replaced ...'

Annala concludes; 'I suppose the combat crews regarded her as a Jonah of sorts and a decision was made to remove all turrets, armour plate and guns and use her as a utility aircraft. After refurbishing she was still slow.' A number of mechanics, including Ed Ware, got their first taste of being a crew chief on the old veteran before she was finally salvaged overseas in March 1945.

Ides of March

Buzz King was reputed to be the fastest aircraft in her squadron. That was always a desirable attribute, particularly in the South Pacific, where single B-17s were called on to fly long, lonely search missions deep into Japanese-occupied territory.

A B-17E, *Buzz King* was originally delivered to the Army Air Forces on 18 April 1942 and assigned to the 303rd Bomb Group at Boise, Idaho, where it was briefly used as a trainer. In early June, when flown to Hawaii, it became one of the nine original B-17Es of the 98th Bomb Squadron, 11th Bomb Group. It departed Hickam on 17 July, piloted by Lieutenant Vincent Crane, and arrived at Plaines des Gaiacs, New Caledonia, four days later.

Although most of its early missions were the long 'security searches', this monotony was occasionally broken. When an enemy naval force was sighted on 13 September 1942 by Lieutenant William Cope in *Madame-X*, an attack mission was planned for the next day. Captain Walter Lucas in *The Skipper* and Lieutenant Eugene Thompson in *Buzz King* attacked the force, which was described as 'two battleships, four heavy cruisers, three light cruisers, six destroyers and two transports'. Considering the size of the enemy force, the bombing was carried out at the comparatively low altitude of 10,000ft, but both aircraft sustained only slight damage from the intense fire put up by the warships, and there were no casualties. They claimed possible hits on the two battleships.

On 25 September *Buzz King*, with Lieutenant Cecil Durbin and his crew, scored a direct hit from 14,000ft on a Japanese cruiser off the southeastern end of Bougainville. As they withdrew they were attacked by fifteen enemy aircraft, and the gunners accounted for three floatplane fighters – two Rufes and a Dave. *Buzz King* 'returned with fuselage unmussed', according to the 98th Bomb Squadron's War Diary.

The 11th Group's B-17Es were heavily armed after their crews had experienced the problem of head-on attacks by enemy fighters. To counter this, General Millard Harmon, the theatre commander, had requested modification of all of his B-17s to a pattern completed on one of his heavy bombers by the Cheyenne Modification Center. This involved installing two 0.50 calibre nose guns and another in the radio compartment, together with new mounts for the waist guns and larger waist ammunition boxes to provide flexible feed. B-17s such as *Buzz King* bristled with fourteen machine guns.

In the middle of October *Buzz King* was sidelined by a damaged wing. So far that month it had flown five security searches, two of them of more than ten hours' duration, but no tactical missions.

Towards the end of October General Harmon could ponder a statistical analysis that showed that 78 per cent of the 11th Bomb Group's total effort was devoted to reconnaissance work, which left little time for strike missions. The B-17s were just too good at the job. He recommended that in future no more than 25 per cent of the total heavy bomber effort should be devoted to reconnaissance, with other types of aircraft taking over most of the task.

Buzz King, piloted by Lieutenant Edwin McAnelly, was one of the force of fifteen B-17s which attacked Japanese transports steaming toward Guadalcanal on 14 November during the frantic, decisive battles for the island. The crew claimed a direct hit and near misses on a transport. They flew a similar mission the following day.

Captain Walter Lucas and *Buzz King*, along with Lieutenant Cecil Durbin in *Omar Khayyam* and Lieutenant Roy Morgan in *Galloping Gus*, took part in the 18 November attack on shipping in Tonolei Harbour led by Colonel 'Blondie' Saunders. All three 98th Squadron aircraft claimed direct hits and near misses on a cargo vessel with their 1,000lb armour-piercing bombs. The bombers were credited with the destruction of six Zeros, Lucas's gunners claiming three of them.

Over the next several months the routine continued, with attacks on the new Japanese airfield at Munda on New Georgia, and strikes against shipping targets around Bougainville. When the 11th Bomb Group moved back to Hawaii in February 1943, its B-17s were passed on to the 5th Bomb Group. *Buzz King* was assigned to Major George Glober's 31st Bombardment Squadron, which operated more or less independently, mounting small night attacks against targets such as Kahili, Ballale, Vila and Munda. One of the 31st's pilots, Captain James Carroll, developed a lasting affection for *Buzz King*, the old B-17E with the ten Japanese flags, twelve little bombs and three ship silhouettes painted on its nose. On 14 March 1943 it was one of nine B-17s ordered to Guadalcanal for 'two or three weeks of prolonged night striking', with Jim Carroll piloting.

Two days later Carroll with *Buzz King* joined Major Glober in *Alley-Oop* for a special mission for which each aircraft was armed with eight 500lb bombs and three new M-26 flares. Their job was to test these new 800,000-candlepower flares to see if they would light up a target sufficiently for accurate bombing, and also diminish the blinding effect of enemy searchlights. Both aircraft made four passes each over the target, Kahili airfield, through heavy flak. The two B-17s were hit by shrapnel but nobody was hurt.

In the evening of 20 March another bold mission took shape, with the 5th Bomb Group commander, Colonel Marion Unruh, leading in *Goonie*. Jim Carroll was to lead one flight of three aircraft, in a plan he thought was 'exquisite in its simplicity'. Nine B-17s and nine 307th Bomb Group B-24 Liberators, their bomb bays full of frag clusters, would parade over Kahili airfield on Bougainville to attract the attention of the searchlights, anti-aircraft positions and night fighters. Meanwhile, US Navy and Marine Corps TBF Avengers would slip in at 1,500ft to mine nearby Shortland Harbour. Jim Carroll remembers:

Preliminaries completed, I checked the magnetos and taxied out to take-off position. With brakes locked, I moved prop and throttle controls to full power position and released the brakes. Ole 124 first trundled, then gracefully lifted off the Marston matting, heading out into the bay towards Tulagi. With gear up, I throttled back to 85 per cent power and turned to a westerly heading for climb-out. Target for tonight was about two hours westerly.

At altitude, I throttled back to 70 per cent power for cruise. Lieutenant Virgil Shepperd, my copilot, and Sergeant Robert Knapp, the flight engineer, synchronized the props to take out the beat. With a flashlight they shadowed the prop arcs to visually reduce the uneven beat to nil, else it would drive the whole crew nutty. En route, chatter was muted. The crew maintained radio silence. Each crew member double-checked his position then settled down to a relaxed alert: relaxed body, alert mind. Alert to any intrusion into the space of the *Buzz King*.

The sky was clear except for a few scattered white fair-weather cumulus clouds. Target areas were also expected to be clear. It was not always thus. Sometimes a crew logged a lot of instrument time getting a mission accomplished. It rained a lot; March weather in the Solomon Islands was always capricious. Also, all of that land-water interface created local weather conditions. Occasionally, the primary target was socked in. Then bombers dropped their bomb load on an alternate target, often Munda. But not tonight. The Southern Cross perched on Ole 124's left wingtip, looked close enough to touch ... The weather was idyllic.

Actually, on a clear night, the route to Kahili from Guadalcanal is direct and rather pretty. Just head out about 315 degrees, can't miss. Just beneath *Buzz King* is the New Georgia Sound, "The Slot" of Japanese warship fame. To our left resides the New Georgia group of islands including Munda and Kolombangara. To starboard loom the islands of Santa Isabel, Choiseul, and Malaita (then rumoured to be the last stronghold of cannibalism – no water landings near there). Dead ahead lay the island of Bougainville, on whose southeastern tip lay the Japanese base of Kahili, whose main runway pointed to Shortland Harbour. Flanking Shortland are the islands of Fauro, Ballale and the Treasuries.

Ole 124 tracked her flight mates by the blue exhaust from the turbo-superchargers. Also, the lead 'plane could be silhouetted against the night sky. And we wondered – how visible was the *Buzz King* with her big tail to Japanese night fighters?

Our crew had flown her enough that we regarded her as our personal aircraft. Whenever we had a choice, we chose Ole 124. She was a proud member of her clan, a pilot's airplane. Easy on the controls, she would lift off on takeoff, not wait to be manhandled or dragged off. She was eager to fly. In flight she was "steady as she goes". She held straight and level flight without autopilot (which did not always work). Some 'planes hunted or wallowed from side to side or up and down. Not the *Buzz King* – she was a dream boat: no slip, no skid.

We, her crew, knew unquestionably that if the going got rough, the *Buzz King* would bring us home – on four engines, or three, or even two, or even on one.

"Treasury Islands dead ahead" sang out the navigator, Lieutenant Fred Sellars. The Treasuries were the Initial Point for assaults on Kahili. Over them we could assemble, join up, or calculate our times over the target. Tonight, the *Buzz King* was not the first to arrive. The main event was in full progress. The B-17 ahead of her was in the full grips of the searchlights. Would he survive? We could see the black bursts of the anti-aircraft and the searching tracers. No night fighters in evidence, yet. Night fighters generated horizontal tracers.

Major George Glober in *Alley-Oop* led them into the target. The operation was timed to the second, so that each aeroplane would be over Kahili for nine minutes, conspicuously displayed to draw all enemy fire and to hold the enemy's attention.

Ole 124 was programmed to phase in just as the preceding B-17 was phasing out. At 150 miles per hour she covered two and a half miles per minute. About two minutes took us out of the effective target area into the rain forest beyond. Nine minutes straight and level took the aircraft twenty-two and a half miles – too far. Most simple were timed dog legs, that is, out two minutes, then back two minutes; or timed turns at two minutes for a 360-degree turn.

Altitude had been preassigned. No collisions over the target area, please! Even a near miss would be distracting. If Ole 124 arrives over the target too soon, she gets in the way of the preceding B-17, too late and the Jap gunners would wise up to the dual operation and go after the TBFs. Those Navy and Marine TBF pilots were gutsy guys. They were sitting ducks even more than were the B-17s. The TBFs were very vulnerable at 1,500ft, and not much defence. If a searchlight picked one up he was in big trouble. Ole 124 planned to keep those searchlights preoccupied.

Our moment approached: six hours of flying for nine minutes of action. But those nine minutes promised to be enough to last out the night. Shepperd counted down "Ten, nine, eight ... We're on!" Sellars, now manning the nose gun, stood up and bowed: "Gentlemen! We are now harassing the Jap!", he proclaimed. The

Right: Pilot Officer Freddie Stokes and 'Digger' Spademan examine the battle damage to AN518 after the running fight with Bf 110s on 22 February 1942. The inflatable dinghies were lost when the stowage lockers (behind Spademan's shoulder) were hit. (F. Stokes)

Below: AN518 lands at LG05 after the abortive sortie to Navarino Bay. (F. Stokes)

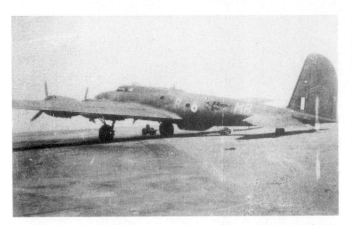

Left: AN518 wearing the markings of No. 220 Squadron detachment shortly before the flight to India. (Frank Taylor)

Right: *Suzy-Q* and her crew – Kiger, Hardison, Stripling, Geckeler, Irons, Fesmire and Bostwick – reunited at Boeing Field in February 1943. (Boeing)

Left: Captain Kenneth Casper crash-landed *The Daylight Ltd.* while returning from the 26 August 1942 Milne Bay mission. (Bud Fletcher)

Bottom left: *Tojo's Physic* was decapitated on Horn Island on 27 July 1942. (RAAF)

Below: The majestic *Chief Seattle* over Washington. (Boeing)

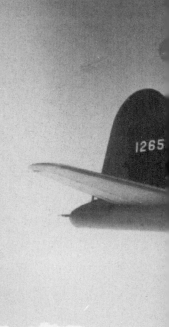

Top: *The Aztec's Curse* after attacking Gizo Island, south of Vella Lavella, on 5 October 1942. (Albert Thom)

Above: Derelict on Guadalcanal, 41-24528 was a victim of the Japanese battleships on the night of 13 October 1942. (Joe Voellmeck)

Left: The remains of 41-9234, smashed against a steep hillside near the head of Black Cat Pass. (Janice Olson)

Above: *All American* comes home from Tunis. (Charles C. Cutforth)

Below: The 97th Bomb Group's *Superman*, flown by Lieutenant John Gallup. (USAF)

Above: *Buzz King*, the fastest aeroplane in the 98th Bomb Squadron. (Phil Gudenschwager Collection)

Left: *Buzz King*'s nose displays her early record with the 11th Bomb Group. (Gudenschwager)

Below left: Sergeant Gerald Bainter at the twin guns mounted above *Buzz King*'s radio room. (Jim Carroll)

Top right: 5th Air Force commander General George Kenney shakes hands with the crew of *Cap'n & The Kids* after the successful parachute invasion of Nadzab, New Guinea. (Kenney)

Right: Sergeant Charles Cole, crew chief, with General Robert Eichelberger's *Miss Em*. (Cole)

Left: The 'official' ceremony in which the selected crew of *Memphis Belle* were presented to Lieutenant General Jacob Devers, senior US military commander in the European Theater of Operations, before the bomber's return to America. Major General Ira Eaker, the 8th Air Force chief, looks on as Devers congratulates Captain Robert Morgan. Crew members lined up for the cameras at Bovingdon on 9 June 1943 are, from the left, Sergeants John Quinlan, Clarence Winchell, Casimer Nastal, Cecil Scott, Robert Hanson and Harold Lock. Lieutenants Vincent Evans, Charles Leighton and James Verinus make up the rest of the line. (USAAF)

Below left: The bulldozed revetments at Seven Mile Strip, Port Moresby, home of the 43rd Bomb Group. (Signal Corps)

Above: Refuelling the 19th Bomb Group's *Blitz Buggy* in a partly completed hangar at Mareeba, northern Australia. (Conrad Marvel)

Below: *The Old Man* after tangling with Japanese fighters over Gasmata on 8 March 1943. (Signal Corps)

Above: Shell cases litter the waist section of *The Old Man*, 8 March 1943. (Signal Corps)

Left: Lieutenant Harry Staley, the man who spent more time than any other in *Black Jack*'s cockpit. (Staley)

Right: *Black Jack*, ditched off New Guinea on 11 July 1943 and finally discovered, totally intact, 43 years later. (Bob Halstead)

Centre right: *Black Jack*'s cockpit after more than 40 years in the deep, warm waters off New Guinea. (Richard Leahy)

Below: *Black Jack*'s crew safely back at Seven Mile: Ralph De Loach in his sarong, to his left Charles Shaver and on his right James Peterson and Herman Dias, wearing the leather jacket. In front are Paul Blasewitz with the cigarette and George Prezioso. Joe Moore took the photograph. (De Loach)

Left: Lieutenant John 'Red' Morgan beside a B-17 at Alconbury in the summer of 1943. (USAAF)

Below: Sergeant George Gronhe, a member of the dismantling crew, examines a cannon-shell hole in the wing root of the wreck that was *Patches*. (USAAF)

Right: Outer wing sections and engines removed, the battered remains of *Patches* rest at Boxted three weeks after the Kassel mission. Corporal John N. Bell looks at one of the many cannon-shell perforations. (USAAF)

Lower right: A crew poses against the tail of *Tinker Toy* at Ridgewell on 1 September 1943. There is a 'flak patch' in the aircraft's number. (USAAF)

Left: Six of the original Ball Boys aircraft. *Screw Ball*, one of the survivors, has a unique form of mission-completed symbol, a miniature form of the screw-through-a-ball insignia. (Via Ken Harbour)

Right: Two 2,000lb bombs being manoeuvred under *Hell's Angels* on 16 July 1943. At this time the aircraft had completed 31 missions, and its gunners were credited with six enemy fighters shot down. (USAAF)

Centre right: *Knock-Out Dropper* on its Molesworth hardstanding three days before flying its 50th combat mission. The 427th Bomb Squadron's S-for-Sugar, one of the runners-up, with 47 missions completed, is the aircraft in flight on the extreme right of the photograph. (USAAF)

Below: A hangar crew at work on *The Duchess* after it had reached its 50th mission in January 1944. The 8th Air Force's first Medal of Honor was a posthumous award to a bombardier who flew and died in the nose of this Fortress. (USAAF)

Right: Jabez Churchill (left) and Billy Cely peer through one of the gaping holes in *Frenesi*'s wings. (USAAF)

Right: A 20mm cannon shell was responsible for removing most of the right elevator on *Frenesi* on 11 January 1944. (USAAF)

Right: The left side of the nose after the 11 January battle, with the skin blasted in several places by cannon shells and bullets. The light-coloured patch is a repair to a hole that *Frenesi* sustained on an earlier mission. (USAAF)

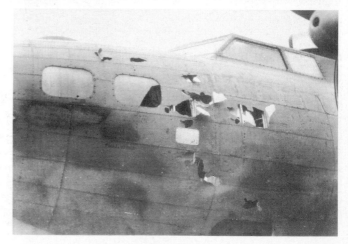

searchlights responded by hitting him full bore with their piercing beams. The bombardier, Lieutenant Nick Milos, began tracking through his bomb sight. Many likely looking bomb targets began to show up.

The glare of the searchlights was very uncomfortable and a bit unnerving. We felt very exposed. Once locked on, the lights were tough to shake; they stayed with us, no escape. The lights were blinding, even at altitude. It was almost impossible not to look out and down, especially in a left turn. Here I was looking out and down to see how the TBFs were doing and whammo! The lights hit me square in the face, completely blinding me, temporarily. Disorientation degenerated to vertigo. *Buzz King* did a wing over. "Take over, Virg! I can't see!", I yelled. We lost 5,000ft before Shepperd straightened things out. Scary, those searchlights.

Tonight the Jap gunners were confused. The mission plan worked wondrous well, the TBFs were having a free run. The B–17s were getting all of the attention, as planned. Early on, the anti-aircraft was wildly inaccurate. As the decoy run progressed, the bursts came closer and closer. Black puffs were appearing right off the wing tip.

The last twenty seconds of our sojourn was the bombing run and Nick Milos was in control of the aircraft. He needed straight and level for accuracy in controlling the bomb drop. Those last few seconds were interminably long. Finally: "Bombs away!" he bellowed as he released his tension along with the bombs. Mission accomplished! Ole 124 leaped upwards from the lightened load. She then hit a steep descending bank to lose the anti-aircraft and made preparations to "get the hell out of here!".

The bomb release also eased the tensions in the crew. There resulted a lot of chatter, a sort of victory dance.

The timing had to be precise, and it was ... the raid was executed to the second, each bomber conspicuously displaying itself for exactly nine minutes above Kahili aerodrome. It was a nice bonus that all bombs hit in the target area, setting fires visible for a distance of 40 miles.

The trip home featured clear skies with the occasional tip of a pretty white cumulus cloud. The Southern Cross smiled off our right wing. The euphoria slowly dissipated to the "relaxed" alert status. No snoozing yet. Guns remained armed. Enemy night fighters were still a possibility. Besides, we had to bring our big beautiful *Buzz King* back to her aerie to land and to rest up. And – What of Washing Machine Charlie? The night was clear; would he be waiting our return? At night, a landing aircraft needs guiding lights which make an inviting target for a marauding bogey. In such an event, the landing friendly circles helplessly in the bay until the bogey departs.

But not tonight. Ole 124 kissed the runway with a hardly noticeable three pointer and taxied to her bunker. The flight crew tended to her needs, then turned her over to the tender loving care of the maintenance crew. Then debriefing and repose. The night was spent and so was the crew – and tomorrow was a repeat performance.

Colonel Unruh's *Goonie*, hit by anti-aircraft fire, had a runaway engine. It was ditched close to the Russell Islands, where all ten men were picked up the next morning. Everyone else returned safely.

The next night's mission, an exact duplicate, again went off without a hitch. With the exception of *Goonie*, no aircraft were lost to any causes on either night. It was a neat little combined operation.

Guadalcanal had been 'secure' since 9 February, but Japanese aircraft continued to carry out small night raids, of mainly nuisance value. These aircraft had become known as 'Washing Machine Charlies' because of the intentionally discordant sound of their engines. On the night of 23 March *Buzz King* was still on Guadalcanal, loaded with bombs for yet another Kahili mission the next day. Jim Carroll recalls:

> Washing Machine Charlie was not to be denied. His bomb struck the *Buzz King* amidships and triggered her bomb load, which ignited her fuel load. She disappeared in one magnificent swoosh!, creating a largish hole on the spot she had occupied. The blast created a hole much more commodious than needed to inter her scattered remains. Salvage was nil.

Well, almost nil. Carroll's camera, an Argus C-3 with a roll of precious colour film, partly exposed, was found. The camera was past saving, but the film was retrieved and processed. Only two prints could be made – one showed *Buzz King*'s left wing and the coast of Malaita, the other was 'weird superimposures, forged in the maw of that explosion'.

So, as Carroll laments, 'Ole 124, she weren't no more!'.

Old Soldier

When the B-17s in the Southwest Pacific were finally 'retired' in late 1943, old *Cap'n & The Kids* had already flown more than 80 combat missions. That was only the beginning. She had left the Boeing factory on 11 June 1942, the 14th of the new model B-17F Flying Fortresses. After final modifications she was flown to Australia by Lieutenant James Murphy, and on 12 August 1942 she became one of the first aircraft assigned to the 63rd Bomb Squadron. The new aircraft and their crews were immediately attached to the 435th Bomb Squadron of the 19th Bomb Group at Townsville, for 'training and indoctrination'.

The 63rd was ready to fly its first independent operation on 14 September 1942, and by then Captain Edward W. Scott and his crew had formed an association with 41-24353, nicknamed *Cap'n & The Kids*. Scott, from Hollandale, Mississippi, had been with the 6th Bomb Group down in Guatemala, flying B-17Es on the never-ending antisubmarine patrols.

Scott and *Cap'n & the Kids* had a field day on 18 October 1942 during an armed reconnaissance of the Buin area followed by a hit-and-run attack on the Faisi seaplane base. The lone B-17 roared in, hitting five four-engined flying boats, while the blast from the bombs knocked out eight smaller floatplanes. The gunners then strafed a 500-ton cargo ship, which caught on fire and was burning brightly as *Cap'n & The Kids* disappeared into the distance. Scott and his crew were credited with the destruction of five flying boats and five of the floatplanes.

On 24 November *Cap'n & The Kids* flew three missions, being in the air at 0700 to bomb enemy positions around Sanananda Point, and returning to the same area three hours later. The third take-off, at 2056, was to attack a reported five Japanese destroyers in the Huon Gulf. The B-17s claimed direct hits on two of the warships, and the destroyer *Hayashio* was sunk.

Ed Scott, along with Major Bill Benn, Captain Ken McCullar and others, was involved in the development of the 'skip-bombing' techniques. Throughout August and September hour after hour had been devoted to trials, the B-17s skipping bombs across the water or aiming them directly at the old wreck in Port Moresby harbour. The 63rd wrote the book on skip bombing, which essentially involved a diving beam attack at between 200ft and 300ft altitude at 200-250mph, dropping a string of two to four bombs starting short of the target. The target needed to be silhouetted by a low moon, flares or fires. It was stressed that under combat conditions surprise was essential, and that the tactic should only be used against merchant vessels and under cover of darkness 'unless the circumstances warrant a high casualty rate'.

Scott piloted *Cap'n & The Kids* on her missions up to 21 January 1943, when the target was shipping in Blanche Bay. Scott chose a merchant vessel and made his first run at 250ft, dropping three 500lb bombs with five-second delay fuses. The first bomb was well short, but the second hit about 10ft from the target and the third landed right alongside it. The ship was 'enveloped in water, observed lifting out of water and rocked violently' according to the mission report. The crippled vessel was later seen creeping toward shore, apparently to be beached.

On 5 February *Cap'n & The Kids* acted as the 'harassing agent' for a night mission against Lakunai airfield at Rabaul. Scott was over the target off and on for a total of three hours, dropping incendiary bombs and flares at intervals, or easing down to strafe searchlights or explore the northwest coast of New Britain for targets of opportunity.

Scott flew a reconnaissance mission on 11 February and the major mission against Rabaul on Valentine's Day. Four days later *Cap'n & The Kids* staged through Milne Bay to attack shipping targets on Bougainville, then she was out for routine maintenance until 10 March, when Lieutenant Bill O'Brien took her to Wewak.

Shortly after midday on 13 March 1943 an enemy convoy consisting of a cruiser, two destroyers and five transports, with fighter cover, had been sighted at sea, almost certainly destined for Wewak. A shadowing aircraft, *Tuffy*, went out at 1445 and *Cap'n & The Kids* with six other B-17s took off at 1700 as the attack force. They were each armed with four 1,000lb bombs, except for Scott's *Cap'n & The Kids* and *Panama Hattie*, flown by Lieutenant Herbert Derr, which each carried eight 500lb bombs primed with skip-bombing fuses. The B-17s were forced to fly through thunderstorms, and one had to turn back owing to severe icing. In the end only three crews were able to find the convoy. Lieutenant Neill Kirby in *The Reckless Mountain Boys* dropped flares, enabling Scott in *Cap'n & The Kids* to make a devastating attack.

Scott made a low-level bombing run from an altitude of 200ft on a 4,000-ton Japanese tanker. Hits were scored, and the enemy ship immediately burst apart and sank. Continuing the bombing run, they then obtained direct hits on an enemy transport, causing explosions on both sides of the vessel. The Scott crew was credited with sinking two Japanese ships on a single bombing run. Kirby and his crew made two runs and were credited with a waterline hit on a transport and a hit on a destroyer.

Over the next couple of months *Cap'n & The Kids* flew thirteen more missions, eight of them reconnaissance flights over the islands and sea lanes.

Cap'n & The Kids had always been a lucky aircraft, and was only shot up badly on one occasion. Lieutenant Everett Sunderman was at the controls on 7 May, flying yet another reconnaissance mission, when the B-17 was intercepted by seven Oscars about 20 miles east of Wewak. On their first pass two of the fighters tried to hit *Cap'n & The Kids* with aerial bombs, but these exploded harmlessly off the right wing. The same two Oscars then made a second pass from twelve o'clock, while a third came in from three o'clock almost simultaneously. Sunderman was wounded slightly in the left thigh as bullets peppered the B-17. He managed to reach some protective cloud at 5,000ft and, with No.2 engine feathered and No.3 running roughly, *Cap'n & The Kids* limped along the north coast of New Guinea to the Allied airfield at Dobodura.

General George Kenney took every opportunity to promote 'airpower' and his beloved 5th Air Force, so it was natural that he would invite the Allied commander, General Douglas MacArthur, to watch what promised to be a spectacular operation – the paratroop invasion of Nadzab in New Guinea. Colonel Harry Hawthorne, commander of the 43rd Bomb Group, organized what Kenney called the 'brass hats flight'. Hawthorne would carry General Douglas MacArthur with him in *Talisman*, while MacArthur's chief of staff, General Richard Sutherland, would be in *The Mustang* with Lieutenant William E. Crawford, and Kenney himself flew with Captain John VanTrigt in *Cap'n & The Kids*.

It was also natural that Kenney would write a letter about it all to General 'Hap' Arnold in Washington, as part of his ongoing plea for more men and aeroplanes for the Southwest Pacific. The letter read, in part:

> You already know by this time the news of the preliminary move to take out Lae but I will tell you about the show on the 5th of September, when we took Nadzab with 1,700 paratroops and with General MacArthur in a B-17 over the area watching the show and jumping up and down like a kid. I was flying number two in the same flight with him and the operation was a magnificent spectacle. I truly don't believe that another air force in the world today could have put this over as perfectly as the 5th Air Force did ...

It was not the last time that *Cap'n & The Kids* would fly 'brass hats', but for the next six weeks she took part in what was the B-17's swansong as the heavy bomber in the Southwest Pacific. John VanTrigt flew it for the next three missions. The aircraft's last mission with the 63rd Bomb Squadron was on 18 October, when Flight Officer Halbert Miller flew her as 'weather ship' for an abortive Rabaul mission.

In November 1943 twelve veteran B-17s were handed over to General Paul Prentiss's 54th Troop Carrier Wing for use as armed transports. The workhorse C-47s had suffered tremendous losses, and some places were simply too hot for them. The twelve aircraft were *Yankee Didd'ler*, *The Last Straw*, 41-2408, *Spawn of Hell*, 41-2665, 41-2657, *Lulu Belle*, *Panama Hattie*, 41-24420, 41-24548, 41-24357 (later named *The Super Chief*) and *Cap'n & The Kids*, which flew with the 433rd Troop Carrier Group, where she was given the 'nose number' 371, painted just behind the cabin under the top turret.

On 19 February 371's nose section and fuselage were damaged when a C-47 taxied into her at Ward's Drome, one of the Port Moresby airstrips. Patched up by the 478th Service Squadron, she was returned to the 69th Troop Carrier Squadron on 23 February, in time to stake her next claim to fame. *Cap'n & The Kids* and *The Last Straw*, the 433rd's other B-17, were ordered to Finschhafen on Detached Service.

The recapture of the Admiralty Islands on 29 February 1944 began as a 'reconnaissance in force' of the Momote airfield area on the eastern side of Los Negros Island, rather than a full-scale invasion. Once hotly defended, there had been no Japanese reaction in the Admiralties since 6 February, and 5th Air Force aircraft were parading over the area without drawing a single shot. However, that was because the Japanese commander had forbidden any firing at Allied aircraft and pro-hibited all movement in the open during the day, in an attempt to convince the Allies that the islands had been abandoned.

General Ennis Whitehead had ordered 'eight ageing B-17s, modified to drop supplies, into Finschhafen in case they were needed'. This proved a prudent move. The first day and night on Los Negros were critical because reinforcements could not arrive until 2 March.

On 1 March the possession of the airstrip was still being bitterly contested, and *Yankee Didd'ler* from the 317th Troop Carrier Group flew a couple of supply drops, and *Spawn of Hell* and the other three B-17s of the 375th Troop Carrier Group dropped twelve tons of blood plasma, ammunition, barbed wire and weapons. *Cap'n & The Kids* and *The Last Straw* made three drop runs over the American lines, then three strafing runs over the Japanese lines.

On 2 March *Cap'n & The Kids* was back with a cargo of ammunition, flying in at about 400ft. The pilots, Flight Officer Ralph Deardorff and Captain A. J. Beck, were in contact with 'Saucepan', a destroyer lying offshore to direct air operations in the area. It was gloomy, with a low ceiling and vapoury, driving cloud which provid-ed the perfect cover for enemy fighters to make hit-and-run attacks.

Suddenly, Deardorff heard the clatter of machine-gun fire in his aircraft and urgent calls on the interphone. There were three fighters. One, a Tony, was overtak-ing parallel with them and slightly higher. When abreast of the B-17 he rolled in to make a firing pass. The right waist gunner got a few bursts off before his gun jammed. The Japanese fighter dived beneath the B-17 and away.

The second fighter, a Zero, attacked from two o'clock, passing under *Cap'n & The Kids* without inflicting any hits. Deardorff raced toward the American war-ships offshore and the umbrella of fire they could provide.

The third Japanese fighter, another Tony, made a pass from about three o'clock high. The radio gunner, Sergeant William Mathis, and top turret gunner Private Brian Marcorelle both fired as it flashed past, before turning to begin another attack from nine o'clock. Sergeant A. C. Crossen, manning the left waist gun, reported:

> I saw bullets hitting the water on our left side and a ship passed under us but I had no chance to fire at him. Another 'plane passed under us from one or two o'clock. A third 'plane, a Tony, passed over

and behind us from four o'clock; he flew straight out level and made a right turn and headed back toward us. After he finished his turn and started toward me, I put several bursts into him in the engine and right wing, and as he came on I put more bursts in him ... he suddenly turned right ... he was smoking as he turned.

The Tony was about 200yd out when it broke off the attack. The tail gunner on *Cap'n & The Kids* squeezed off a few rounds at it as it flashed by. The Japanese fighter hit the water and there was a huge flash of flame and a plume of black smoke. It was all over in less time than it takes to tell, no more than a minute. More fighters were lurking in the scudding cloud, but by this time *Cap'n & The Kids* had retreated to the protective range of American destroyers.

As soon as it was safe the B-17 headed back to Momote, where possession of the airfield was still in dispute. The Japanese were on the western edge of the strip, and the Americans in the jungle along the east, only a couple of hundred yards from the beach where they had landed. The B-17 made two drop runs and turned and flew back along the length of the strip, firing into the Japanese positions while the Americans on the ground raced to retrieve the precious boxes from the exposed runway. *Cap'n & The Kids* landed safely at Finschhafen at 1400 with two bullet holes in her tail and an antenna shot away.

On 22 April *Cap'n & The Kids* and *The Last Straw* left the 69th Troop Carrier Squadron for an 'extended mission' with the 317th Troop Carrier Group, which provided five B-17s for a 'special operation' in support of the landings in the Hollandia area of the New Guinea coast. The infantry moving inland was running short of food and ammunition, and had to call for air supply until Cyclops airstrip was ready to receive aircraft on 28 April. The first dropping mission over Hollandia was carried out on 26 April by the five B-17s, and a high average of 'hits' was obtained in the dropping zone.

The following month *Cap'n & The Kids* was dropping 7,000 pairs of combat boots to infantrymen who were burning and blasting the enemy out of a maze of caves, holes and fissures on the small island of Biak, in Geelvink Bay.

On 10 August 1944 the aircraft was transferred to Depot No.2 at Ward's Strip, her career as an armed transport over. But the old B-17F was unstoppable. When the US Eighth Army was activated in September 1944 its commander, Lieutenant General Robert L. Eichelberger, needed transport, and *Cap'n & The Kids* had a new job.

Major Charles Downer, a veteran of the 43rd Group's 403rd Squadron, assigned as the General's pilot, remembers:

> I could not have dreamed up a more interesting assignment. The general needed to keep in touch with his ground combat operations scattered along the route leading to the re-occupation of the Philippines.

The airplane assigned to him was 124353, one of the most note-worthy veterans of combat in the 43rd Bomb Group. As the *Cap'n & The Kids* it had been used to pioneer skip-bombing tactics in the 63rd Bomb Squadron, and in the course of 81 missions it had been credited with eight enemy vessels sunk and eleven fighters shot down. It was taken down to Australia and modified for use by General Eichelberger. He renamed it *Miss Em* for his wife Emaline, and had her favourite flower, a big red rose, painted close to the little rows of bombs, ships and rising suns.

I picked up the airplane at Townsville on September 11, 1944, and flew up to Hollandia a few days later. Our airfield was at the west end of twenty-mile-long Lake Sentani, and the Army head-quarters, where we were billeted, was at the east end. The setting was beautiful. Native villages were scattered along the south shore, some of them extending into the lake with scores of grass huts built on stilts.

General Eichelberger and his staff welcomed us with open arms. The general was a big, fatherly man with a good sense of humour. Unlike his boss, General Douglas MacArthur, Eichelberger showed that he liked people and he assumed that they liked him. Although both generals were products of West Point and both had served there as superintendent, respect for General Eichelberger was tinged with affection, rather than fear.

My aircrew, after some early changes, included copilot Captain Sidney Webb, navigator Captain Thomas Porada, crew chief and flight engineer Master Sergeant Charles Cole, radio operator Staff Sergeant Alfred Goldman, assistant engineer and tail gunner Staff Sergeant Brian Marcorelle, and waist gunners Staff Sergeant John Branciforte and Sergeant Francis Sullivan.

The enlisted crew members, who were also the ground crew, did a superb job of maintenance. During the next eleven months we flew without an engine failure or a serious mechanical delay.

Charles Cole remembers:

Miss Em was one of my better assignments while in the service ... the general and his staff were super as were our flight crew officers ... we all had a family relationship. *Miss Em* was a very reliable aircraft. Never once did it ever abort a flight in its almost daily schedule. We did the regular maintenance and inspections and always had the 'plane ready. When General Eichelberger arrived for a flight the crew always lined up at attention by the tail and saluted. The general would say, "Are we ready boys?"

Downer continues:

The general lost no time in putting the airplane to use. There were many trips to airfields along the north coast of New Guinea, to islands such as Wakde, Biak and Morotai, and an occasional trip to Australia as far as Sydney. In November we began flying to the Philippines, stopping en route at Angaur Island or Peleliu Island in the Palau group, where artillery continued pounding the well-dug-in Japanese during the night. At Tacloban airfield on Leyte, where Navy and Marine Corps fighter bombers were being serviced and sent back out in rapid order, we were allowed only 45 minutes to deplane our passengers, refuel, file our clearance and be off the ground, under threat of being bulldozed into the ocean. Every square foot of apron was needed for the urgent combat turnarounds, and plenty of unserviceable airplanes ended up in that wet graveyard.

Not long after my arrival in the Eighth Army, the general had given me an additional duty as aide-de-camp. He had other aides with specialized duties covering all of his real needs, so my extra duties were mostly to accompany him when he visited his combat outfits and to assist in entertaining his visitors. Because he believed in getting as far forward as he dared in order to encourage his troops, and because he had lots of visitors at his headquarters, my aide work was an unexpected treat for a bomber pilot. Other pilots of B-17 command aircraft – including General George Kenney's and General Walter Krueger's – outranked me. Not to be outdone, the general promoted me to Lieutenant Colonel on 30 January 1945.

On 1 February we moved to the Philippines, with our headquarters on the beach at Tanauan, about ten miles south of Tacloban, and with our airfield nearby. From there we flew out to observe a great variety of combat operations, including a number of amphibious landings. On one of these, on 19 February on the island of Samar, the general asked me to make a low pass just offshore from the landing beach. Then he grabbed one of our waist guns and added to the suppressive fire against possible targets hidden by the trees. As we broke off to seaward, a large explosion occurred on the water ahead of us. Evidently a Japanese artilleryman was trying his luck as an anti-aircraft gunner.

The most spectacular of all the operations we observed was the recapture of Corregidor on 16 February 1945. In Japanese hands since May of 1942, the little island fortress at the mouth of Manila Bay was garrisoned by about 8,000 troops. General MacArthur's promise to return and take it back had been at the centre of his strategy throughout the war. The place had been dive-bombed, level-bombed, napalmed and strafed daily for ten days, more thoroughly than any other two square mile area in the Pacific. That preparation continued until just before our troop carrier aircraft came over and dropped more than 2,000 paratroopers. At the same time, a 1,000-man amphibious force landed on the north shore.

Circling overhead, we were high enough to take in the entire scene at once and low enough to see the individual participants. Although the intended paratroop drop site was the old parade ground, a stiff breeze from the north caused many to be dragged across the roofs of buildings and slammed into concrete fire walls. Others were carried beyond the tops of the cliffs at the south side and dropped into the ocean. The white, curved wakes of PT boats laced the surface as they dashed frantically to pick up the men, weighted down with guns, grenades and ammunition.

The overall operation was a great success. General MacArthur did return shortly after, and Manila Bay could be entered safely once again.

On 23 May we made an early morning flight to Valencia, along the main north-south road through central Mindanao, to reach a regiment engaged in clearing out scattered pockets of enemy resistance. Upon landing we were told that the airstrip at Malaybalay, twenty miles to the north and closer to our destination, had just been captured and might be usable. An observation pilot flew me up to take a look. A mowing machine was clearing the runway of high grass and had not struck any mines. Everything seemed all right so we went back and brought the general and his party up in the *Miss Em*. We drove out to a company that had experienced a banzai attack just before dawn. The men were busy cleaning their weapons. Machine guns, carefully sighted-in the evening before with overlapping fields of fire, had served them well during the attack, mowing down the unseen, desperate enemy on their screaming approach. Eighty bodies were sprawled where they fell. Our losses were three men, killed because one Japanese soldier reached their foxhole with a grenade.

Charles Cole remembers this flight, too; 'Downer could set *Miss Em* down where no self-respecting C-47 would dare to land. One such airstrip was on Mindanao where we depended on a dip in the grass strip to get airborne ...' Downer continues:

On 6 August I flew the *Miss Em* for the last time – a two hour trip from Tanauan, past the smoking cone of the Mayon Volcano, to Nichols Field at Manila. I was being sent to the States on leave to get married and also to pick up a brand-new B-17G being modified for General Eichelberger. The former *Cap'n & The Kids* had been kept busy in the eleven months since joining the Eighth Army, making 160 flights on 141 days. Eastern Air Defense Force Headquarters had classified 63 of them as combat missions.

So the war was finally over for *Cap'n & The Kids*. It had been a long haul, and the old warrior was finally scrapped at Tacloban, Leyte, in April 1946.

The Most Famous

Undoubtedly the most well-known of all Flying Fortresses, *Memphis Belle* is also the subject of much myth. Its fame stems largely from the wartime documentary of that name, featuring the crew's 25th mission in the bomber, and the later fictional Warner Brothers' film also entitled 'Memphis Belle'. The wartime feature led the city of Memphis, Tennessee, to acquire the aircraft for permanent exhibition. It remains the only surviving B-17F that saw combat.

Memphis Belle is frequently stated to have been the first B-17F to complete 25 combat missions, which is not correct. Rather, it was the first 8th Air Force B-17 credited with 25 missions to be returned to the USA. Other inaccuracies connected with the bomber's record continue to be promoted, prominent ones being that the original crew flew all missions of their tour together in *Memphis Belle*, and that none of them was wounded.

Boeing B-17F serial number 41-24485 is recorded as 'rolling out' of the Seattle factory on 2 July 1942 and being officially turned over to the USAAF on the 15th of that month. It was then flown to Dayton, Ohio, for modification and fitting-out for combat use. The 91st Bomb Group received the aircraft on 31 August at Dow Field, Bangor, Maine, where the unit was being equipped with 36 new B-17Fs before movement to a combat zone. The bomber was assigned to Captain Robert K. Morgan and crew in the 324th Bomb Squadron. Morgan's fiancé, Margaret Polk, was from Memphis, and he decided to name his new charge *Memphis Belle* in her honour. He arranged for a civilian to paint a pin-up girl on the nose, the figure being based on one of the George Petty prints featured in *Esquire* magazine.

The Group air echelon was ordered overseas in late September 1942, and the Morgan crew and *Memphis Belle* started their movement on the 25th and arrived at Kimbolton, England, on 1 October. The 91st Bomb Group soon removed to the more comfortable Bassingbourn, Cambridgeshire, and it was from this airfield on 7 November 1942 that the Group flew its first combat mission, *Memphis Belle* being one of the fourteen B-17s despatched and the second aircraft to become airborne. Six aircraft aborted and flak was encountered over the target, the Brest submarine pens, but *Memphis Belle* was not one of the eleven that were damaged.

Two days later it was in a fourteen-strong formation sent to St Nazaire to bomb at half the normal altitude. Although no 91st aircraft were lost, all were damaged, the *Belle* collecting about 60 small shrapnel holes and later having to land at Exeter, short on fuel. After refuelling, one engine refused to start and, against all the rules, Morgan began the take-off on three, hoping that the windmilling propeller on the errant engine would bring it to life. This proved successful, and the aircraft and crew returned safely to base. St Nazaire was again target for *Memphis Belle* on 17 November, when it collected a large hole in the left wing. The aircraft took part in three heavily contested missions in December, escaping unscathed.

On 3 January 1943 it was St Nazaire yet again, and *Memphis Belle* and the Morgan crew were selected to lead the Group and the task force. Flak and fighter opposition was encountered, but only a few holes were found when the aircraft put down at St Eval. The Group lead position was also assigned to the aircraft for the next mission, to Lille on 13 January, when Colonel Stanley Wray, the 91st's CO, flew as co-pilot.

It was back to the U-boat pens on 23 January, when Fw 190s of JG2 made head-on passes at the 91st formation. *Memphis Belle* was raked with cannon and machine-gun fire in the tail, collecting large holes in its fin and rudder. Several bullets narrowly missed tail gunner Sergeant John Quinlan. Repairs took some days, and the bomber was not to attempt another mission until 14 February, when extensive cloud caused this operation to be abandoned over Holland. St Nazaire brought more battle damage on 16 February, including a cannon shell hit on No.2 engine. Morgan brought the Fortress back to Bassingbourn, where it was grounded again until the mission of 4 March. This was the first successful 8th Air Force attack on Hamm marshalling yard, but *Memphis Belle* suffered mechanical trouble and had to turn back.

On the 6th, following a long haul to Lorient, the 91st's aircraft were low on fuel and diverted to Davidstowe Moor, near the southwest coast of England. All, that is, except *Memphis Belle*, which, with Robert Morgan and squadron CO Haley Aycock at the controls, made it back to Bassingbourn with only a few minutes' supply of fuel remaining on landing. Apparently Morgan did not want to miss a party being held at the station that evening! The aircraft was scheduled as Group lead two days later, but mechanical problems caused a turn-back while it was still over England.

The Morgan crew and *Memphis Belle* had another close call and the first casualty on the bomber's 16th mission, on 28 March. The rail centre at Rouen was the target, but poor weather and a failure to rendezvous with the Spitfire escort allowed enemy fighters to conduct effective interceptions. During an attack from the rear a 20mm shell exploded against the tail guns, putting a fragment into Sergeant Quinlan's leg, and other hits perforated the tail surfaces. The damage was soon repaired and, on the last day of the month, *Memphis Belle* was the Group lead to bomb Rotterdam docks.

An aborted mission on 4 April left *Memphis Belle* still under repair when the Group flew to Antwerp next day. Twelve days were to pass before the Morgan crew and *Memphis Belle* were despatched on another combat mission, to strike an aircraft factory at Bremen. This proved to be the most heavily contested and costly raid so far for the 91st. Six B-17s, all from one squadron, were shot down, and most of the 28 Fortresses of the Group that went over the target returned to base with some battle damage.

By early May *Memphis Belle* was one of half a dozen B-17s at Bassingbourn that had survived twenty or more missions. At this time Captain William Wyler, the former Hollywood film producer, was making a documentary on VIIIth Bomber Command operations for the USAAF. Much of the filming had been carried out at Bassingbourn, and the plan was to build the narrative around one particular crew and aircraft. *Memphis Belle* and the Morgan crew were tentatively selected for this purpose.

On 13 and 14 May *Memphis Belle* was flown on missions by other crews, probably because Morgan and three other members of his crew were in London for radio recordings. Next day the Morgan crew were in *Memphis Belle* when the Group bombed Heligoland as a target of opportunity. Eighth Air Force Public Relations was now intent on promoting the *Memphis Belle* movie venture, and when HRH King George VI and the Queen visited Bassingbourn on 16 May, it was the *Memphis Belle* crew who were introduced to them.

On 17 May Captain Robert Morgan and several members of his crew flew their 25th mission. However, *Memphis Belle* had only 24 to its credit. The storyline of the Wyler documentary now centred on the final mission of a 25-mission tour, with the crew being sent back to the USA – although Morgan and his men were not told of this at the time. Eighth Air Force Public Relations established this as 17 May, but on 19 May *Memphis Belle* was sent to Kiel with another crew to authenticate the 25 missions claimed.

With crew and aircraft secure, there was some hectic cinematographic photography at Bassingbourn over the next few days, with Morgan and his crew simulating various activities connected with a combat mission. A special review of the aircraft and crew was arranged at Bovingdon, where Lieutenant General Ira Eaker and General Devers, overall commander of the US forces in Europe, addressed the crew on their departure to the USA. All of these proceedings were filmed for Wyler's documentary.

After their return to the United States, the crew and aircraft toured the country for bond-raising promotions, starting in Washington on 9 June. Wherever they went they were feted by the media. In the autumn of that year the aircraft was overhauled and modified at Spokane, Washington, before being flown to the B-17 training base at MacDill Field, Tampa, Florida. It served at this airfield and nearby satellites until the spring of 1945, the *Memphis Belle* insignia remaining on its nose throughout this period.

In June 1945 41-24485 was put into storage at Altus, Oklahoma, and in October it was released for disposal. Mayor Chandler of Memphis had requested the bomber as a war memorial for his city soon after its return to the USA from England, and had restated this interest in the summer of 1945. Despite the usual obstacles of governmental bureaucracy, Walter Chandler persisted and was able to purchase the aircraft for $350 in March 1946. Flown to Memphis Airport on 17 July 1946, it then languished there for four years, a victim of procrastination regarding its final disposition.

In the summer of 1950 *Memphis Belle* was partly dismantled and reassembled on a concrete pad in the Memphis National Guard armoury. Although it was fenced in, the aircraft became a target of souvenir hunters and juvenile vandalism over the next two decades. In 1977 the National Guard were required to sell the site, and at this time the *Memphis Belle* Memorial Association, headed by local enthusiast Frank Donofrio, arranged for the aircraft to be temporarily stored at the city airport. Fund raising and refurbishment took place over the next few years, culminating in *Memphis Belle* being removed to a permanent, specially constructed pavilion on the city's Mud Island park by the Mississippi. The dedication took place on 17 May 1987, with Robert K. Morgan, Margaret Polk (they never married) and surviving members of the original crew present.

William Wyler's *Memphis Belle* documentary, although basically propaganda for a cause, avoided the inflated patriotism of wartime and was skilfully dramatic. It remains one of the best US air feature documentaries of the Second World War.

Forty-five years later, Wyler's daughter, Catherine, embarked on a fictional version of the *Memphis Belle* storyline with producer David Puttnam and Warner Brothers. Filmed in England in 1989, five surviving flyable Fortresses participated. Part of the contract agreement with the owners of these aircraft was that, after filming had been completed, each Fortress would be finished in *Memphis Belle* insignia to display at airshows over a period of some months. The film was described as a 'Saturday night movie', and although it took considerable liberties with fact, it undoubtedly helped to reinforce the legend of *Memphis Belle*.

The Old Man

One of the first B-17Fs to reach the 19th Bomb Group in Australia was serial number 41-24403, accepted by the Army Air Forces on 26 June 1942. By the end of August it was at dusty Mareeba in Queensland, assigned to the 30th Bomb Squadron, where the name *Blitz Buggy* was neatly lettered on both sides of its nose.

In the afternoon of 15 September 1942, Captain Cecil Knudson and his crew flew from Mareeba up to Port Moresby in *Blitz Buggy*. Briefed, fed and rested, they took off from Seven Mile Strip at 0015, bound for Rabaul. In his report, Knudson calls it an 'individual mission', and everything went smoothly. After gaining altitude over Hood Point, near Port Moresby, Knudson crossed the Owen Stanley Mountains at 14,000ft, then began a slow descent. They were at 8,000ft by the time they reached New Britain.

Knudson reported:

> The target area was covered with a dark overcast extending 25 miles west of the target, the base of which was at 10,000ft ... Our approach was entirely over land which may have been one reason we caught the Japs unaware, for as we came to the target area we could see lights both on Vunakanau aerodrome and in the town. They may have thought it was one of their 'planes for several ships in the harbour were signalling to us as we were making our bombing run.

Knudson's bombardier could pick out the runway at Vunakanau, and the lights there were just going out as the bombs tumbled from *Blitz Buggy*. All bombs were on target as Knudson made a diving left turn and headed west at 0423.

Back at Seven Mile they found one shrapnel hole in the side of the bombardier's compartment. Captain Robert L. Williams, also from the 30th Squadron, was not so lucky. He had been shot down over the target in 41-24427. The Knudson crew and *Blitz Buggy* remained at Port Moresby, flying another mission to Rabaul that night.

On 5 October 1942 *Blitz Buggy* was again one of a force of B-17s attacking Vunakanau airfield. In the cockpit were Lieutenant Fred Wesche and his copilot, Lieutenant Arthur McMullan. The navigator was Lieutenant Francis Sickinger, and he tells the story. 'We took off about 0220 and flew in formation to St George's Channel and turned toward Vunakanau at 0650. About half of the airport was closed in so we made a big circle to start our run. Some of the crew saw the Zeros taking off on our first pass.'

The mission was led by Major John Rouse, commander of the 30th Bomb Squadron, whose aircraft was hit and his bombardier blinded, causing their bombs to go wide of the target. This formation was intercepted by about twenty Zeros, and so began a running fight that would last for more than 50 minutes. The Japanese fighters attacked from all angles and shot down 41-9196, flown by Lieutenant Earl Hageman.

In *Blitz Buggy* the bombardier, Lieutenant Bernard Anderson, had dropped when the leader did, so their bombs were also wide. Sickinger continues; 'Andy handed me the bomb sight and was just ready to charge the 0.30 when he was hit across the back. I was trying to man both side guns and my oxygen hose wouldn't stretch to the right side. Consequently I was on oxygen only about half the time.'

A bullet whizzed past Sickinger's ear and shattered the radio compass. 'I was sweating, and because the glass caused me to close my eyes I thought, "I'm hit! I'm bleeding!" and it was just the sweat running down my face."

Anderson had been hit but was still manning his gun, so Sickinger, although temporarily blinded, felt his way around and supplied the wounded bombardier with ammunition for his nose gun. In spite of his wounds, Anderson managed to run two cans of ammunition through his 0.30-calibre gun during the battle. When Sickinger had removed the glass fragments from his eyes and was able to see again, he went back to his own guns. 'Sergeant Albert Kennedy, the top turret gunner, and I blew one Zero apart, one of his wheels hit our wing as we ducked under him,' Sickinger later wrote in his diary.

Anderson's father was a veteran of the First World War who had been paralyzed from the waist down, and the bombardier had once told Sickinger, 'If I get hit, just leave me alone, I'm going to kill myself.' Sickinger continues:

> So the first thing I did was to take his .45 away from him. And then, after I got his parachute off, I saw that gash across his back and I got out the first-aid kit. He said it wasn't hurting too much. He had a very broad Scottish brogue – anyway, I gave him a shot from one of the syrettes of morphine. They were like a toothpaste tube only with a needle in the end. They had an alcohol swab packed in with them ... Fortunately, he was not bleeding so we left the wound open. We left Andy at the hospital in Moresby and came back to Mareeba.

Anderson recovered fully, but he never flew another combat mission.

Lieutenant Chester Kennedy had flown to Australia as co-pilot with Captain Dave Hassemer in *Hoomalimali*, the first B-17F to arrive at Mareeba. On 31 October 1942, when the various crews were assigned to squadrons of the 43rd Bomb Group, he was listed as copilot on Lieutenant John Frost's crew, but Frost was shot down while attempting a bombing run on a Japanese destroyer on 22 November. Kennedy was concerned that he might end up with one of the inexperienced new crews, but his luck continued to hold and in the middle of December he was assigned to Lieutenant Glen Lewis, a veteran of the 28th Squadron.

On 18 December they flew *Blitz Buggy* up to Port Moresby, and their first combat mission was a three-aircraft strike against Japanese coastal shipping at Finschhafen. There was absolutely no opposition on a mission which Kennedy called 'duck soup'. After bombing the ships the B-17s went in low to strafe, and the vibration from the guns of the top turret cracked the Plexiglas panel over Kennedy's head. This was whipped away by the slipstream, and it made it a very cold ride back over the Owen Stanleys at altitudes up to 15,000ft. The damage to *Blitz Buggy* was repaired in an hour at Port Moresby.

On Christmas Eve 1942 they attacked a tanker at Gasmata, then three days later flew a night mission against Rabaul. On 16 January they claimed a transport in Simpson Harbour. On 22 January the target was Lakunai, and the bomb load incendiaries and fragmentation bombs.

At some time in January 1943 someone decided to paint over the name *Blitz Buggy* and replace it with a painting of a cheerful Uncle Sam and a new name, *The Old Man*.

On 24 January 1943 Lewis and Kennedy were off to Rabaul again, and the copilot recorded the events in his diary:

> Gee! I do get tired of writing about missions! Several weeks ago I resolved that I was not going to say very much about them except when something unusual happened. You see, by now they are pretty much the same, at least for the most part. Writing of them each time as they occur thus becomes somewhat monotonous and iterative and just routine.
>
> Before I go further let me take issue with my own remark that they are "just routine". They are, I suppose, in a way of speaking; but I must quickly add that I get the hell scared out of me on an average of about three times per mission. Each exists only for a brief time or for about two hours or more. Even being scared by ack-ack, by mountains, or by very bad tropical thunderstorms can become routine, though, believe it or not. I suppose what becomes dangerous to one's existence is a state when he no longer is scared or when he loses respect for the weather or the ack-ack.
>
> I can't skip last night's mission of seven hours and fifteen minutes, again in *The Old Man*, regardless of how tiresome writing of them becomes. Over the target I just steel myself against what's happening. I watch most intently for the target ahead, whether it be shipping, or airdrome, or town; I see the searchlights as they sweep the skies from horizon to zenith in nervous little jerks; I watch them all converge on

us almost immediately after one has found us; I see occasional bursts of anti aircraft fire ahead, above, and to our sides; I keep my eyes the while glued on the cockpit instruments that I can sooner discover anything amiss with an engine; I brace myself for the time when we will be hit; and I prepare my thoughts so any action in that eventuality will be orderly and well arranged. During all of this, however, I don't really think; instead, I seem to go through this sort of routine in a kind of suspended animation, but at this time I don't feel fear at all.

It's in the minutes before going into the run and in the minutes after the completion of the run that get to me. Last night was a bit different however. We were to hit shipping in Simpson Harbor. The moon was directly overhead and thus at such an angle that there was no "slick" on the water – just a big spot. Too, the Japanese must have dispersed their ships along outlying coastlines and small islands. At any rate, three separate passes over the middle of the harbour revealed no more than a half dozen ships and these only after we were directly over them. Of course, that was much too late for a bombing run.

On each of these attempts the searchlights picked us up early and followed us all the way across the harbour. To escape them we dived and turned corkscrew fashion, and thus on our next attempt we went in about 500ft lower. After the third run we were down to 5,000ft, and on each run the ack–ack would paint the sky all about us.

Failing to find a suitable target after this third run, we again dived and turned and headed up the nearby shore to escape the ack–ack and the searchlights and to position us differently for still a fourth run at 5,000ft ... more quickly than usual the searchlights got us. I s'pose I'd never seen ack–ack previously! I never want to see it again, not like it was this time. They had our altitude, and all of it was bunched right out my window and off the right wing of old 403. Suddenly there was a tremendous tearing, ripping sound, and the 'plane momentarily staggered and seemed actually to stop in mid-air. We had received a direct hit! The engines seemed all right; but, needless to say, we wasted no time in getting away from there.

As we were manoeuvring to escape, Sergeant Leon Gossick, our radio operator, started frantically calling that he and James Harris, our ball turret gunner, were wounded. This decided matters for us; we went on over Vunakanau on the opposite side of the harbour and dropped our thousand pounders right up the dispersal bays alongside the runway. From there we headed home to assay our damages and to take care of Gossick and Harris, whose wounds proved not serious. *The Old Man* performed as if nothing had happened to her. And an ambulance raced with us down the runway at Jackson as we landed.

Closer inspection revealed that a five-inch shell had burst in our right wing just behind the gasoline tank and off the fuselage. Also, another shell, probably a three-incher, had burst in or near the radio room. The resulting holes of ingress and egress of the five-inch shell were about a foot in diameter and there were dozens and dozens of tiny holes in the skin all around the large hole. The shell in the radio room had blown the top out of it, and shrapnel from that burst had entered the rear part of the fuselage and the ball turret. Old 403 had gone through it all just as if nothing had happened. All of us were, indeed, most lucky that we were all right, and Gossick and Harris will also be all right in about two weeks or so.

Do you see what I meant when I earlier remarked that I couldn't skip last night's mission? I couldn't even wait to write it up before "hitting the sack". I'm very drained and sleepy now, it's already 1000 hours. If there's need I shall sleep until this time tomorrow morning; and, in so doing, dream of entirely other things. Thus, when I do awake, the events of last evening will have been an impossibility and I shall again just go on my way marking time until I'm again home.

The Old Man was repaired quickly, having suffered no structural damage. Glen Lewis and Chet Kennedy took her on the St Valentine's Day mission to Rabaul, and flew her again on the night of 21 February, but the town and harbour were totally socked in.

The next real test for *The Old Man* came when it found more trouble over Gasmata on 8 March 1943, on what was supposed to be an easy mission. It began as a long but routine reconnaissance mission for Lieutenants Melville 'Dutch' Ehlers and Joe 'Indian' Cochran and their crew. It was the first mission they had flown in about three weeks, since the big Valentine's Day mission to Rabaul. On that one they had run into heavy anti-aircraft fire, and navigator Lieutenant Warren 'Doc' Bryant and bombardier Lieutenant Lloyd 'Breezy' Boren had been wounded, mostly by splinters of Plexiglas in their arms and faces.

Lloyd Boren takes up the story:

After that, we were sent to Sydney on leave. The squadron had an unofficial custom of sending a crew just returning from leave on a 12-hour recce mission, presumably to sober up.

We took off with one bomb bay tank and four five-hundred pounders. The flight was uneventful, and we approached Gasmata at about 4,000ft. We spotted what looked like bomb craters in the runway, so felt reasonably safe until we saw 'planes taking off over the painted craters. We started climbing fast, and I salvoed the bombs and bomb bay tank. We were hopped by thirteen Zeros, and had about a ten-to-fifteen minute running fight with them. They made nose passes every time, and we were probably saved by some thick clouds we were able to reach.

Breaking out of the clouds, they caught up with us again ... I had three guns, one pointing ahead, and one on either side of the nose ... I remember using the centre gun on a Zero which was going the same way we were when we broke out of the clouds. I called to Dutch to follow him, and used a whole can of ammo trying to hit him. Never did know whether I even touched him, but couldn't have been more than a couple hundred yards away ... two of them got hits in both the nose and cockpit area of our 'plane. We had gotten five 'planes downed by this time.

Only the four officers were wounded, the nose and cockpit took the bulk of the hits. Dutch was shot through the upper leg, and a flesh wound across the lower back. The Indian was hit in the left side of the neck by fragments when the bullet which hit Ehlers exited and burst against the panel, Doc was hit with fragments across the face and neck, and I was hit in the left knee, left wrist, right arm and shoulder, and right cheek.

We again made for cloud cover with the copilot and engineer flying the 'plane. We got away and made for Dobodura, landing with the Indian flying the ship. Dutch and I were shipped via the hospital ship *Manunda* to Sydney, and two weeks after we had left Sydney on leave, we were back in Sydney at the Royal Prince Alfred Hospital.

The Old Man had one more narrow escape, on the night of 12 June 1943. Lieutenant Lewis Sutton, navigator on Major William A. Smith's crew, remembers the strike as 'the roughest mission we flew'. He recorded it thus in his diary:

Took off 2330 for Rabaul (Vunakanau airstrip again). Weather good all way. Flew contact. Got to the target at 0245 morning of the thirteenth. The 403rd Squadron hit before us. We saw some of the flashes. While we were 75 miles away yet. We got over target area and started on our run. Interphone system went haywire making it necessary for another run causing every searchlight in Rabaul area to turn on us. There must have been at least forty. They were signalling their night fighters at the same time.

The Old Man ran the blinding gauntlet, and four 1,000lb bombs and 60 20lb frags tumbled from her bomb bay. Lewis Sutton continues:

The lights stayed on us for at least five minutes. We were at 5,500 and went down to 4,000 and strafed the searchlights. Most of the guns went out during this. My 0.50 cal was OK. I fired 250–400 rounds –

later found out I probably burned the gun up (but who cares).

We got a large 37mm cannon hole in our left wing from the top. This exploded and blew 40-50 holes in the bottom side of the wing. One small calibre hole between Nos.1 and 2 engines near gas tank. One large – two inch – hole in radio room just creasing the radio man's hair. Three or four in central fuselage between radio room and tail section. One 37mm into tail gunner Harold Poland's position was spent causing it to tear only his new flying suit and scratching his tail again. We left the target area at 0325.

Once again *The Old Man*'s luck had held. Japanese Irving night fighters from the 251st Kokutai had been prowling in the darkness. Superior Flight Petty Officer Shigetoshi Kudo and his observer, Lieutenant (jg) Akira Sugawara, had spotted a B-17 trapped in the lights at 0314, and set it afire. They reported that the American bomber crashed northeast of Ubili airfield at a place named Ulamona, on New Britain.

After arriving back at Port Moresby at 0615, Lewis Sutton noted; 'One of our ships did not return. It was seen to crash 15 miles south of Vunakanau. Crews that saw him go down 0330 think perhaps they might have had a chance to jump. Some hope to pick them up later.'

The lost B-17 was the 65th Squadron's *Georgia Peach*, another veteran of the old 19th Bomb Group, piloted by Lieutenants John Woodard and Russell Emerick. Sadly, only two men got out. Lieutenant Jack Wisener, the bombardier, survived as a prisoner of the Japanese. Navigator Lieutenant Philip Bek escaped from the doomed aircraft but was killed by his captors.

It was Lewis Sutton's last combat mission in B-17s, but any cerebration was dampened in the early morning of 14 June when *The 'Jersey Skeeter'* was taking off on a routine reconnaissance mission. Sutton recalls:

> We were awakened by a terrific explosion. Later at breakfast we learned that Lieutenant James A. Pickard (one of our best friends) had crashed on take-off. The explosion was a bomb bay tank of gas and oxygen tanks. Later one of four bombs exploded. Two enlisted men were alive.
>
> A horrible accident and most of us believe it was due to these worn out old B-17s we have to fly. It is nothing less than a crime to have to fly in those old ships. How long we can continue to take this kicking is beyond me. Phenomenal results are expected of a few battered crews and still fewer B-17s.

The B-17s were being replaced by B-24 Liberators in the 43rd Bomb Group, squadron by squadron, and the diminishing band of B-17s was gathered in Major Folmer Sogaard's 63rd Bomb Squadron. *The Old Man* flew her first mission with the 63rd, an attack on supply dumps in the Bogadjim area, on 23 July, piloted by Lieutenant Henry Evans. She flew a number of missions through July and into August; mostly tactical strikes. The last mission was a Wewak strike on 18 August 1943, with Lieutenant William Crawford.

The B-17, even war-weary, was always popular with the senior officers as a personal transport, and the Southwest Pacific Theatre was no exception. General Douglas MacArthur had his specially-built XC-108, the *Bataan*, with its chromed nose gun, General George Brett had used the veteran B-17D *The Swoose*, General Robert Eichelberger had *Miss Em*, Major General James L. Frink, Services of Supply commander in the Southwest Pacific, had *USASOS War-Horse*, General George C. Kenney had one of the old 19th Group B-17Es, now stripped of paint and nicknamed *Sally*, Lieutenant General Walter Krueger of Sixth Army had *Billy*, the one-time *Tojo's Jinx*, and General Ennis Whitehead, commanding Advon, Fifth Air Force, got *The Old Man*.

The name and the painting of Uncle Sam on the nose were too appropriate to change, but there were other alterations. The radio compartment was modified for passengers, with two seats facing each other on the starboard side. Aft of the radio-room bulkhead there was a separate compartment with a bed. *The Old Man* was still well-armed, the top turret, waist guns and tail turret being retained, but there was a 24V refrigerator where the ball turret had been, useful for cooling Australian beer.

General Whitehead's original pilot was Captain John Glyer. His copilot was Captain Waldo Schauweker, and the flight engineer was Sergeant Ernie Vandal. All were veterans of the 43rd Bomb Group.

When Glyer was sent home, Schauweker took over. He remembers Whitehead fondly and well:

> He was a rough but a fine gentleman. He had a big heart! Ennis normally flew copilot for me on some "look-see" flights. He was an old World War I fighter pilot – he flew *The Old Man* the same way. One thing that I remember well – when General George C. Marshall toured the Pacific, I flew him on a tour of New Guinea. He was a good passenger —also had General Kenney and a few Admirals on board. Had plenty of P-40 fighter cover.

Schauweker was with the crew for about six months, and last flew the old B-17 in June 1944. His copilot had been Captain Glenn Ream, who now took his turn in the left seat. Schauweker, on a visit to the Townsville Depot, had found Sergeant Jerry Hein, who had worked for his father in Bowling Green, Ohio. He requested him and put him on the crew as 'chief cook and bottle washer' to 'keep the rank happy'.

Sergeant Gordon Bavor was a radio operator who had joined the 43rd Bomb Group's Communications Section at Nadzab in March 1944. A year later, at Clark Field, he 'somehow heard about the chance to work on General Whitehead's 'plane'. His section chief in the 43rd Group asked him if he would like the job, and Bavor was taking a code test at Fifth Bomber Command the next day. His association with *The Old Man* was short and sweet:

> The first time I saw the 403 was 18 April 45, at Clark Field. The crew gathered and we test hopped the ship over Manila and Corregidor. Seems that we flew to Leyte in the 403 on 2 May 45. I believe we transported some Red Cross girls and some officers to Tacloban. The last time we flew on the 403 was 13 May. We found out that we were going to the States, as was General Kenney's crew, to pick up new airplanes.

So the final crew of *The Old Man* was Major Glenn E. Ream, pilot; Captain Raymond E. Crawford, copilot; Captain Frederick W. Epplen, navigator; Technical Sergeant Frederick A. Kleinfelder, flight engineer; Sergeant Gordon F. Bavor, radio operator; Technical Sergeant Leonard J. Lawson, assistant engineer and Staff Sergeant Gerald A. Hein, tail gunner. The Ream crew took delivery of a gleaming new B-17G, 44-83555, at Topeka, Kansas, and flew it to the Philippines. *The Old Man* never returned home, and the last record of her whereabouts was Clark Field on 9 July 1948.

Black Jack's Last Mission

Rod Pearce operates the charter boat *Barbarian* out of Lae, and is one of the most experienced scuba divers in the Southwest Pacific. Over the years he has developed an obsession with the Second World War relics which lie forgotten on the seabed around New Guinea and the neighbouring islands. In 1986 a couple of his friends, David Pennefather and Richard Leahy, came to him with a fascinating tale. Villagers at the tiny hamlet of Bogaboga, near remote Cape Vogel in the Milne Bay Province, had told them a story about a 'very big' aircraft crashing into the sea right in front of their village during the war. Pennefather and Leahy were a little sceptical, knowing the Melanesian's desire 'to tell you what he thinks ought to have happened, or what he thinks you want to think happened'. Yet somehow this story had the ring of truth.

Although only a handful of elders could actually have seen the event, the details were intriguing. The aircraft had crashed on a Sunday morning they said, because they had been on their way to church when it passed overhead. The women and children, terrified by the deafening roar and the crash, had hidden in the jungle. Ten or more Americans had escaped from the sinking aeroplane, and the villagers had helped them ashore.

It was the middle of 1986 when Pearce first heard the story, and he was hooked. A fully-equipped search expedition was planned, and Pearce and Pennefather were joined by Bruce Johnson, chief pilot for Richard Leahy's Kiunga Airlines. Their most reliable witness seemed to be a little old man named Valentine, who was quite positive about where the aircraft would be. It was a starting point, so the divers allotted themselves specific search areas and slipped into the warm blue water.

Working their separate ways down the fringing coral reef, Pennefather and Johnson encountered only moderate visibility and a few coral outcrops. Pearce, 150ft down and nearing the end of his air supply, was almost ready to give up when he saw a dark shape that did not quite fit, something looming out of the solid wall of blue water before him. As he swam closer the outline grew clearer. Lying on the white coral sand, deep in the warm blue waters off Papua New Guinea, was a Boeing B-17 Flying Fortress, fully armed and totally intact. Pearce could hardly believe his eyes as he swam toward the old bomber, resting on the ocean floor as if ready for take-off on some ghostly mission of long ago.

When the three divers surfaced, Pearce said nothing at first, vainly trying to control a silly grin as the others reported their uneventful searches. Then he said, as slowly and as calmly as he could, 'It's a B-17'. That was 27 December 1986.

Pennefather immediately made a 'bounce dive', staying near the bottom only long enough to wonder at what he was seeing and to tie a guide line to one of the B-17's twisted propeller blades. That night on *Barbarian* they celebrated with French champagne.

The next day visibility had improved, and the divers inspected the old bomber more closely. There was no apparent battle damage, but the starboard tailplane had been bent upwards against a coral outcrop and the nose was crushed. The fabric covering of the control surfaces had rotted away long ago, but the twin tail guns still moved freely in their mounts. The spine of the aircraft was twisted and the skin buckled above the ball-turret stanchion. The Fortress was totally intact, cocooned by a light growth of coral, and wherever the beams of the divers' flashlights touched it, it glowed in a surreal display of yellow, crimson, pink, mauve and purple. Brilliantly coloured tropical fish darted through the skeletal remains of her control surfaces.

Entering the B-17 through the gaping waist windows, the divers found the ball turret forced up into the fuselage, with live ammunition still in the tracks to the guns and scattered over the fuselage floor. In the radio room the machine gun had been slid back to its stowed position, and was locked there for ever by coral and corrosion. A receiver was still suspended above the collapsed frame of the radio operator's table. Beneath the silt in the aeroplane's shattered nose was a twisted sextant, and the cheek gun which would have been manned by the navigator was still in position.

Bruce Johnson decided it was worth the risk to attempt to get inside the cockpit. Removing his air tank and bulky buoyancy vest, he steered them ahead of him into the cramped bomb bay. Edging forward in almost total darkness, he manoeuvred through a maze of twisted wires and broken control cables, emerged under the top turret and squeezed between the pilots' armour-plated seats. Placing his air tank on the right seat, he became the first man to sit in the pilot's seat in more than 40 years.

The instrument panel lay under a veneer of coral, but the divers were eventually able to locate the small brass plate which carried the aircraft's radio call number. Back aboard *Barbarian* they carefully scraped away the coral crust to reveal the numbers etched into the metal – 124521. *Black Jack* had finally returned from her last mission.

The old B-17 was no stranger. One of a production block of 36 B-17F-20-BOs produced at Seattle in July 1942, the aircraft passed through the Lowry Modification Center in Colorado and was flown to Hamilton Field, California. At the end of August she headed out across the Pacific carrying Lieutenant William O'Brien and his crew, bound for Australia and General George C. Kenney's 5th Air Force. On 7 September 1942 the aircraft was assigned to the 63rd Bombardment Squadron of the 43rd Bomb Group.

Captain Ken McCullar selected 124521 as his regular aircraft. One glance at the last two digits of the serial number made the choice of a nickname easy – *Black Jack*. While Sergeant Ernie Vandal painted the name and design on the nose,

Technical Sergeant Tony DeAngelis and his ground crew took care of another personal touch. They rigged up a fixed 0.50 calibre machine-gun in the nose, with a firing button on the pilot's control wheel – McCullar's answer to the head-on attacks becoming favoured by Japanese fighter pilots.

Husky and genial, McCullar was a totally fearless pilot. With squadron commander Major William Benn, he spent hours taking *Black Jack* as low as 50ft above the sea, perfecting the 'skip bombing' tactic by bouncing 100lb bombs into the hulk of the SS *Pruth* in Port Moresby harbour. *Black Jack* and McCullar became a team, and it seemed as though there was some magic which always got them home. Copilot Lieutenant Harry Staley's diary gives a glimpse of the events and the times; 'We changed the engine ourselves (worked all night under flood lights) at Mareeba just in time to get in on the big show ... we were the second ship over the target and we really caught hell ... Mac did a half roll to get out of the searchlights ...'

The association between Ken McCullar and *Black Jack* ended on an epic note on the night of 24 November 1942, when the B-17s were sent to attack five troop-laden Japanese destroyers in the Huon Gulf. Allied pilots attacking these fast, heavily armed warships at night knew the score. When all you could see was a solid sheet of flame, you could be pretty sure you were right over the target.

The Fortresses took off from Port Moresby's Seven Mile Strip and flew into bad weather which forced them to cross the towering Owen Stanley mountains on instruments. They located their quarry easily, silhouetted against the moonlit sea. *Black Jack* was at about 3,500ft when McCullar selected a target and chopped his throttles back to make his first skip-bombing run from 200ft at 255mph. The B-17 roared through the silky darkness, now dotted with blobs of flame as the warships put up a curtain of fire.

McCullar's bombs hit just off the stern of the ship, but the return fire hit an ammunition can in the aircraft's tail, exploding about 70 rounds and starting a fire. Tail gunner Sergeant Harvey Bancroft did his best to smother the outbreak with a blanket and some heavy flying clothes until extinguishers were rushed back and the blaze was put out.

A second skip-bombing run resulted in hits directly on or very near the warship, starting a fire in the starboard bow. On this run the radio operator, Sergeant Edward Welcome, and two other crewmen were injured, but not seriously.

As *Black Jack* flew through the bursting shells for a third low-level attack the left outboard engine was hit. The oil cooler was blown completely out of the leading edge of the wing, letting the oil pour out before the propeller could be feathered. McCullar was forced to climb to 1,500ft and then make another bomb run from 1,200ft. Again the bombs hit close, but *Black Jack* took more punishment. Up in the nose, Lieutenant Bob Butler, the bombardier, and navigator Lieutenant Ken Beckstrom were feeling very exposed, but had to grin and bear it, not firing their guns lest they pinpoint their aeroplane's position.

McCullar took the B-17 up to 4,000ft on the three good engines and made a fifth and final run, dropping the last of his eight bombs. This time the right inboard engine, hit in the fuel system, cut out. McCullar was able to feather the propeller, but could not maintain altitude on the remaining two engines. The crew jettisoned all the loose equipment, while the radio operator began sending out their position and course, because things looked bad. The shot-up engine on the left, glowing cherry-red in the darkness, could catch fire and explode at any moment. Butler and Beckstrom were ordered to the rear in case the propeller spun off and slashed through their nose compartment.

Eventually the propeller, grinding loose from the engine, spun off into the darkness, and the motor began to cool down. The pilots were able to restart the damaged engine on the right, drawing at least partial power from it, but it took more than two agonising hours for the B-17 to struggle up to 10,000ft, just enough for McCullar to thread his way through a mountain pass and get safely back to Moresby. And this time it had been worth it; later that night an Australian Beaufort crew reported seeing the destroyer *Hayashio* explode and sink.

McCullar was the genuine article – he concluded his fairly detailed but matter-of-fact report with the words 'landed OK and forgot about it'. *Black Jack* was out of action for nearly two months, and perhaps after that she was living on borrowed time. McCullar had flown other aeroplanes and got into more trouble. He took *Tuffy* out on 8 December and brought her back with more than 100 bullet holes and a couple of cannon hits. Then he moved on to command of the 64th Bomb Squadron and his regular copilot, Harry Staley, took over the repaired *Black Jack* with a mostly new crew of his own. The Staley crew flew only five missions in the aeroplane before getting badly shot up over Rabaul on 14 February 1943.

In his diary Staley wrote:

Got back this morning about 0730 after a hectic, rough mission. Starting off, I got in prop wash at one hundred feet and luckily missed a hill. Arrived at the target thirty minutes before bombing time, so decided to make a run over the town and throw out some small frag bombs and incendiary sticks. Made the run, and was just pulling out when they got me in the searchlights. A few seconds after that, an ack-ack shell hit us, and went through the No.3 engine supercharger, and up through the nacelle. It got the oil lines and all control levers to the No.3 engine. I feathered the engine, and waited my turn to bomb our area. We finally bombed, dropping eighteen 100-pound wire-wrapped daisy cutters, and three 300-pound demo. Besides all the little stuff. We made our run and dropped the bombs thru the target area starting several small fires. When we started home, there were numerous fires – some of them visible over sixty miles away. On the way home No.2 supercharger went out, leaving about half the normal power, so we returned. Luckily on two and a half engines. My 'plane will be out for approximately two weeks so I'm going to try and get another.

Staley and his crew completed their missions, mostly in the aeroplane known as 'Pluto', and went home.

Black Jack was flying again in April, but from then on her crews read like a roll call of the 63rd Squadron, with thirteen different crews in fourteen missions.

At 0030 on the night of Sunday, 11 July 1943, four B-17s roared down the runway at Seven Mile Strip. As they gathered speed the lights along the runway briefly lit the names painted on their noses – *Talisman*, *Cap'n & The Kids*, *Tuffy* and *Black Jack*. The ten men aboard *Black Jack* that night had never all flown together as a crew before. The pilots, Lieutenants Ralph De Loach and Joe Moore, had originally come to New Guinea as copilots on other crews. Navigator Lieutenant Charles Shaver and bombardier Lieutenant Herman Dias had arrived as replacements. Ironically, the flight engineer and top turret gunner, Technical Sergeant Delbert Smith, had an old relationship with the aircraft. He had flown in it from Hamilton Field as a waist gunner on Lieutenant William O'Brien's crew the best part of a year before. Sergeant George Prezioso was in the radio room. Waist gunner Private Dan Clinton was flying his very first mission that night. The other three crew members had all been transferred from the 403rd Squadron in May; waist gunner Corporal James Peterson, ball-turret gunner Sergeant Joseph Wilson and tail-turret gunner Sergeant Paul Blascwitz.

Their target was Vunakanau, 500 miles to the north on New Britain. *Black Jack* was carrying a mixed load of explosives designed to cause the greatest possible damage to an airstrip – fourteen wire-wrapped 300lb bombs, two dozen 20lb fragmentation bombs and sixteen clusters of incendiaries.

The B-17s headed southeast to Hood Point, to circle and gain height before crossing the mountains. It was not long before things started to go wrong. De Loach would later report:

> While crossing the Owen Stanley range the flight gyro started to go out due to bad weather ... decided to push on with gyro working intermittently and took a course which brought us out in Kimbe Bay, thence a straight course to Rabaul. When about 1½ hours out of Rabaul, and encountering severe weather, Nos.3 and 4 engines began malfunctioning. The oil pressure on No.3 dropped to 50 pounds and the engine began to vibrate violently. No.4 engine dropped rpm and began to vibrate also when about ten minutes from the target. This engine then ran away and was immediately feathered. Quick loss of altitude and a drop of the right wing resulted but we continued, making our bomb run, and the bombardier toggled out all of our bombs. When No.4 was feathered we dropped from 14,000ft to 10,500ft doing 120mph at which altitude we bombed, then turned sharply to the left, still losing altitude, with No.3 engine vibrating worse.
>
> We knew we must maintain our altitude of 8,000ft in order to get over the range of mountains on New Britain, so we started No.4

engine but were unable to draw more than 25 inches of mercury, due to threat of running away. At the time we were forced to throttle No.3 back to 20 inches to keep it from shaking the nacelle off. Lieutenant Moore, the engineer and myself worked every moment to keep the ship in the air.

They were flying into a massive tropical storm and the radio compass was going haywire. It was impossible to maintain a straight course as *Black Jack* floundered through the darkness and blinding rain. De Loach says; 'At 0500 our altitude was approximately 5,000ft and we were in the midst of heavy weather. It was impossible to climb to altitude to get above the storm, so we were forced to stay in it which resulted in our becoming completely lost.'

It was about 0530 when Prezioso began trying to contact anyone, anywhere, for a fix on their position. Smith was crouched behind the top turret, transferring fuel as fast as he could from the right wing tanks to the good left engines. It was a slow, laborious task. Forty-five minutes later they were still in the storm and down to 2,000ft. At about 0630 Prezioso sent out the first SOS. The prospect of ditching the aeroplane in the terrible weather conditions was a nightmare, but it seemed inevitable. Baling out over the sea was unthinkable. Clinton and Peterson unbolted the waist guns from their posts and threw them overboard, along with the spare ammunition. In the radio room Prezioso shredded the pages of his lead-covered code book before it, too, was thrown into the darkness. Convinced that they were over Japanese-held territory, Blasewitz tied a Thompson sub-machine gun to a Mae West.

Then, at 0700, as if by a miracle, they broke out of the storm into clear weather, and they could see the coast. Figuring they were close to Japanese-held Lae (well to the northwest of their actual position), they turned southeast. In fact they were close to the Allied airstrip at Dobodura on Oro Bay, but they had no way of knowing this.

Following the coast past a succession of small native villages, De Loach and Moore searched for a broad stretch of beach where they could land, but without success. Fuel was running dangerously low. One red warning light flashed on, then another, and they knew that they would have to put *Black Jack* down in the sea. The pilots tightened their safety harnesses.

Standard procedure required everyone but the pilots to move into the radio room, but there simply was not enough space for eight men. Smith, Wilson and Clinton settled on the wooden walkway that ran around the ball turret and braced themselves against the bulkhead between the waist and radio room. Everyone had parachutes and seat cushions to protect themselves.

The pilots planned to put down in the shallow waters of the fringing coral reef. They hauled back on the controls to keep the nose up, and the bomber hit the water in a torrent of spray. Instead of decelerating, however, *Black Jack* shot forward into the air again, slamming into the deep water beyond the reef with a sickening impact. The ball turret erupted into the fuselage under the three men huddled there. Smith's back and shoulder were broken, and Clinton and Wilson were both badly hurt. Water surged in through the shattered nose and the bomb bay doors, swirling through the aircraft. The wounded were bundled out through the radio room hatch and on to the wing, and Blasewitz pulled the liferaft release handles.

In the cockpit the pilots were already in water up to their knees. De Loach went out through the side window, but his flying suit got caught. He struggled free and swam to the rest of the crew.

The rubber liferafts did not release from their compartments, so Peterson pulled one out and it inflated. The water was lapping at his ankles as he stood on the wing. With only the one liferaft serviceable, the wounded were laid in it, and the others clung to the sides and kind of pushed it along. *Black Jack* stayed afloat perhaps 45 seconds, then sank nose first.

The paddling airmen could see the shore, but their raft was drifting out to sea with the current, and Wilson was bleeding so badly that they began to worry about sharks. Then they saw outrigger canoes making toward them, and they were soon safely ashore at the tiny village of Bogaboga. They were still in sorry shape, but their luck was holding. Hidden on a hilltop a few miles up the coast were two Australian coastwatchers, Eric Foster and Tommy Syme. *Black Jack* had roared out of the west, heading straight for their position, and their first anxious thought was that the Japanese had homed in on their radio. Then they saw the big white star under the aeroplane's wing, and minutes later heard the tremendous crash. They hurried along the bush track towards Bogaboga.

By the time they arrived things had settled down a little. Smith had been given morphine to ease his agony, De Loach had fashioned a sarong from a parachute, and village women had heated water to wash the airmen's' wounds. With the help of the villagers the injured men were carried back to the coastwatchers' position, and an urgent radio call brought a quick response. Flying Officer Ronald Bonython of No.1 Rescue and Communications Squadron picked up the three wounded men in a RAAF Seagull and flew them across the channel to Vivigani airstrip on Goodenough Island. The rest of the crew were picked up later and taken to Goodenough by motor launch, then down to Milne Bay, where they boarded a C-47 for Port Moresby.

De Loach was flying again in August, and finished his tour with a weather reconnaissance flight over Wewak in *Tuffy* on 6 September 1943. Prezioso was aboard *Talisman* on the morning of 5 September 1943, when General Douglas MacArthur observed the parachute invasion of Nadzab from the aircraft. Blasewitz went on to fly another seventeen combat missions. Bonython, the rescue pilot, was lost two months after the *Black Jack* ditching while searching for a Beaufighter crew down near New Britain.

For 43 years *Black Jack* lay on the ocean floor, washed by the warm current between New Guinea and Goodenough Island. The discovery of the old bomber led to a search for the crew, and slowly, after many blind alleys and dead ends, six were traced. The first was Joe Moore in Pennsylvania, then the flight engineer, living in a trailer park in Arkansas. They were followed by the radio operator in New Jersey, the tail gunner in Florida, a waist gunner in Minnesota and the pilot, Ralph De Loach.

When De Loach learned of the discovery of his B-17 he thought it was about time he went back to New Guinea to visit the little village where his life had hung in the balance all those years ago. In December 1987 the white-haired pilot stepped ashore and was met by the little group of village elders who still recalled that Sunday in 1943, and the memories flooded back. Standing on the beach and staring out to sea, where a bobbing orange buoy marked *Black Jack*'s last resting place, he summed it all up. His rich voice brittle with emotion, he said, 'I think the way *Black Jack*'s ended up now, sitting under the sea encrusted in coral, is one of the finest endings it could have had ... a very proper ending for a very gallant aircraft'.

Ruthie II

Of the many acts of gallantry and fortitude involving the crews of Fortresses, probably none surpass that which occurred in the 92nd Bomb Group's *Ruthie II* on 26 July 1943. The happenings of that flight became famous, and were even accorded reference in the opening scenes of that most authentic of films about the operations of the 8th Air Force, the 1949 20th Century Fox release 'Twelve O'Clock High'.

In the last ten days of July 1943 a period of clear weather settled over northwest Europe, allowing VIII Bomber Command an opportunity to press home its campaign of daylight precision bombardment against German industry. There was a shortage of replacements for bomber losses at this time, but although B-17F 42-29802 had reached the UK early in April, 3½ months appear to have elapsed before it was employed in combat. On 22 July it was sent to the 92nd Bomb Group at Alconbury, and was received that day in the 326th Bomb Squadron. It was taken over by 1st Lieutenant Robert L. Campbell, whose previous aircraft had been badly shot up and declared salvage earlier in the month. Campbell had named this aircraft *Ruthie* after his girlfriend, an American nurse from the Second Evacuation Hospital at Diddington, near Huntingdon. On the replacement B-17 he bestowed the name *Ruthie II*.

After a day of preparation and inspection the newcomer was ready to go to war. In the early dark hours of the 26th, Campbell's crew was one of those attending a briefing at Alconbury. They learned they were to be part of a force attacking a rubber plant at Hanover. A 21-plane group formation was desirable, but the 92nd could muster only 19 Fortresses, two of which were YB-40s, the experimental, heavily-armed escort version that carried no bombs.

Campbell had lost some members of his original crew through wounds and indisposition, and his co-pilot for this mission was Flight Officer John C. Morgan, who wore RAF wings above the right-hand breast pocket of his tunic. A month away from his 29th birthday, the laconic Morgan had been something of a rolling stone and adventurer. Four months before the United States became involved in hostilities he joined the Royal Canadian Air Force, and after flight training he went to England, where he served with a Canadian bomber squadron as a Sergeant Pilot for seven months. Transferring to the USAAF in late March 1943, Morgan was given the rank of Flight Officer in lieu of a commission, and joined the 92nd Group in May. This was to be his fifth mission with the Group, and thereafter he was promised his own crew. Both Campbell and Morgan were well-built men, over six feet tall and weighing approximately 185lb and 200lb respectively. Morgan had a mop of auburn hair and was inevitably known as 'Red'.

The Fortresses took off into a bright sunlit morn, and Bob Campbell moved *Ruthie II* into position as the left-hand wingman in the Group's three-aeroplane lead element. A Spitfire escort was present for part of the journey over the North Sea, and when these friendly fighters departed the gunners were apprehensively alert for unfriendly attention. Their foreboding was met from out of the sun as the task force approached the Fresian Islands.

Focke-Wulf Fw 190s came through the 92nd formation from between 1 and 2 o'clock high. The rate of closure was so fast that Red Morgan, who had just relinquished the controls to Bob Campbell, saw only the blink of a fighter's guns when, with a violent explosion, the windshield in front of him instantly became a blind of cracks and distortions completely obscuring his view. He was aware of a concussion and the aircraft rocking. Turning, he saw Campbell slumped forward over the controls, the back of the right side of his head a mass of blood and the brain exposed. With brute strength Morgan grasped the mortally wounded pilot by the shoulder and pulled him backwards in his seat.

> There was no time for trauma – it suddenly got very busy. There was blood all over the cockpit, all over me. The shattered windscreen obscured my vision. I could not see anything ahead at all. I could look out of the window above and the only thing I could do to keep in formation was to watch an aircraft above.

Morgan's complete attention was now focused on flying the bomber and keeping Campbell away from the controls. As the initial shock subsided, Morgan realized that he had been hit by fragments of metal, although nothing appeared to have penetrated his flight clothing. A check on the instruments showed no problem with the engines, and the aircraft appeared to handle normally.

An attempt to call other members of the crew revealed that the intercom had been put out of action. Hearing a shout and taking a quick glance to the rear, he saw the top-turret gunner stagger into the hatch that led to the nose compartment. Blood on the equipment suggested he had been wounded. Now and again the guns in the nose compartment were fired in response to further fighter attacks, so Morgan knew that the navigator and bombardier were still at their posts, but hearing no fire from the rear he suspected that the men stationed there had baled out. For the time being he had to concentrate on the controls, and on fending off the crazed actions of the pilot.

The burst of fire that had struck the cockpit included a 20mm cannon shell which had penetrated the windshield, and a 7.9mm bullet which had entered through the side window, passing in front of Morgan's face to strike Campbell. Another 7.9mm bullet and a 20mm shell had penetrated the base of the top turret, striking the top-turret gunner, Staff Sergeant Tyre C. Weaver, in his left arm just below the shoulder, and the explosion had severed the limb. Weaver was knocked out of the turret and fell down the hatch into the nose compartment.

Seeing the stricken, blood-drenched man, the navigator, 2nd Lieutenant Keith Koske, immediately grabbed a first aid kit and attempted to apply a tourniquet, only to find it was impossible because the arm was severed too close to the shoulder. An attempt to give Weaver a shot of painkilling morphine was also unsuccessful because the needle bent. Although the extreme cold at the altitude at which they were flying, 24,500ft, helped check the flow of blood, and although he had done what he could with dressings, Koske realized that unless Weaver received the right medical attention fairly soon he would probably bleed to death.

The estimated time of arrival back in England was 1530, and it was not yet noon. Koske decided that the only hope for Weaver was to parachute him into Germany and take a chance that he would be quickly found and treated. Releasing the nose hatch door, he fixed a parachute on Weaver, placed the release ring firmly in the gunner's right hand, and was in the process of manoeuvring the stricken man's legs through the open hatch when the pilot 'chute suddenly whipped out in the updraught. In his dazed and pained state Weaver had pulled the ripcord ring. With great presence of mind Koske grabbed the pilot 'chute before it pulled out the canopy and bundled it under Weaver's good arm. Holding the arm as a clamp over the 'chute, he persuaded Weaver into a crouched position and then toppled him out. Koske noted that they were approximately 25 miles from the target at this point. He then returned to navigation duties and manning a nose gun while bombardier 2nd Lieutenant Asa J. Irwin prepared for the bomb release. As the B-17 appeared to be under control, if occasionally engaging in what they took to be evasive action, the two officers in the nose compartment had no reason to suspect that all was not well in the cockpit.

All was far from well, for John Morgan now had a test of endurance on his hands. Unable to communicate with other members of the crew but knowing that some, if not all, were still aboard, his hope was that soon one of them would come to the cockpit. The crazed actions of the dying pilot continued:

> Bob was a strong, big, old Mississippi boy who just didn't know he was dead. He would fall forward and grab the wheel. When this happened the 'plane would nose down and I had to get him by the shoulder and pull him away. Under the circumstances you didn't really know what he was trying to do; he was waving his arms about, hitting me in the face and mouth – blackened my eyes. He was constantly falling forward so that I had to keep my left hand on his shoulder most of the time.

After the target, the men in the nose continued to man the guns, and although the B-17 formations were frequently under attack, most passes were now from the tail end and there was little opportunity to fire. Although they could not obtain any response over the intercom, the bombardier and navigator assumed all was well, as there was the occasional burst of firing from elsewhere in the aircraft.

Some 15 minutes out from the enemy coast, Koske decided it was safe to leave his gun position and check with the pilot. As he ducked down and came through the hatch on to the flight deck he met a scene of carnage. Frozen blood was splattered everywhere, and Morgan was holding off the still struggling pilot with one hand while flying the aeroplane with the other, as he had been doing for more than two hours. Koske immediately went to Morgan's assistance, and was told that they would have to remove Campbell from the left seat as the bomber could not be landed from the right side because of the shattered windshield and side window.

With what assistance Morgan could give, Koske attempted to remove the struggling pilot, but finally had to seek additional help. On making his way back through the bomb bay to the rear of the aircraft, he discovered that the tail, waist and radio gunners were in a state of semi-consciousness owing to insufficient oxygen, and some were also badly frostbitten. Apparently, part of the system in the rear of the aircraft had been damaged during the first pass by the fighters. Only the ball turret gunner, with a separate supply, had remained in action.

Returning to the flight deck, Koske managed to undo the pilot's retaining straps. The still-resisting Campbell was removed from the left-hand seat, and with the aid of one of the revived gunners Koske managed to get the mortally wounded man down into the nose compartment, where Lieutenant Irwin had to keep hold of him to prevent him slipping out of the open nose hatch. Morgan moved into the pilot's seat for the final hour and a quarter of the flight to England, with the fuel gauges showing a rapidly diminishing supply. The radio was inoperative, but Morgan had already decided to land at the first airfield seen after crossing the Norfolk coast.

When England was reached they flew some miles before sighting an airfield, which was an RAF station at Foulsham. Several other B-17s were already circling to land, so Morgan ordered red flares to be fired, indicating wounded on board, and then cut into the landing pattern. Tail gunner Staff Sergeant John Foley assisted by lowering the wheels and flaps as the approach was made. Despite the loss of hydraulic fluid, *Ruthie II* was brought safely to the end of its landing run. An RAF ambulance was waiting when the engines were finally cut. Campbell was carefully lowered through the nose hatch on to a stretcher. As the doctor leaned over him, the dying man was still strong enough to bring his feet back and kick the RAF doctor in the chest. Campbell lived for another hour and a half.

What of the exhausted Morgan, free at last from his ordeal in the deafening, shaking, freezing environment that was a Fortress at war? 'I was all right. Sore all over, I'd taken a physical beating. We went back to the base that night and I was scheduled to fly next day. However, apparently I'd been talking in my sleep that night and Doc Shoemaker came to the briefing room and said, "No way, he goes to the flak house".'

In fact, Red Morgan did not return to combat for some weeks. The following spring he was to have a miraculous escape from a B-17 shot down over Berlin, and spent the last 14 months of the war as a prisoner. They gave John Morgan the highest award his country has for gallantry, the Medal of Honor, although he would deflect praise by insisting that Koske was the real hero. Indeed, Koske's action did save Weaver's life. The parachute was seen to open by other airmen in the 92nd Group formation, and when Weaver landed in a field a nine-year-old German girl saw him and fetched some soldiers, who immediately got him to a hospital. Weaver made a full recovery and was later repatriated to the USA.

Ruthie II, holed in several places including a fuel tank, remained at Foulsham for repair. Someone had the gruesome task of washing all traces of blood from the flight deck and nose. The aircraft never again flew in combat with the 92nd Bomb Group. Instead, in September 1943 it was transferred to the 379th Bomb Group at Kimbolton, one of three groups in which B-17s without long-range fuel tanks were being concentrated. Assigned to the 527th Bomb Squadron, the bomber flew its first mission with its new operators on 16 September. Over the next six months it participated in sixteen combat sorties with fourteen different crews, all of whom were probably unaware of the dreadful drama that had been played out in the bomber on its very first combat mission.

Following a mission on 19 March 1944, *Ruthie II* was retired from combat, and on 7 April was taken over by the service command for overhaul. Eight days later it was returned to the USA, and spent the rest of its days mostly at a replacement training centre, in use by replacement crews, before becoming yet another of the many veteran aircraft dumped at Kingman, in the Arizona desert. There it became just another source of aluminium scrap.

Robert L. Campbell was eventually laid to rest in the US military cemetery at Madingley, England, where his grave can still be seen.

The Saga of Patches

During the last ten days of July 1943 a high-pressure area extended over much of northwest Europe, providing the clear skies vital to the daylight precision bombing practised by the US 8th Air Force. The sun blazed, ripening the grain crops in East Anglian fields, and farmers began to gather a harvest. Some time after noon on the 30th, a boy watching farm workers hitching a binder to a noisy tractor was startled by a shadow speeding across the canopy of uncut barley.

Looking up, he saw a Fortress at some 500ft, passing between the sun and his hand-shielded gaze. Momentarily he saw a flash of sunlight through a wing and then, silhouetted against the sun's glare, the ragged outline of the tailplane, from which huge pieces were missing. The wounded aircraft staggered rather than flew through the air as it made a curving descent towards a nearby airfield. Later, village rumour held that several dead were removed from the bomber, which had returned on a proverbial 'wing and a prayer'. In reality there were no fatal casualties, but what happened that day to the 384th Bomb Group's *Patches* was one of the classic combat survival actions in which B-17s were involved.

Patches was one of nine B-17Fs that the 547th Bomb Squadron brought to England in May 1943. At first it was simply known as '848', the last three digits of its serial number. At the 384th Bomb Group base it was allotted the individual radio call sign R-Roger, and the recognition letters SO:R were painted on its fuselage.

Selected to fly on the Group's first mission, on 22 June, '848' was despatched with Lieutenant D. P. Ogilvie's crew. The target was the docks at Antwerp, and this shallow penetration of hostile airspace which should have been a low-risk introduction to combat was, unfortunately, otherwise. Inexperience delayed the formations, and they arrived in the target area without fighter escort. Three Fw 190 Staffeln intercepted on the target approach over the sea off Sans Van Gent, their frontal attacks causing one Fortress to go down and severely damaging others. These included '848', which took cannon strikes from cockpit to tail that wounded the ball and tail gunners.

Coming off the target, the lead B-17 of '848's' flight apparently suffered engine failure through battle damage, and began a gradual descent towards the sea. Ogilvie and the other wing aircraft of the flight followed for several thousand feet to give fire support. Fortunately there were no enemy interceptions, and Ogilvie and the other wing B-17 pilot eventually realized their leader was doomed. Back at Grafton Underwood they were reprimanded for breaking formation; separation meant vulnerability.

Fortress 42-5848 required a lot of work that took nearly a month to complete. It was found to have some 40 holes, which were covered by riveted sheet-alclad patches. On completion of the work it was obvious that the bomber would henceforth be known as *Patches*, and this name was painted on the side of the nose. While the bomber was under repair the 384th Bomb Group undertook two more costly missions, and before *Patches* was returned to combat a quarter of the Group's original strength was gone.

Then came Blitz Week, as it was later called. Starting on 24 July, six missions were flown in seven days, and some were very rough indeed. *Patches* flew its second mission on the 28th and came back short of fuel, having to put down at RAF Oulton. On the next day *Patches* went with the Group to Kiel, where cloud foiled the raiders and targets of opportunity had to be attacked. On the last day, 30 July, the 384th could muster only thirteen bombers for a raid on the Fieseler aircraft works at Kassel.

Second Lieutenant William R. Harry's crew were to take *Patches* on this mission. Like their charge, it was to be their fourth foray into the dangerous skies over Hitler's *Festung Europa*. Drawn from right across the United States, they had an unusually wide age range. Radio operator Technical Sergeant Edward Simpson and tail gunner Staff Sergeant Leroy Parent were only 19, in contrast to ball turret gunner Staff Sergeant John McKenna, the 'old man' of the crew at 33. The two waist gunners were also well above the average for combat aircrew, Staff Sergeant Thomas Wheeler being 28 and Staff Sergeant Willard Cronin 30. The engineer and top turret gunner, Technical Sergeant Curry Reed, was 22, the same age as Harry and navigator 2nd Lieutenant David Black. The other two officers, co-pilot Ivan Rice and bombardier Charles Mannka, both 2nd lieutenants, were 25 and 24 respectively.

Not a single cloud sat in the blue of the morning sky as the 384th's small formation rose high above England to join with others. Mechanical troubles forced two of the Fortresses to turn back before the Dutch coast was reached, but while the 384th was only eleven strong, it was part of a force of more than 100 Fortresses briefed for the same target. For Bill Harry and his men the flight was untroubled until about 0900, as the formation prepared to bomb. Up to that time surprisingly little had been seen of enemy fighters, and the gunners were beginning to tire of continually searching the sky, peering towards the sun.

Just after bombs away *Patches* shuddered, and the men in the forward part of the aircraft heard the sound which was usually likened to a handful of pebbles thrown on a tin roof. A near miss by an exploding flak shell had peppered the rear fuselage with splinters, wounding both waist gunners in the arms and legs, Willard Cronin being the more seriously injured. Calling for assistance, Charles Mannka made his way back to the rear of the aircraft to administer first aid and help Edward Simpson get the injured men into the more sheltered radio room. At this time tail gunner Leroy Parent reported that his electrical flying boots had failed and he believed that his feet had become frostbitten.

Leaving behind the flak barrage over the target, the formation headed home. Still there had been no attacks by enemy fighters, and some cherished the hope that this would be an occasion when the Luftwaffe did not appear in the sky. It was not to be, for, as they neared the Dutch border, Fw 190s came swiftly out of the sun. One of the interceptors bracketted *Patches* with its fire. Two strikes on the top turret put a bullet through the left thigh of Currie Reed, causing him to half fall out of his turret and fracture a leg. Even so, Reed climbed back and stuck to his guns, later claiming an Fw 190 destroyed. During the same pass Harry was struck in the right hip by a bullet, and other hits in the cockpit area caused co-pilot Rice to be slightly wounded by flying fragments. It was also found that the oxygen system had been damaged, and loss of pressure at several stations threatened to induce anoxia. The situation did not allow the use of the emergency walk-around bottles, and Harry had no option but to drop out of formation and descend to an altitude where his men would not be dependent on oxygen. *Patches* would become a straggler, and the hope was that they would escape the notice of enemy fighters.

Alone and 200 miles from home, *Patches* was highly vulnerable. The crew waited for the enemy fighters to appear, but hoped their attention would be directed to the formations high above and ahead. It was not long before a gunner called in 'Focke-Wulfs attacking'. Harry immediately started evasive action, jinking the Fortress up and down. Hits were sustained but no serious damage was done. He asked the crew to report each fighter approach so that he could take evasive action and, as every attack was called in, he and Rice threw the aircraft around. The attacks continued for 20 minutes, and *Patches* was hit repeatedly by 20mm shells and rifle-calibre bullets. Despite this, the pilot's violent manoeuvring of the aircraft minimized the damage sustained in the fighter passes, which continued well out to sea. Eventually the Focke-Wulfs disappeared, presumably because of fuel or ammunition exhaustion. Only then did Bill Harry turn over the controls to Ivan Rice and have his wounds dressed. *Patches* was nursed across the North Sea, making a landfall on the Essex coast.

The first airfield to come into sight was Boxted, a B-26 base near Colchester. It took both pilots to nurse *Patches* into a landing, as the throttles were jammed and the flight control surfaces severely damaged. Despite their best efforts it was not possible to line up *Patches* to touch down directly on the main runway, and, when the wheels finally hit, *Patches* immediately veered off to the left because the tyre on that side was flat, having been hit by enemy fire. After careering across two runways the bomber finally came to a standstill at nearly 90° to its original landing approach. Ambulances were soon on the scene and removed the six wounded. Bill Harry, Currie Reed and Willard Cronin remained in the base hospital for a few days, but the other wounded were able to return to Grafton Underwood that afternoon.

It is said that they counted a thousand holes in *Patches*. Fortresses were in very short supply at the time, and an aircraft was never scrapped unless it was totally beyond economical repair. The mobile repair and reclamation people came and looked, as did the 384th Bomb Group engineering officers. *Patches* was in one piece, but all agreed that there were just too many perforations and that, apart from the man-hours that would have to be expended to make the aircraft flyable again, it would simply be nothing but patches. A week after its last landing, *Patches* was declared salvage. It languished at Boxted for several weeks, its dismemberment appearing to be a low-priority task for the mobile recovery and reclamation people.

William Harry and Ivan Rice returned to combat with a re-formed crew, only to be shot down on the disastrous Schweinfurt mission of 14 October 1943. Rice was killed, and Harry escaped with wounds. Fate was indeed fickle.

Jinx Ship?

On a damp autumn day in 1943 a British telephone engineer performing maintenance work at Ridgewell airfield, Essex, got into conversation with a USAAF mechanic. The civilian remarked on the nickname of the Fortress standing nearby, and the gist of the American's reply was, 'That's the jinx ship of the Group. Some guys refuse to fly in her.' The name of the B-17 in question was *Tinker Toy*.

Exaggeration and rumour were commonplace in personal communication on a bomber station. The facts suggest that *Tinker Toy* was no more a 'jinx ship' than several other B-17s that were involved in bloody incidents, but there were certainly many 381st Bomb Group men at Ridgewell who had no hesitation in condemning the aircraft in those terms. The Group medical officer wrote in his records that *Tinker Toy* was viewed with a mixture of horror and pride by men of the base, and there is no doubt that this Fortress qualifies as either famous or infamous in 381st Bomb Group history.

Boeing B-17F-25-VE serial number 42-5846 was built by Lockheed's Vega factory at Burbank, California, early in 1943. It was delivered to the fledgling 381st Bomb Group at Pueblo Army Air Base, Colorado, in April of that year. On 21 May the aircraft, carrying the CO of the 533rd Bomb Squadron, departed the United States for an overseas destination which proved to be the UK and the 8th Air Force. It was assigned to the 535th Bomb Squadron and flew its first combat mission, to Villacoublay with 1st Lieutenant Frank Chapman's crew, on 26 June. Two days later 1st Lieutenant Robert Holdom took *Tinker Toy* to St Nazaire, and over the next three months nine different crews went into battle in the bomber. Unavailability of the aircraft owing to battle damage or mechanical problems often led to its regular crew being assigned other aircraft for missions.

On 26 July the 381st sent eighteen B-17s to Hamburg. Lieutenant Frank Chapman's crew was given *Tinker Toy*. Lieutenant Bill Hodge, Chapman's regular navigator, was unable to fly, and his place was taken by Lieutenant Sidney Novell, recently arrived at Ridgewell, this being his first combat mission. Some flak was encountered returning from Hamburg and, although no Group aircraft was seriously damaged, a shell fragment sliced through the nose Plexiglas of *Tinker Toy* and struck Novell in the head, fatally wounding him. *Tinker Toy* was the first B-17 in the squadron to bring a dead man back to Ridgewell.

On 17 August the 8th sent its bombers on a double strike, the 1st Wing to Schweinfurt ball-bearing plant, and the 4th Wing to a fighter factory at Regensberg. Poor visibility delayed the take-off of the 1st Wing force, disrupting the carefully planned timing aimed at splitting the enemy fighter opposition. The 381st was the low group formation of the leading combat wing attacking Schweinfurt, and suffered the loss of eleven B-17s. *Tinker Toy* and 1st Lieutenant Charles Dowell's crew survived, but ball turret gunner Staff Sergeant Ward Bathrick was seriously wounded. Hit by splinters from a 20mm round which exploded outside his turret, he remained at his post, refusing treatment until the battle was over. Bathrick was credited with shooting down the Fw 190 which had wounded him. Later in the month this crew made a radio broadcast from London, telling of their experiences on the Schweinfurt raid.

Tinker Toy was loaned to the 533rd Bomb Squadron on 6 September 1943 and flown by Lieutenant Paul Gleichauf's crew. The briefed target was Stuttgart. While crossing the Channel, the crew discovered that the oxygen system on one side of the aircraft was leaking, but there seemed good reason to believe that if the leaking system was used first there would be sufficient oxygen to sustain the crew through the rest of the trip. Even so, the problem grew worse and some of the crew were reduced to using auxiliary oxygen bottles, and the ball turret station had to be abandoned by the gunner. Some crew members at times became disorientated through lack of oxygen, and one man inadvertently released his parachute, which became snagged while he was passing through the bomb bay.

Unfortunately, high cloud foiled the raiders, and the search for targets of opportunity made the mission unduly prolonged, with the result that many Fortresses were critically low on fuel when leaving the French coast. *Tinker Toy* was one of these, but Gleichauf fortunately found a small RAF fighter field on the south coast. The landing was made with fuel gauges reading empty.

The 381st had been flying in the low group position of the lead wing formation on the first Schweinfurt raid, and in a similar placing on 8 October it was again decimated by enemy fighters near Bremen, seven B-17s failing to return. *Tinker Toy* was one of the survivors, but what occurred in it that day undoubtedly gave substance to the jinx legend.

A replacement crew captained by Lieutenant William Minerich, which arrived in September, had been assigned *Tinker Toy*, and most of the men were on their fifth mission. Approaching the Initial Point, the 381st formation came under vicious attack by Fw 190s. An enemy fighter attacking from the 10 o'clock position scored several cannon-shell strikes on *Tinker Toy*. One 20mm shell smashed through the nose Plexiglas, wounding bombardier Gordon Stickel. Another detonated under the navigator's position, wounding navigator 2nd Lieutenant Henry Palas, who had to be helped to one side for protection from the icy blast entering the shattered nosepiece. Two other cannon-shell strikes in the same fusillade hit the left-hand windshield framing and entered the cockpit. One exploded under the pilot's face, decapitating him, and the other detonated beside Lieutenant Thomas Sellars, but despite its proximity he sustained only a moderate wound in the left arm, although he was severely shocked. The flight deck was a scene of carnage, and blood from the dead pilot sprayed over everything and immediately froze.

The top turret gunner, Technical Sergeant Henry T. Miller, suddenly found that the lower part of his turret had turned crimson. The shock to Sellars and Miller is not difficult to imagine, but the co-pilot did his best to keep the bomber under control. Miller, realizing that Sellars had wounds to his left side, helped manipulate the throttle controls on the return flight. Other battle damage included hits on the right wing engines, but despite his horrific situation Sellars was able to bring *Tinker Toy* back to Ridgewell and make a good landing.

Those who went to the aircraft soon after it landed encountered what they described as 'the smell of death'. In recognition of his ordeal, Tom Sellars was later awarded the DSC, his nation's second highest award for valour, and Henry Miller was awarded the DFC. The fact that Sellars did not return to combat for three months gives some idea of the traumatic effect the mission had on him.

Two weeks after the 8 October mission, navigator Henry Palas's bride of three months, Carmen, learned that he had been wounded and obtained some details of the fateful mission. The *Los Angeles Herald and Express* published her comments; 'I wondered why he didn't write these past two weeks. Usually he writes every day and I write to him twice a day. In his last letter he asked me to send him a fruit cake – that's his favourite kind of cake.' Henry Palas did not receive the cake, as it proved too heavy to send through the mail, but his pretty young wife did advance her confidence; 'I have no fear for Henry. He'll always come through okay.' Sadly, her faith was not honoured. Henry Palas started flying combat missions again in November, but on 30 January 1944 the crew with which he was flying had to ditch in the North Sea. There were no survivors. Palas's name appears on the Wall of the Missing at Madingley, England.

At about this time the Hollywood movie 'Hers to Hold' had reached England. It was a typical, sentimental, patriotically flavoured tale of the period, and featured songstress Deanna Durbin doing her bit for the war effort. Someone in the 381st noticed that a scene shot in the Burbank factory showed B-17s coming off the production line, and one aircraft that formed a backdrop for Miss Durbin's presentation carried the tail number 25846. Thus *Tinker Toy* had gained public attention from a very early date.

Tinker Toy was then put in the hands of Lieutenant Lee Smith and crew, who flew it to Paris on 5 December and Emden on the 11th. The Henslin crew taking it to Bremen on 13 December 'lost' No.2 engine. It was Bremen again on 16 December, and again on the 20th, when 1st Lieutenant Dorman Lane and his men flew it. The 381st had a 'rough trip', and four bombers did not return. One was *Tinker Toy*. An enemy fighter, probably hit by defensive fire, sliced a wing into the bomber's rear fuselage and both aircraft tumbled out of the sky. *Tinker Toy* was seen to disintegrate as it went down, and three parachutes were counted. It was just another bomber, another crew, in the bloody air war of the time, but *Tinker Toy* remained something of a legend with the 381st.

There is another aspect of *Tinker Toy*'s record that would have given some credence to the jinx tag, had its advocates known the details. There was not a single crew which, having flown a mission in *Tinker Toy*, did not have at least one member, and usually more, lost in another bomber in a subsequent mission.

The Ball Boys

All military units with esprit de corps strive for distinction through their insignia, but of the 1,500 flying squadrons formed by the USAAF during the Second World War, few can rival the 511th Bomb Squadron. Not only did the approved squadron insignia feature a ball motif in acknowledgement of the unit's original commander, Clinton F. Ball, but an amazing conformity of aircraft nicknames containing the word 'ball' was maintained throughout the unit's two years of overseas deployment.

The 511th Bomb Squadron was the fourth squadron of the 351st Bomb Group, formed in November 1942 at Geiger Field, Washington, where Clinton Ball assumed command. He was then a 1st Lieutenant with a West Point commission, but was soon elevated to the rank of Captain. When the squadron began to receive its combat aircraft in March 1943, Clint Ball had *Linda Ball* painted on both sides of the nose of his command B–17F, No.42-29849, in honour of his baby daughter of the same name. The other flying officers discussed the naming of their aircraft, and 2nd Lieutenant William R. Smith proposed that all nine of the new B–17s should have nicknames with a 'ball' suffix. Thus the names *Cannon Ball*, *Eight Ball*, *Foul Ball*, *Spare Ball*, *Screw Ball*, *High Ball*, *Fire Ball* and *Snow Ball* soon graced the noses of the bombers.

The squadron made a direct flight across the Atlantic from Gander, Newfoundland, to Prestwick, Scotland, on 16 April, and after refuelling moved on to its wartime station at Polebrook, Northamptonshire. Here another B–17 and crew were assigned, raising the strength to ten, and this aircraft was promptly named *Speed Ball*. It was with these ten B–17Fs that the 'Ball Boys', as they were dubbed by public relations, began combat operations on 13 May 1943. The fates of the original aircraft and of their crews is typical of B–17 squadrons joining battle in the spring of 1943. It was, to quote Clint Ball, 'tough and rough'. Grim would be a more appropriate adjective.

The first 511th Bomb Squadron Fortress to be lost was *Spare Ball* on the Group's third mission, a raid on Emden docks on 15 May. After bombing, *Spare Ball* was seen to drop back gradually from the formation, presumably through some loss of power, as it was believed that the aircraft had sustained flak damage. It was then reported to have entered a slow spiral, to have been attacked by enemy aircraft and eventually to have disintegrated before plunging into the sea about 40 miles northeast of Borkum. Parachutes were reported, but there were no survivors from 1st Lieutenant Joe Meli's ten-man crew.

Four days later the group went to Kiel and came under attack from fighters on the bomb run at 26,000ft. First Lieutenant William R. Smith's *Fire Ball* took hits, a 20mm shell exploding in the rear fuselage and severing oxygen lines. The left waist gunner, Technical Sergeant Lewis Baker, apparently thought the aircraft doomed, and in attempting to bale out released his parachute prematurely. The canopy snagged on the door, suspending his body outside to thump against the fuselage. Deprived of oxygen, the other gunners lost consciousness, and it was only when they failed to respond to intercom calls that the forward crew realized that something was amiss. The gunners were revived with walk-around oxygen bottles, but nothing could be done for Baker as the slipstream defeated all attempts by crew members to haul in his body. Lieutenant Smith brought *Fire Ball* down at RAF Sculthorpe with Baker's body still dragging behind; a harrowing experience for all of the crew.

Lieutenant Carl Wilson's *Eight Ball* came close to being lost on the next mission. Difficulty with the propeller speed on No.2 engine developed into complete control loss as the Fortress neared the enemy coast. The windmilling propeller caused severe vibration and, unable to feather the blades, Wilson decided to abort. Fortunately the aircraft was not intercepted by enemy fighters, although the major concern was the intense vibration and its effect on control. A ditching in the North Sea seemed very likely. By flying just above stalling speed the pilots were able to keep *Eight Ball* in the air. Eventually the reduction gear assembly disintegrated, and although the errant free-wheeling propeller remained, the vibration was substantially reduced.

Eight Ball was flown back to Polebrook and landed safely, although soon after touchdown the No.2 propeller separated from the engine and struck the left-hand nose station gun, as well as removing the area of skinning on which the aircraft's name was painted. Fortunately no one was seriously hurt, but *Eight Ball* spent several weeks in the hangar undergoing an engine change and repairs to the wing and nose. As the aircraft had itself disposed of the name *Eight Ball*, it was re-christened *No Balls At All* by some humorist.

The squadron came under fighter attack on the 11 June mission. No aircraft were lost, but a 20mm cannon shell from an Me 109 exploded in the nose of *Foul Ball*, killing the navigator, 2nd Lieutenant Fred Angel. At St Nazaire on 28 June the Ball Boys were set upon by Fw 190s of JG2. When the leader of the second element of three B-17s decided to manoeuvre to a better defensive position, one aircraft, *High Ball*, was caught in turbulence and dropped 1,000ft before its pilot, 1st Lieutenant Robert Adams, the squadron Operations Officer, could regain control. The isolated *High Ball* was then set upon by enemy fighters. Cannon shell strikes in the waist killed both waist gunners, the ball gunner and the radio operator. Number 3 engine burst into flames and defied all efforts to extinguish it. Adams ordered the men to bale out. Four members of the crew were taken prisoner by German troops soon after descending, but co-pilot George Gloudeman and navigator Joe Normile were sheltered by French patriots and eventually returned to the UK via Spain. The 351st Bomb Group lost three other bombers that day.

A mission to hit a tyre factory at Hanover on 17 July was frustrated by adverse weather conditions, and while withdrawing over the Dutch coast the formation came under determined fighter attack. No aircraft fell during the combat, but 1st Lieutenant William Peters' *Snow Ball* was badly damaged. In a head-on attack the bombardier was wounded and the navigator, Lieutenant Fred Wattles, was killed by cannon shells which shattered the nose. First No.4 engine was put out of action, and then No.1. Probably seeing their victim heading for the sea and guessing that the bomber was running low on fuel, the enemy fighter pilots turned away. With no hope of keeping *Snow Ball* airborne, Peters alerted the crew for a ditching. Although the aircraft struck hard and sank in an estimated 45 seconds, all living members of the crew escaped. After an hour on liferafts, one of which was damaged, they were spotted by an RAF reconnaissance aircraft, and rescue by Walrus amphibians came some 50 minutes later.

First Lieutenant Max Pinkerton's *Cannon Ball* was the next to be lost. Flying as tail-end charlie, the bomber suffered repeated fighter attacks and No.3 engine caught fire. *Cannon Ball* fell out of formation, but all of the crew were able to bale out successfully, although co-pilot Flight Officer Herbert Berreau was apparently killed on landing. The others were all taken prisoner. *Cannon Ball*, one wing a mass of flames, plummeted into the ground near the Black Forest. This was on the 17 August Schweinfurt mission, when 60 Fortresses failed to return.

On 6 September 1943 the 8th Air Force set out to bomb the Bosch factory at Stuttgart. Bad weather thwarted this attack, and through spending too long in hostile airspace many bombers were desperately low on fuel on reaching the English Channel. Lieutenant C.F. Norris watched the gauges register empty on *Foul Ball* and managed to glide to within 100 yards of Beachy Head for a perfect ditching. All of the crew were able to get safely ashore.

Depleted fuel supplies again caused concern for pilots on 15 September, when the 351st Group went to Romilly-sur-Seine air depot near Paris. The distance was not great, but on this occasion each Fortress carried a 1,000lb bomb under each wing, in addition to a 6,000lb load in the bomb bay. Fuel consumption was therefore heavy, and on return many emergency landings were made at airfields in south and east England. The only aircraft to come to grief was the Ball Boys' lead ship, a replacement B-17F received in June and fitted with British Gee navigational equipment. It was originally named *Meat Ball*, but this had been changed to *Major Ball*, presumably to acknowledge the aircraft's status.

On this occasion it had been loaned to the 508th Bomb Squadron and was being flown by its CO, Major James T. Stewart. Darkness had descended when the formation reached Polebrook and, after two thwarted attempts to land, *Major Ball* ran out of fuel on the next approach and crashed in a field just short of the runway. The crew quickly extricated themselves, there being no serious injuries. The recently promoted Lieutenant Colonel Clinton Ball hurried towards the crash scene in a Jeep, only to end up in a ditch after swerving to avoid another vehicle on a narrow English road. A few days later Clinton Ball became Group Operations Officer, turning over command of the 511th to Captain Harry Morse, the pilot who had flown *Linda Ball* across the Atlantic.

A replacement aircraft was the next loss for the 511th, when Lieutenant Dan Nauman's *Minor Ball* went down in a flak barrage over Frankfurt, but he and several members of his crew survived. Nauman had been the regular pilot of *High Ball*, which had been lost with another captain and members of Nauman's original crew on 28 June.

Losses of 8th Air Force B-17s were running at over 10 per cent of sorties flown in early October 1943. Fighter opposition on the Anklam mission of 9 October claimed two more 511th replacement aircraft, *Spit Ball* and *Cue Ball*. The latter was flown by Captain Morse's crew, all of whom parachuted safely and were taken prisoner.

Lieutenant Elmer Nardi's *Speed Ball* was the subject of much curiosity at Polebrook when it returned from the mission. Part of an enemy air-launched rocket was to be seen embedded in its wing.

The only 511th and 351st Bomb Group loss on the infamous Schweinfurt mission of 14 October was a replacement crew and aircraft, *Onda Ball*. The sixth of the Ball Boys' original B-17s to be lost was *Fire Ball*, with Elmer Nardi's crew. On 3 November, Nardi and three other members perished when the aircraft disintegrated after being struck by cannon shells. The other crew members were able to bale out and were taken prisoner. The squadron complement was now increased to fourteen aircraft, leaving the remaining originals very much in the minority.

The last day of 1943 proved to be one of the Polebrook group's most disastrous days. Flak and fighters in the area of the target, an aircraft assembly plant near Bordeaux, claimed six of the 31 B-17s despatched. *Speed Ball*, on its 24th mission, survived the debacle in the target area only to be shot up by enemy fighters over the Brest Peninsula. Two engines were disabled, and Lieutenant Albert Jones was forced to ditch near Guernsey. Nine men managed to get on to the liferafts, but one later died of exposure. During the night the rafts grounded on rocks off Guernsey. Only two members of the crew eventually reached the Guernsey shore alive, suffering from severe exposure.

The last of the original Ball Boys aircraft to be lost was *No Balls At All*, on its 22nd mission. After attacking Schweinfurt on 24 February 1944, damage to No.2 engine caused the aircraft to fall behind. Continually losing height, 2nd Lieutenant Walter LeClerc was unable to get any further than Holland, where a crash-landing was made, ending up in a drainage ditch. All of the crew were taken prisoner.

The survivors of the ten B-17Fs with which the 511th had begun operations in May 1943 were *Screw Ball* and *Linda Ball*. Ironically, *Screw Ball* had been the assigned aircraft of Joe Meli's crew, who brought it to England and were then the first crew to be lost, in another aircraft. After completing its 34th mission late in March 1944, *Screw Ball* was retired to Burtonwood. On 10 April the aircraft departed for the United States, where it was employed in training new crews. The B-17Fs with their hydraulically actuated turbo-supercharger controls were gradually being taken out of combat service and replaced by the far less troubled B-17Gs with their electronic system. *Linda Ball* was also retired with 34 missions to its credit in March 1944, eventually to be returned to the United States. Both surviving veterans ended their days in the post-war aircraft graveyards at Altus in Oklahoma and Walnut Ridge in Arkansas, respectively.

Of the original crews of the 511th, only that of Lieutenant Carl Wilson survived in its entirety to finish a 25-mission tour. When *Eight Ball* was under repair they flew most of their missions in *Pistol Ball*, an earlier replacement that was to endure for 36 missions. Clinton Ball remained as a command pilot with the 351st Bomb Group to the end of the war, with 32 missions to his credit.

The Ball Boys tradition was continued throughout the hostilities, and a listing of more than 100 'ball' names were drawn up, from which those for replacement B-17s could be selected. A final claim to fame for the 511th Bomb Squadron is that the sole surviving B-17 that actually flew combat with the 8th Air Force, albeit for only eight missions near the end of the war, and was still flying 50 years later, was a Ball Boys aircraft.

The Early Champions

In the first year of 8th Air Force combat operations, the average life of a B-17 was short. Four pioneer Fortress groups came to England in the autumn of 1942 with a nominal 32 aircraft apiece, and by the following November the 91st Group had five of its original aircraft remaining, the 303rd had seven, the 305th four, and the 306th just one. This also reflected the fortunes of the respective groups. However, it was a relatively slow period of operations, with a total of about 75 to 85 missions flown per group.

Only 35 per cent of crews had a chance of completing their 25-mission tour during this first year, and, by the same yardstick, no individual B-17 was liable to survive much more than 30 combat sorties. But the fortunes of the air war were such that a few of these originals endured despite all of the Luftwaffe's efforts and other operational hazards. Those in the 303rd Bomb Group at Molesworth, Cambridgeshire, were undoubtedly the most starred.

The announcement of a 25-mission tour for a combat crew, before non-operational duties or return to the United States, focused attention on who would be the first to achieve this goal. The situation that developed in the winter of 1942–43 militated against all ten members of any one crew completing 25 missions together, because of illness, separation to fly with other crews, and many other reasons. In fact, one lone individual, an engineer/gunner in the 306th Group, was the first to complete a tour. Because 25 missions was the goal for aircrew, it was natural that the figure should also become the point of interest as far as the bombers that carried them were concerned, an interest fanned by 8th Air Force Public Relations, which was prohibited from releasing too much information on aircrews for fear of supplying the enemy with too much information on the rate of attrition.

In the early spring of 1943 several 8th Air Force B-17s were approaching 25 missions, although there appears to have been some variation in what constituted an officially acknowledged combat sortie. However, VIII Bomber Command decreed that the first to reach this figure was a 303rd aircraft named *Hell's Angels*, serial number 41-24577, which had also achieved this without once having failed to complete a raid owing to turning back because of crew or mechanical failures, known in the air force terminology of the time as aborting. The 25th mission occurred on 17 May 1943, although the 8th Air Force Public Relations news release erroneously gave the date as 14 May, the day the pilot, Captain Irl E. Baldwin, and several members of his crew reached the ends of their tours. Interestingly, a 91st Bomb Group Fortress, *Delta Rebel No. 2*, carried 25 bomb symbols on its nose before this date, but for reasons not recorded in official records was apparently not accepted as the champion.

Hell's Angels was named after the Howard Hughes movie of First World War aerial combat, and, following the publicity connected with the Fortress's tour, the 303rd Group started to refer to itself as the 'Hell's Angels Group'. *Hell's Angels* flew on the 303rd's first mission, on 17 November 1942, and was somewhat fortunate in collecting only one bullet hole and a few flak fragments during the ensuing six months. While there were no casualties during this time, two members of the original crew were lost while flying with other crews. However, the first member of the 303rd to become a prisoner of war arrived via *Hell's Angels*. During an air battle over France he misunderstood a pilot's instruction and baled out.

Under the care of the 358th Bomb Squadron crew chief, M/Sgt Fabian Folmer, *Hell's Angels* continued to live a comparatively charmed life. On 6 September it completed its 41st mission, again an 8th Air Force record, but then suffered its first abort. But only one mission behind was the 359th Bomb Squadron's *Knock-Out Dropper*, alias 41-24605, another 303rd original. Unlike *Hell's Angels*, *Knock-Out Dropper* had given its diligent ground crew, headed by Sergeant Stanley Jacobs, plenty of work, and the bomber had a number of abortive missions in its record. Nevertheless, after a trip to Norway on 16 November 1943, a day short of the anniversary of its maiden mission, *Knock-Out Dropper* became the first B-17 in the 8th Air Force to fly 50 missions. At this date *Hell's Angels* had 47 missions to its credit, as had another original, the 427th Bomb Squadron's 41-24619, unnamed but known by its call sign, S for Sugar.

When received in the 359th Bomb Squadron, *Knock-Out Dropper* was assigned to Lieutenant Jack Roller's crew while they were in the last phase of training at Battle Creek, Michigan. They brought the bomber to Molesworth and flew eighteen missions of their tour in it, including their last and the bomber's 25th, on 22 June 1943. Thereafter, *Knock-Out Dropper* was taken into battle by several different crews – seventeen, to be precise. No major battle damage had been sustained, its worst resulting from a 20mm cannon shell strike in the tail during one of the Schweinfurt missions. In assessing *Knock-Out Dropper* to have been the first B-17 to complete 50 missions, a blind eye was evidently turned to some twelve abortive trips, albeit mostly recalls owing to adverse weather.

Hell's Angels flew only one further mission, thereafter being retired from combat. It had been decided by 8th Air Force HQ that the return of a veteran bomber to the United States with six members of its original ground crew would aid the re-emphasizing of the 8th Air Force's campaign. This would be achieved by touring major US city airports to encourage the purchase of savings bonds. To enhance the bomber's battle service, any man at Molesworth was allowed to paint his name or signature on the Fortress. A dossier of *Hell's Angels'* service was prepared which listed details such as sixteen engine changes, five sets of brakes, three landing gear changes, and several superchargers and oil coolers in the course of 450 hours of operational flying. Its weathered camouflage paint covered with graffiti, *Hell's Angels* began its return flight to the United States on 20 January 1944.

Knock-Out Dropper soldiered on until 27 March 1944, when it became the first 8th Air Force Fortress to complete 75 missions and was then retired. At this time it had a little over 675 combat hours, not an exceptional amount for a B-17, but by this date so many refinements and improvements had been made to the B-17 that this early F model was considered obsolescent for combat operations.

Only one other original 303rd aircraft remained at Molesworth. This was *The Duchess*, in which Lieutenant Jack Mathis had been mortally wounded over his bombsight, later to receive the posthumous award of the 8th's first Medal of Honor. On 10 May 1944 *Knock-Out Dropper* was returned to the United States, followed by *The Duchess*, veteran of 59 missions, on 6 June. Both aircraft, along with *Hell's Angels*, spent the remainder of the war at Florida and New Mexico replacement training centres.

To the trainee aircrews who flew in them they were just old, worn B-17s which had faced the enemy. For obvious reasons the odds of completing a tour as a member of a bomber crew were not put to these men. In any case, they were probably unknown to their tutors. Thus there is unlikely to have been any appreciation of the fact that these Fortresses had endured well beyond what had proved to be the average lifespan of their kind in the European Theatre of Operations; of just what 49, 59 and 75 bomb symbols accrued during the first year of 8th Air Force operations had entailed. Rather, these veteran Fortresses were curiosities, good for a photo call with the subject standing beneath the nose and its fading decor. Ultimately, in 1945, all three ended their days in the junk yard. The early champions were just as much scrap metal as the old B-17s that had never left the United States.

Poppa's Gonna Take You Home

An oft-told anecdote highlighting the risqué names with which some USAAF air-craft were adorned during the Second World War concerns a Fortress at Bury St Edmunds airfield in Suffolk. One evening a GI took his English girlfriend to see *Frenesi*, one of the most renowned B-17s on the base, which had returned despite extraordinary battle damage. The girl eyed the name and the nude painted on the aircraft's nose, turned to her companion and addressed him gravely, 'You don't fool me, Yank. That doesn't say "Fren-esi", it says "Free an' easy". And get this straight, I'm not!'

The veracity of this story is unknown, but there is no doubt that when 1st Lieutenant William Cely decided to name this B-17 after the instrumental number recorded and popularized by Artie Shaw, the convenient *double entendre* was not lost on the crew. For when navigator 2nd Lieutenant Floyd MacGowen painted *Frenesi* on the right side of the aircraft's nose, he added a rather stark female nude.

Frenesi started life as serial number 42-39775, one of the first B-17G models to come off the production line at Burbank, California, in August 1943. In October it joined the much needed flow of replacements to the 8th Air Force, and in the follow-ing month arrived at Bury St Edmunds and the 94th Bomb Group. Here it was assigned to the 333rd Bomb Squadron, whose personnel sometimes irreverently mocked themselves as the 'Tough Shit' outfit, having been issued with the squadron code letters TS to paint on their aircraft. The individual call sign K-King was given to 42-39775 on its assignment.

Like their bomber, the Cely crew were a replacement team fresh from the training fields in the United States. Bill Cely was a short, slightly-built man of 27, some six years older than the average age of the rest of the crew, and because of this he was dubbed 'Poppa'. *Frenesi* and the Cely crew fared well during their first few missions, but the operation of 11 January 1944 was a very different tale.

On this date the unreliable north European winter weather was forecast as clear skies in many areas. A maximum-effort mission was laid on to strike at targets in the priority category, German aircraft production. The 3rd Bomb Division was given the task of attacking targets in the Brunswick area, and 243 aircraft set off in an increasing build-up of clouds. With doubts about the ability of escort fighters to make rendezvous with a somewhat disorganized bomber stream, coded recalls were issued. But by this time the leading combat wing, with the 94th Bomb Group in the van, was only 25 miles from its briefed objective, the Me 110 assembly plant at Waggrum, and the sky ahead looked clear. With an opportunity for visual bombing, the wing leader decided to continue. Unfortunately, there was difficulty in identifying the target in the snow-covered terrain far below, and the formations had to circle back before the lead bombardier could set up his bombsight for what proved to be an accurate and destructive pattern of strikes.

Devoid of friendly fighter support, the wing's 47 Fortresses drew the Luftwaffe's attention in full measure, the German fighter controller vectoring in the Me 110 *Zerstörer* armed with cannon and rocket launchers. The assault on the 94th Bomb Group was such that seven B-17s in its formation of seventeen failed to return, and of those that did, only one was devoid of battle damage. *Frenesi*, on its eleventh mission, was leading the second element of three.

After the B-17s had bombed the target, a fusillade of air-launched, proximity-fused rockets exploded around them, one burst peppering *Frenesi*'s fuselage and wounding gunner Sergeant Warren Becker in his left side. Then either a flak burst or another rocket detonation crippled No.2 engine and put more holes in the fuselage and wings. The pilots were unable to feather the propeller and, as it seemed that it might separate from the engine at any moment, Cely told bombardier Al Bender and navigator MacGowen to leave the nose. At the same time the pilots saw that the crew oxygen system had failed.

As *Frenesi* could no longer stay with the formation and anoxia would soon affect the crew unless a lower altitude was reached, Cely warned the crew and put the bomber into a dive, descending from about 20,000ft to 10,000ft. What Cely did not realize at the time was that, in addition to the oxygen lines, the intercom had also been shot out, and the crew did not hear his warnings. Consequently, several men thought that the bomber was out of control. The navigator and bombardier went out of the nose hatch, as did the shot and bleeding Sergeant Becker. In the rear the ball gunner, radio operator and a cameraman also baled out. During the dive *Frenesi* was apparently pursued and shot at by Fw 190s which continued to harass the damaged bomber despite Cely's evasive action. In a desperate bid to evade the enemy attacks, Cely again put *Frenesi* into a dive, heading for the clouds at about 4,000ft, where he again levelled off. The Focke-Wulfs did not follow.

The confusion and apprehension among the crew members, devoid of intercom communication during this drama, can be well imagined. Right waist gunner Staff Sergeant Everett Hudson's account, as reported by the 94th Bomb Group PRO, states:

> Everything was all right until we hit the target ... It was then that I saw 15-20 twin-engined ships circling to our rear. They got sort of abreast and then came in, letting go their rockets. Gee, they were bursting all around, like light bulbs blowing up, and I could see fragments flying all over. I heard the tail gunner say he'd got one, just after the cameraman took him some more ammunition. After we left the target, the sky just filled up with Fw 190s from out of nowhere. My interphone went dead then, and I tapped the other waist gunner

to call them out as I pointed at them. They queued up on us, a whole nest of them and I saw our right wingman go down in smoke, and when I looked out of the other waist window, our left wingman was gone too. I tried to let the other waist gunner know that both our wingmen were gone and we were completely open from the rear, but he just didn't understand my gestures in the heat of the fight. We went into a terrific dive then, it seemed we were going to crash for sure, so fast we went. I was being thrown all over the ship, half the time I was on my head, or hitting the top of the ship, or the turret. It was like a cyclone inside the ship. I saw one fellow bale out and I knew others had gone before him. God sure was with me. I tried three times to make the door, but each time the ship and evasive action threw me somewhere else. Finally got to the waist window and was going to jump when I noticed my 'chute had been ripped open. I was bruised all over and my left shoulder felt as if it were gone. Then the plane levelled off a little. I took my 'chute off and made my way to the pilots' compartment. The radio room was a mess. Everything was torn up and thrown around – every movable piece was smashed and strewn all over the place. I told the pilot I didn't have a 'chute and he said, "That's all right, Poppa's going to take you home", and he did too. He's the best damned pilot in the world.

Tail gunner Staff Sergeant Clifford Prater had been busy firing at the frequent fighter attacks launched at the rear. One Fw 190 pilot's fire blasted away large portions of the tailplane, but Prater escaped injury. Recounting what followed, he said:

Right after this I looked around and saw the fellows putting on their 'chutes. I tried to call the pilot to ask him if we were supposed to jump but my interphone was out. So I stuck to the guns. At this time we were going into a steep dive and I was thrown all over the place back there. It was knocking hell out of me, so I crawled up in the waist and tried to ask the fellows if the pilot told us to bale out. Some had gone out already and we sure thought the ship was a dead one. The cameraman was the last to jump ... and just before he went out a 20mm hit beside the waist door and got me in the left arm and both legs – fragments. Then I saw the cameraman jump, I think he must have been injured some, he was so close to me. The ship started diving again and I was slung around again. I hit the top and landed on the ball turret. Fighters were still after us yet. We got into clouds and the pilot levelled off. You could hear the plane cracking in the radio room.

Despite the battle damage they could see and the windmilling propeller on No.2 engine, Cely and co-pilot 2nd Lieutenant Jabez Churchill decided they had a good chance of flying *Frenesi* home. Left waist gunner Pearson had gone forward to tell Cely that the tail gunner was wounded. Churchill took over the controls while Cely went back to see if Prater was badly wounded, and then sent Pearson back to administer morphine and render first aid to the tail gunner. Pearson reassured the wounded man: 'Hold on for 45 minutes pal and we'll be home. We're at the coast now.' Although Cely was prepared to make an emergency landing, *Frenesi* handled sufficiently well for him to fly to home base and make a good landing. When Cely dropped out of the exit door he was seen to put both hands on the ground and exclaim 'Ah'.

The battle damage to *Frenesi* was considered the most extensive seen at Bury St Edmunds. Number 2 engine was devoid of cowling and completely wrecked. There were two enormous, gaping holes in the right wing where cannon shells had exploded, fortunately either side of the outer fuel cells, both elevators had been shredded and there were numerous shell and splinter holes all over the airframe, including the nose Plexiglas. The wounded Cliff Prater remarked, 'Boy, those pilots were on the ball. How they ever managed to bring that wreck of a crate back is beyond me.' After inspecting both interior and exterior, the group commander, Colonel Frederick Castle, endorsed this with, 'It's the best job of piloting I've ever seen. It is inconceivable how that ship could fly.'

They towed *Frenesi* to a hardstand, where the immediate verdict was that the aircraft was only good for salvage. The fuselage was still in fair condition, but the wings and tailplane were beyond reasonable repair. An estimated 80 per cent of the elevator surfaces was destroyed. When the aircraft was turned over to the 453rd Sub-Depot (the base engineering organization), its inspectors shook their heads. It was a pity, but *Frenesi* would have to be junked.

Then fate took a hand. In the early hours of the following morning, 12 January, fire broke out in the nose of the 410th Bomb Squadron's *Belle of Baltimore*, serial 42-31289. Flares took light, and when the flames were finally extinguished the whole nose back to the flight deck was burned out. A suspected electrical short was the cause, and it seemed like another salvage case. Then the 453rd Sub-Depot engineering officers had an idea. Why not take the wings and tailplane from *Belle of Baltimore* and install them on *Frenesi*'s fuselage? One good Fortress from two wrecks.

The challenge was taken up, and 1,955 man-hours later the task was completed. The most difficult work was still to be done, for *Frenesi* was a Vega-built B-17G-1-VE series model and the *Belle* had been a Boeing-built B-17G-10-BO with entirely different instrumentation. *Frenesi* had so-called autosyn instruments, whereas the wings and engine nacelles from the other B-17 contained plumbing for the newer pressure operated types. *Frenesi* had oil-operated superchargers, while the *Belle* had the new electronic version. The Sub-Depot's Sergeant Rosen scavenged parts. In fact, three men spent three days visiting salvage yards such as that at the old airship hangar at Pulham St Mary to find out what was required to rework the instrument panel and lines. Even then, all of the tubing still had to be manufactured by the Sub-Depot. Taking into account this additional work in acquiring and making parts, a grand total of nearly 4,000 man-hours was expended to give *Frenesi* new life.

At last, on 4 April 1944, the bomber took off from the main runway on a test flight. There were no problems, but some further work had to be done on the instrumentation. On the afternoon of 27 April *Frenesi* returned to combat, flying as a spare to bomb a target at Le Culot. As its old squadron, the 333rd, had become a Pathfinder unit, *Frenesi* was transferred to the 332nd, and on 29 April Lieutenant Williams took it to Berlin and back. Early in May, Lieutenant Israel and his men became *Frenesi*'s named crew, and beginning on 13 May they flew 12 missions in a row with it. The crew went on to fly 20 missions of their 30-mission tour in this bomber, finishing up on 26 August.

Several other crews flew it during the next few weeks, and all went well until the morning of 1 November. As *Frenesi* was lined up on the runway, awaiting take-off, it was rammed from behind by *Ice Cold Katie* (serial 43-38183). Most of the rear end of *Frenesi* was demolished, fortunately without injuring anyone. Once more the Sub-Depot men surveyed the wreckage, but this time *Frenesi* was beyond economical repair. On 3 November 1944 it was declared salvage, whereas *Ice Cold Katie*, being fairly new, was repaired and eventually returned to combat in January 1945. Some parts from the nose of *Frenesi* were used in the reconstruction work, and the rest of the hulk became a ready source of spares for other B-17s. The fuselage of *Frenesi* remained beside a hangar for cannibalization for several weeks.

In the 1980s a prewar civilian house that stood within the Bury St Edmunds airfield boundary, and had served as an engineering office and store during the war, was turned into a public house. The landlord owner, Keith Allchin, thought it fitting to name the new inn in acknowledgement of the bombers that once inhabited the surrounding acres. *The Flying Fortress* is a unique public house, and has a traditional inn sign swinging in the breeze beside the country road. The sign depicts a B-17 of the 94th Bomb Group, and that B-17 is *Frenesi*.

Sweater Girl

After a year of combat the 99th Bomb Group, the 'Diamondbacks', could boast that 13 of their original 35 aircraft still survived. The lucky 13 B-17s had an average of 95 missions between them, and four had achieved 100 missions or more. Of that illustrious quartet, *El Diablo*, flown overseas by the group commander, Colonel Fay R. Upthegrove, was crewed by M/Sergeant John Beaver; *Bugs* was crewed by M/Sergeant Frederick Ruffin; and *Robt. E. Lee*'s crew chief was M/Sergeant Peter Bezek. His B-17 had started out as the raunchier *Balsanal* before a name change in honour of Robert E. Lee Goad, who had been shot down in another aeroplane in May 1943. The fourth aircraft was *Sweater Girl*, and her ground crew was headed up by M/Sergeant Chester A. Smiechowski from Chicago.

The new B-17F which would later be named *Sweater Girl* left the Boeing factory on 16 December 1942 and went to the Continental Airlines Modification Center at Denver. In early January she was flown to Salina, Kansas, where the 99th Bomb Group was in its final training phase. Although at least seventeen different pilots flew 42-29472, she is rightly claimed by three crews as 'their' aircraft. Lieutenant Keith Windrum was her original pilot, and in his diary entry for 3 March 1943 he noted that his bombardier, Lieutenant Don Hemmingsen, 'Is working on a nose gun ... attracting a lot of attention'. Hemmingsen and another of the crew had simply walked into a hangar dressed in coveralls, picked up an 0.50 calibre machine-gun and walked out with it. It was installed in the nose to fire straight ahead, even though the cone of fire was small. The as yet unnamed *Sweater Girl* was the first in the group to have a nose gun, although Colonel Upthegrove's *El Diablo* was soon similarly armed.

The 99th Bomb Group air echelon left Morrison Field, Florida, bound for the 12th Air Force in North Africa. Their route took them first to Borinquen, Puerto Rico, then on to Atkinson Field in British Guiana, Belem in Brazil, Natal, and across the Atlantic to Bathurst in Gambia. The final stop before North Africa was Marrakesh, Morocco.

The 99th completed its preliminary combat training at La Senia in Oran, and towards the end of March moved up to its own field at Navarin, Algeria. One veteran described Navarin as little more than 'a wheat field levelled off for airplanes to take off and land'. *Sweater Girl*'s first mission, an attack on the port area of Naples on 4 April 1943, was completed successfully. On the second mission, flown the next day, the ball turret operator, Sergeant Gerald Meier, burned out his electric suit and froze his feet badly. On 12 April the Windrum crew had its second – and final – 'casualty' when Technical Sergeant Jack Williams, the engineer, started urinating blood. Windrum aborted the mission, and it was subsequently discovered that Williams had a kidney stone.

Sweater Girl suffered major damage while being flown by another crew on the 14 April 1943 mission to Monserrato in Sardinia. The target was an enemy airfield, and an estimated 30 fighters intercepted the B-17s. Two runs were made over the target, although some of the aircraft had successfully bombed on the first run. *Cotton Eyed Joe*, *B.T.O.* and *Sweater Girl* all suffered major damage, and the War Diary noted 'steps are being taken to assure no repetition of two runs over the target'.

While the repairs were carried out there was time for other things, and on 17 April a painter started work on the billboard on the big tail. It showed a busty blonde in a yellow sweater, blue skirt and white shoes. 'We all had a part in naming her' says Keith Windrum, who recalls that the tail artwork cost $20.

The mission of 3 May was memorable for all the wrong reasons. Although the weather had been bad for days, a briefing was held at 0900. At 1100 the combat crews were told to go and eat. At 1300 they were assembled again, and finally at 1500 they were ordered to attack a reported 150 barges and tank landing craft in Bizerte harbour. They were airborne at 1555 and passed the rendezvous point at 1625, flying into thickening weather.

As Keith Windrum later recalled, 'We were to bomb heavily laden ferries in Lake Bizerte. At the briefing, our weather officer suggested that the field would be closed in upon our return. Over the target, we could see through the clouds and there were no ferries in the lake.' Upthegrove, flying the lead B-17, was furious. He said 'Let's get the hell out of here and go home', but it wasn't going to be that easy. Of the 25 B-17s reaching the target, only three returned to Navarin. The others were scattered all over Africa.

Windrum continues:

Upon the return flight, we were flying *Sweater Girl* on the extreme left position of the group. We came to the front and were circling very tightly. I neglected to switch my radio over on 'command', and did not hear Colonel Upthegrove's directions to separate and each be on our own. However, the circles were getting tighter and tighter. I was at the bottom of the vortex and I was unable to maintain my position and was forced to pull out of the formation. At that moment all of the 'planes were dispersing. Prior to pulling out of the formation, I had happened to notice a railroad track through a small hole in the underlying clouds. I dove for this hole, flying parallel with the railroad tracks. At my speed I was unable to push the nose down fast enough to hit the hole. However, as it was getting dark and since I was flying parallel with the railroad track, I proceeded through the clouds and came out with about a two hundred foot ceiling.

We proceeded along the railroad tracks for a few minutes and came over a small airdrome that had no runway, as I recall it, but was grass. There were a few galvanized shacks and one or two Hurricane airplanes. We managed to land. We were greeted by the pilot who had flown the recon flight that morning. He informed us that he had reported that there was nothing in Lake Bizerte.

We were just east of Constantine, approximately thirty-five miles from our home base. Two of the men were left as guards and we made it home that evening.

There was disbelief at the 99th base. As night fell, 50 trucks and jeeps, all the vehicles that could be found, were parked around the runway with their headlights on.

It was too late; six B-17s and seven men were gone. *Stars and Stripes* crash-landed at Ain M'Lila and was later scrapped. *Whizzer* crash-landed in a salt lake at Zebkret o Zenouil and was written off because recovery was impossible. The crew abandoned *War Bird* in the air. Lieutenant Edward McLaughlin, flying 42-29469, 'made a perfect bombing run and dropped most of his men down the main street' of a North African town before he and the others also parachuted to safety. Lieutenant Sid Buck in *Lady Luck* wanted his crew to bale out, but they elected to stay. A 'lucky lightning flash' revealed a suitable landing place and they got down safely. Colonel Leroy Rainey ditched 42-29496 about ten miles off Bone, but only one liferaft inflated and just four of the crew of eleven were saved, the others drowning or dying from exposure.

Sweater Girl flew the series of missions to Pantellaria, and Windrum's terse diary entries sum it up.

> June 9: Went into Pantellaria today. No excitement involved. June 10: Went on two raids over Pantellaria today. I never saw so many 'planes. We bombed the daylights out of them. June 11: Made another raid on Pantellaria. Watched the navy shell it. We went in at 12,000! While we were on the way home they surrendered.

Windrum continues:

> Gerbini was in an area in which we had been ordered not to drop bombs, even scuttling them. On July 5, we were to make two massive raids into this area. We were to have P-38 escorts, fly over Malta to pick up Spits for escorts. The P-38s missed us. Therefore we had only the Spits. Approaching Sicily we could see the dogfighting ahead. Swarms of fighters. Reminded me of bees. When we approached this swarm we had no more escort. There had to be over one hundred German fighters left. I assume they were all Me 109s. I know they had the desert camouflage. I remember our first contact with the fighters was the "snaking" through our squadron of three or four – seems like

four – of the fighters. They came from the front and above, and dived through. From our 'plane not a shot was fired. Shortly thereafter, for at least twenty to thirty minutes the firing never stopped. It was quite an air battle! I remember that the waist section was several inches deep in spent casings when the battle was over. I understand the bomb pattern was perfect.

In my own mind I felt that we had air superiority from then on, although we had some tough raids over Messina, Naples and Foggia.

On July 16, 1943 we had a forced landing on the way back, at Souk-el-Arba in Africa. No fault of *Sweater Girl*. Had fine sand in the gas and two engines quit before we got down ... All 'planes, as I remember, had to start refuelling by straining gas through chamois.

Sweater Girl flew her 50th mission on 7 September 1943, to Foggia.

The second pilot to fly *Sweater Girl* regularly was Lieutenant Joseph Trentadue. He wound up his missions in the aircraft on 8 December 1943, when the 99th attacked shipping at Porto San Stefano from 3,500ft. There were no fighters or flak and the gunners had a field day strafing.

Lieutenant Bob Braungart was pilot of the third and final crew to lay claim to *Sweater Girl*. He flew the first of a dozen missions in her on 14 December 1943, against targets in the Athens area.

She was a veteran now, but crew chief Smiechowski and his men were still able to keep *Sweater Girl* in the air for seven straight days of missions. On 13 January Lieutenant Monte Eydenberg flew her to the Guidonia airfield near Rome, through heavy flak and a score of fighters. On 14 January Bob Braungart flew her to attack Mostar aerodrome in Yugoslavia, running into intense heavy flak. On 15 January the Eydenberg crew went to Arezzo marshalling yards; no fighters, no flak. On 16 January Braungart took her to Villaorba airfield near Udine, Italy. On 17 January Lieutenant G. R. Wiren and his crew flew *Sweater Girl* to the marshalling yards at Prato, Italy, again encountering no fighters or flak; on 18 January Braungart flew her to Poggibonsi marshalling yards, no fighters, no flak, and the week ended with another mission to the Rome area, Centocella aerodrome, no fighters, no flak, with Lieutenant Ralph Chamberlain.

Bob Braungart flew his final mission in *Sweater Girl* on 29 January, but no bombs were dropped at the primary target because of heavy overcast. The bombers went to the secondary target, the Fabriano marshalling yards, but missed it completely, their bombs landing in hills to the southeast.

With the arrival of the 483rd Bomb Group and their brand-new B-17Gs (most of which were handed over to the 99th), old warriors like *Sweater Girl* could be given a rest. The aircraft flew only three missions during February, four in March, none in April, and four in May. *Sweater Girl* flew her final mission on 14 May 1944 with Lieutenant Dennis Gaeth and his crew. Their target was the airfield at Piacenza, Italy.

Having completed her missions, the old B-17 continued to serve as a 'weather ship' at Tortorella. After the war she was flown back to Walnut Ridge, Arkansas, in the United States, where she was reduced to salvage.

Nothing much happened to *Sweater Girl*, really. She was not a flak magnet; she was never singled out by the fighters. She just flew 111 missions with no member of any of her crews being killed or seriously wounded flying in her. She is remembered fondly.

How Big Mike became Frenchy's Folly

The USAAF operating in Europe classified aircraft damage in four main categories, designated by a letter. Category A damage was that which could be repaired within 36 hours by the operating unit itself. Category AC was damage taking 36 or more hours and requiring the attention of a major service unit on the base. Category B was severe damage needing the skills and equipment of a major repair depot, whether the work was performed on the home station or elsewhere. The final Category was E, which was applied to aircraft for which the damage was assessed as being beyond economical repair. Category E meant the aircraft was to be scrapped or, in the terminology used, salvaged.

There are many examples of heavily damaged aircraft assessed as Category E that were reprieved and put back in the air. In such cases the records were amended. And there were a few Category E wrecks that were written off only to be unofficially rebuilt; unofficially because, on paper, they had ceased to exist. A prime example is a B-17 put together by Technical Operations at Bovingdon. The commanding officer, Colonel Cass Hough, flew it back to the United States and used it for several weeks while often engaged in his Company's business. As official records held that this B-17 had been reduced to scrap in England, to avoid explanations the aircraft was simply abandoned when Cass Hough retired from the service.

One Fortress rescued from Category E by extraordinary effort was the 381st Bomb Group's 42-39997. This aircraft arrived at Ridgewell, Essex, on 13 January 1944, and was given to the 533rd Bomb Squadron, whose personnel were later to bestow on it the name *Big Mike*. Starting on 21 January, *Big Mike* endured for 29 missions with little hurt from the enemy. Then, on 29 April, Lieutenant Ned Renick's crew took it to Berlin. The flak was heavy and *Big Mike* took a few fragments. One smashed through hydraulic lines, and no hydraulic pressure meant no brakes. On return to Ridgewell, Renick put *Big Mike* down as close to the start of runway 28 as he could, but a brakeless Fortress needs more than a mile to slow down.

Big Mike did not slow down; it kept on rolling, clean off the end of the runway to the northwest, over the airfield boundary and 75 yards across a sloping field of young wheat. All might have ended well, but for a hedgerow bank and a six-foot-deep ditch alongside. *Big Mike*'s left main wheel ran over a tree stump in the old hedgeline and then dropped violently into the ditch, smashing its left wing into the ground and bending the propeller blades on Nos 1 and 2 engines. At the same time the whole aircraft skewed slightly left, the fuselage coming to rest on the stump and the ball turret being partly crushed. The right main wheel also dropped into the curling line of the ditch. None of the crew was hurt, but it looked as though *Big Mike* would never fly again.

The 2nd Strategic Air Depot inspectors, whose job it was to assess and categorize damage, came and shook their heads. Category E and salvage for spare parts was the verdict. The engineering officers of the 448th Sub-Depot at Ridgewell had other ideas. Apart from the left wing and buckled skin on the under-fuselage, the aircraft was in good condition. While it would not be possible to complete repairs in the time allowed for Category B classification, they felt confident that the bomber could be put back in the air. Agreement was reached that, for the present, *Big Mike* would not be classified Category E, and that 448th Sub Depot mechanics on the base could undertake repairs only when not required for other work.

The first task was to remove *Big Mike* from the Essex ditch. It might have been possible to dig away the ditch bank under the aircraft, but for the fact that it was pinning down the large tree stump. Some 40,000lb had to be lifted vertically six feet and then moved back three feet so that the landing gear was on level ground. First the crumpled left wing section outboard of the engines was removed, and then all fuel was drained from the tanks and moveable equipment taken out to lighten the aircraft as much as possible. Balloon jacks, British pneumatic devices, were placed in excavations under each inner wing section. These were then inflated to their maximum, with the result that the right main wheel was raised sufficiently to clear the top of the ditch, but the left was still not high enough. It was decided that an attempt would be made to get the right landing gear back on level ground by attaching cables to that side and giving a steady pull with Cletracs.

Gradually *Big Mike* was swung on the balloon jacks until the right wheel was clear of the ditch. Getting the left landing gear out was now the problem, and the only way was to reduce the bank of the ditch directly behind the wheel and hope there would be enough give in the balloon jacks to carry the wheel on to the slope. It was essential that, once the Cletracs started pulling the cables harnessed to the left gear, they did not stop. Pull would be exerted on the right side at the same time to ensure that the aircraft was brought well clear of the ditch. When this phase of the operation was started it appeared successful, but as *Big Mike* began to be rolled well away from the ditch the left landing gear suddenly collapsed. This was caused by the main longerons in the engine nacelle containing the landing gear giving way.

Once more *Big Mike* was down on its left wing, but this time it reposed in a level wheat field. Balloon jacks were put under the left wing and a 25ft aircraft trailer was driven on to the field and carefully reversed under the wing between the balloon jacks. The jacks were deflated and *Big Mike* was once more on the move, towed backwards by the Cletracs and supported by a truck trailer under its left side and rolling on its own right main wheel. This procession edged back on to the airfield perimeter track and made for the nearest hangar, No.2.

The 448th Sub-Depot Engineering Officer, Captain Mitchell Hall, and his assistant, Lieutenant Larry McGhehey, then made a thorough inspection of the

Above: The 99th Bomb Group's *Sweater Girl* over Tunisia. (Mark C. McIntire)

Below: *Sweater Girl* forms the backdrop for a 'March of Time' crew filming the returning B-17 crews. (Joseph Kellerman)

Above: *Big Mike* after the removal of all damaged components. (Via Dave Osborne)

Below: B-17G 42-39997 outside No.1 hangar and ready to resume combat under a new name. (Via Dave Osborne)

Above: Forty missions and still going strong. *General Ike* at rest at Bassingbourn in October 1944. (USAAF)

Below: The *Tail Crazy* crew: Bill Tatler is standing on the right below the name, John Rice is next to him, and Thomas O'Connor is standing on the left. (Tatler)

Above: The cannon-armed *Tail Crazy* in June 1944. (Charles F. Hollenberg)

Below: The tail cannon installation on the 97th Bomb Group's *Miss Windy City*. (Morley L. Russell)

Top right: The 97th Bomb Group's *Opissonya* over Capri. (Don Hayes Collection)

Bottom right: *Hustlin' Huzzy*, one of three 97th Group aeroplanes lost on the 23 June 1944 Ploesti mission. (USAF)

Left: *Mizpah* over Budapest on 14 July 1944. (Robert W. Toombs)

Below: Lieutenant Ewald Swanson, pilot of *Mizpah*, and seven of his crew survived as prisoners of war. (Swanson)

Right: *Hard Luck* at Thorpe Abbotts. (100th BG Memorial Museum)

Below right: *Snake Hips* at Woodbridge, showing the extensive damage to the fuselage and right wing. (USAAF)

1	2	3	4	5	6	7	8	9	10	11	12	13	14	15	16	17	18	19	20	21	22	23	24	25

Perſonalkarte I: Perſonelle Angaben *SWANSON* *E.A*

Beſchriftung der Erkennungsmarke: Nr. *0801*

Kriegsgefangenen-Stammlager: *E.A* Lager *Krgsgefle.d.Lw.3*

Name: *SWANSON*

Vorname: *Ewald A.*

Geburtstag und -ort: *3.12.1919 Michigan*

Religion: *Prot.*

Vorname des Vaters:

Familienname der Mutter:

Staatsangehörigkeit: **U. S. A.**

Dienſtgrad: *1. Lt.*

Truppenteil: *USAAF* Komp. uſw.:

Zivilberuf: *Angestellter* Berufs-Gr.:

Matrikel Nr. (Stammrolle des Heimatſtaates): *O-753 823*

Gefangennahme (Ort und Datum): *14.7.44 Near Budapest*

Ob geſund, krank, verwundet eingeliefert:

Des Kriegsgefangenen

Lichtbild	Nähere Perſonalbeſchreibung		
	Größe	Haarfarbe	Beſondere Kennzeichen:
	1.83	*dkl.braun*	

Fingerabdruck des rechten(!) Zeigefingers

Name und Anſchrift der zu benachrichtigenden Perſon in der Heimat des Kriegsgefangenen **133**

Mr. Nels Swanson
1129 Stephenson Ave
Escanaba, Michigan

1089 *SWANSON, E.A 0801*

Above: A close-up of the mangled bomb bay area. (USAAF)

Top right: The graffiti bomber in flight. (USAAF)

Right: *Pelia Tulip* safely down at Debach on 14 October 1944. (USAF)

Bottom right: *Big Tin Bird* at Kings Cliffe, summer 1945: the first 8th Air Force Fortress to put its nose into enemy controlled airspace, and at the time of this photograph the oldest of its type in the ETO. (Via Royal Frey)

Right: An object of much curiosity: *5 Grand* shortly after arrival at Snetterton Heath. (Via Geoff Ward)

Above: The open-cockpit *Gremlin Gus II* takes off from Honington. (R. Sturges)

Left: 'Mac' McKinney leans against the tail-gunner's compartment of *Mary Alice* on its Deenethorpe pad, autumn 1944. By this time most of the original olive drab and neutral grey rear end had been replaced by unpainted parts, and even those have several battle damage patches. (H. B. McKinney)

Left: Navigator Victor Bonomo smiles through his office window following *Fortress McHenry*'s 27th mission. Bonomo was the first officer of the 94th Bomb Group to complete two combat tours. (V. Bonomo)

Below: Dan Knight, pilot of the first crew assigned *Mary Alice*, who named the bomber after his mother, surveys the damaged tail turret in a Beccles hangar following the 13 July 1944 mission to Munich. (USAAF)

Bottom: *Ol' Gappy* (left) and *Swamp Fire* at Kimbolton in the winter of 1944–45. (USAAF)

Above: *Swamp Fire* with 24 mission symbols on 1 May 1944. The assigned crew are, rear row, left to right: Sergeants Berj Bejian, Roy Avery, Andrew Stroman, John Rose, Elijah Lewis and Edward Przybyla. Front row: Lieutenants Matthew Scianameo, Byron Clark, Joe Korstjens and Harvey Harris. Korstjens holds Scragg, the ground crew's pet. (Byron Clark)

Below: *Ol' Gappy* with 115 missions completed, photographed in late January 1945. The bomber was unusual in that the symbols for missions completed were duplicated, being painted on both sides of the nose and stretching back along the fuselage. (S. C. Ellis)

Above: Rollin Davis pretends to touch up the 120th mission symbol, and the rest of the ground crew look busy to give the cameraman the desired atmosphere, February 1945. (IWM)

Below: Captain Henri Perrin (second from left) with the air crew and the German mechanics who serviced *Bir Hackeim* while it was based at Wahn. (Perrin)

Left: The disfigured nose after the accident at Wahn. (Perrin)

Below: *Shoo Shoo Shoo Baby* at Bulltofta, Sweden, in the summer of 1944. (Torbjorn Olausson)

Right: Broken down into manageable pieces, *Shoo Shoo Shoo Baby* was loaded aboard a C-5A for the airlift to the USA. (USAF)

Below right: The 'production line' at Dover Air Force Base, site of the largest aircraft restoration project ever undertaken outside a major museum. (Mike Leister)

Above: Built to last. *Shoo Shoo Shoo Baby* shortly after her arrival at Wright-Patterson Air Force Base, Ohio. (AFM)

Below: *Sally-B* in her TV role for 'We'll Meet Again'. A visual bonus derived from this employment were the 'plastic' gun turrets. (George Pennick)

wreck. The task of repair was more daunting than had originally been thought. In addition to a complete new wing on the left side, the outboard wing section on the right side would have to be replaced, as well as all four engines and the left tailplane. More damage to the fuselage was discovered, and there was renewed debate as to whether or not the work should be undertaken. However, the Technical Sergeant who had been put in charge of the operation, Charles Barbier, popularly known as 'Frenchy' because of his origins, was enthusiastic, so the decision was made to go ahead.

The major and most difficult task was the fitting of a new left wing. The B-17 wing was fabricated in three sections – the inner, containing the engine nacelles; the outer; and the wingtip. The inner and outer sections were secured by taper pins and, while it was not difficult for a service unit to replace the outer section on an airfield, an inner section replacement was a task for air depot work, although it was rarely undertaken there because a special jig was essential.

Undeterred, Frenchy and his men stripped the engines and accessories from *Big Mike*'s left inner section and removed it, supporting the remainder of the aircraft with a cradle and jacks under the fuselage. There were several left inboard wing sections at Ridgewell, salvaged from other B-17s, but none were from a B-17G of the same model and from the same manufacturer, Vega, as *Big Mike*. The best alternative was a B-17F wing from a Vega-built aircraft, but it would need much modification.

To overcome the problem of installation without a jig, two cradles were built and placed on top of an aircraft trailer, and jacks were positioned under the corners of the cradles. The section of wing was then craned on top of the cradles and the trailer was manoeuvred into place. A balloon jack was placed between the two cradles to take the bulk of the wing's weight while the hydraulic jacks under the cradles were raised as required to line up the tongues on the ends of the wing spars with the yokes in the wing roots. Once the tongues were in position, the old taper pins were inserted temporarily to hold the wing section in place while new taper pins were machined. It was essential to the security of the wing that this coupling was a precision fit, so each hole was reamed as each new taper pin was fitted.

With the new wing in place, the left landing gear was installed and *Big Mike* was towed to hangar No.1 on the technical site, which had better facilities for continuing the work. The B-17F and early B-17Gs had hydraulically-operated turbo-supercharger regulators, and the system had a habit of failing at high altitude owing to freezing and congealing oil. *Big Mike* had the superior electric controls, so it was necessary to remove the hydraulic lines in the B-17F wing and fit electric cables. With the change to electronics on the B-17G, the factories had altered the position of associated equipment, and it was necessary for the complete turbo-supercharger induction system to be revised on the replacement wing. Junction box changes in the wing and rewiring of the engine nacelles consumed more man-hours, but eventually the three sections of the left wing were completely installed and refurbished.

Meanwhile, the sheet metal men were renewing the skin on the underside of the fuselage, and some major repairs had to be carried out between stations 5 and 6, the radio compartment, where the main longeron (longitudinal support beam) had been bent. A longeron from a scrap fuselage was obtained and installed, and it was also necessary to splice and rivet a stringer which had failed at station 6. The crushed ball turret was removed and replaced, along with its supports inside the fuselage. Fortunately the supports had not been forced up far enough to break the spine of the aircraft, which often happened in crashes, distorting the rear fuselage beyond repair. The chin turret, also crushed, was replaced.

The landing gear was removed, checked and reinstalled, as were the bomb-bay doors. Four new engines with propellers were hung, and new fuel tanks, radio equipment and armament were installed. Recent modifications were incorporated. Doors and hatches, often distorted and ill-fitting after a crash, were replaced. Eventually, on 3 July 1944, Sergeant Barbier was able to report that 42-39997 was complete and ready to fly. The task had taken 3,307 man-hours in the course of 65 days. The work had been undertaken only when there were no other pressing jobs on other B-17s, and there had never been more than six men working on the aircraft, and usually only two or three.

During the complex task of virtually rebuilding the aircraft, the project had jokingly been referred to as 'Frenchy's folly' by some of the men on the airfield. As almost half of *Big Mike* had been replaced, it was decided that it would be appropriate to change its name in honour of the crew chief who had been largely responsible for the project. Thus, when the 381st Bomb Group Air Executive, Lieutenant Colonel Conway Hall, lifted 42-39997 from a Ridgewell runway at 1330 on Independence Day, the name *Frenchy's Folly* was emblazoned on its nose.

On take-off the co-pilot, who had only been informed that he was required for a B-17 test flight, expressed surprise and puzzlement on seeing a large crowd of mechanics and others on the technical site to witness the event. Until that moment, apparently, he had no idea of the significance of the flight. Among those aboard for the test hop were Sub-Depot commander Major Raymond Jolicouer and his engineering officers, to show faith in their men's work. After landing, Colonel Hall stated that the Fortress handled beautifully and was one of the best-trimmed of her kind he had piloted.

After checks, *Frenchy's Folly* was back on combat status in the 533rd Bomb Squadron. During the following nine months it completed more than 70 combat missions, finishing its toil for Uncle Sam on 4 April 1945 with a total of over 100 sorties to its credit. The aircraft had certainly vindicated the men whose time and effort were put into returning it to flying condition.

Named for Ike

When the 91st Bomb Group was notified that the Supreme Allied Commander, General Dwight Eisenhower, was to visit their station on 11 April 1944, a proposal was made that a newly received Fortress should be named in his honour. This was taken up by 8th Air Force Public Relations, and approval was obtained for the General to conduct a christening ceremony. The visit was part of Eisenhower's review of his air forces before Operation Overlord, the cross-Channel invasion. Apart from the 91st's distinguished record, the selection of Bassingbourn was probably due to its good facilities, it being the only prewar RAF station occupied by a US heavy bomber group in England.

A display of ordnance and equipment was laid on for the distinguished visitor before three Fortresses, one each from three of the Group's squadrons. These three were B-17E *Yankee Doodle*, which had conveyed General Eaker on the Eighth's first combat mission on 17 August 1942 before being relegated to target-towing duties with the 322nd Bomb Squadron; *Chennault's Pappy*, a veteran B-17F serving with the 323rd Bomb Squadron but inherited from the 306th Bomb Group the previous summer, and *Just Nothing*, a B-17G of the 324th Bomb Squadron, with its name derived from its serial number, which ended 000.

The fourth squadron of the Group, the 401st, contributed the bomber to be christened by the General. The appropriate name selected and painted on the left nose side by Bassingbourn's most esteemed artist, Corporal Tony Starcer, was *General Ike*. The aircraft, officially 42-97061, a B-17G-40-BO, had been accepted by the USAAF at Seattle on 24 January 1944, and was one of the first to be delivered in natural metal finish. After modification, it left the USA for the UK on 22 February, and was assigned first to the 457th Bomb Group on 13 March, only to be reassigned to the 91st three days later. After further modifications it reached the 401st Bomb Squadron at the end of the month and was put in charge of Master Sergeant Alton D. McDaniel's ground crew.

A platform to allow General Eisenhower to break a bottle over the left chin turret gun barrel was positioned close to '061's' nose, the aircraft being drawn up outside a Bassingbourn hangar. According to Public Relations sources, the bottle contained Mississippi river water, available because a combat airman on the base who brought the liquid from the United States with the intention of drinking it on completing his missions had, sadly, failed to do either.

Two days after the christening ceremony *General Ike* was despatched on its first combat mission, with Schweinfurt as the target. Captain John D. Davis was the pilot, the aircraft flying squadron lead. The formation was intercepted by fighters before the target, and a flak barrage was encountered which put a few small holes in *General Ike*'s fuselage. The Davis crew had previously been assigned two Fortresses which they nicknamed *Buckeye Boomerang* and *Buckeye Boomerang II*, both of which had been lost with other crews. They had now acquired the first 'silver' B-17 in the squadron.

Because of its prominence, *General Ike* was frequently selected as a group and squadron lead ship. It was serving in this capacity when Captain Robert S. Roberts and crew took it to Oranienburg, near Berlin, on 18 April. Group Bombardier Captain Charles Hudson was riding in the nose that day, and asked the pilot to take the formation down 3,000ft to enable him to bomb visually below a cloud bank. Captain Roberts finished his tour when he piloted *General Ike* as Group lead to attack Avord air depot on 28 April. Riding as an observer on his first combat mission was Colonel Frank Hunter, CO of the recently arrived 398th Bomb Group at Nuthampstead. On 29 May *General Ike* led the whole 1st Combat Wing and collected a few flak splinter holes in its wings for the trouble on this 10 hour 40 minute round flight.

D-Day, 6 June, required bombing in accordance with the release of an H2X radar equipped lead ship, but *General Ike* flew in the deputy lead position ready to take over if visual conditions occurred. Lieutenant John L. Black was the pilot, and recently arrived Lieutenant Colonel Lewis Ensign, who would eventually become 91st Bomb Group's CO, made his first combat mission as an observer with the crew.

Although *General Ike* was the assigned aircraft of Captain Davis, its selection as a lead ship led to other crews using it on several occasions. During early missions these included Captains George Heileg, Thomas Gunn and William B. Smith. However, Captain Frank Varva, the 401st lead navigator, made more trips than anyone else in this bomber.

So far, *General Ike* had suffered only minor damage from enemy fire, but when 1st Lieutenant William Hanna and crew took it to Toulouse on 25 June an 88mm shell registered a near hit under the left wing, badly damaging a wing spar, and splinters put the radio and part of the oxygen system out of action. The crew escaped unhurt, but the bomber was out of action for a few days while a section of wing was changed.

Returned to service, *General Ike* frequently continued to be selected as the Group lead ship. John Davis, who was eventually promoted major and CO of the 401st, said of the aircraft, '"Ike" is a mighty sweet plane – perfect for a lead ship. She's not hot or fast, but moves along steadily. You don't want a fast aircraft for a group leader.' This statement reflects the fact that, although they were supposedly identical, some B-17s were faster than others at specific power settings.

By 28 July, when *General Ike* returned from its 21st mission, it had 366 hours' flight time and no aborts. During August and September it frequently flew as Group lead, although it suffered a turn-back on one mission.

By the autumn of 1944 B-17s with H_2X radar were becoming more plentiful, and were taking the role of leadships. *General Ike* was then relegated to deputy leader. During the critical period of the German Ardennes offensive, *General Ike* was to have been part of the largest bomber force ever despatched on a single mission, on Christmas Eve. Unfortunately, an engine failed soon after take-off and 1st Lieutenant Menford Borgenson had to make an emergency landing at Ridgewell.

The bomber was then assigned to 21-year-old Captain William T. Carter, who flew 22 of his 35 mission tours in the aircraft. On one occasion Carter found himself leading the whole 8th Air Force to bomb a submarine concentration at Hamburg when the lead pathfinder carrying the Group CO, Colonel Terry, had to abort owing to an oxygen leak.

General Ike was not without its misfortunes during the Carter crew's tenure, once having a wheel break through the taxiway surface and getting stuck while moving out for a mission. The most damaging incident of the bomber's career occurred on its 65th mission, when Gelsenkirchen was attacked on 16 February 1945. The propeller on No.3 engine would not feather, and windmilled. Eventually it separated from the engine and slashed into the right side of the nose, nearly decapitating Tony Starcer's portrait of Eisenhower. Carter brought the bomber safely home, where it underwent repairs that kept it grounded for some weeks.

Returned to the squadron, *General Ike* served to the end of hostilities, flying its last mission on 25 April, when it was loaned to the 324th Bomb Squadron and flown by 1st Lieutenant John L. Hatfield's crew.

With other 91st Bomb Group aircraft it left for the USA on 8 June 1945, and, after temporarily parking at Bradley Field, Connecticut, was eventually ferried to Kingman, Arizona, as surplus, there to stand under the desert sun awaiting the breakers.

Tail Crazy

Lieutenant William D. Tatler and his new crew took delivery of their new B-17G at Hunter Field, Georgia, in late December 1943. The aircraft had been accepted by the Army Air Forces on 8 December, and had gone straight to Continental's Denver Modification Center and then to Georgia. Built under licence by Douglas at Long Beach, the camouflaged aeroplane had staggered, enclosed waist gun positions, a significant improvement on earlier models of the Flying Fortress and one warmly welcomed by combat crews.

The Tatler crew left Morrison Field, Florida, on 29 January 1944, their destination Italy via South America and Africa. Bill Tatler tells the story:

> One of our scheduled stops was at Belem, Brazil, where we spent the night. The following morning when we went to depart we found our B-17 surrounded by more than six inches of mud, caused by the previous evening's rain. In order to get out of the mud, I had to use a lot of throttle and brakes to keep it moving. Approaching the taxiway and climbing out of the mud took even more throttle and brakes.
>
> As I neared a B-26 awaiting take-off just ahead of us, I started to use the brakes and got no response. I pulled the emergency brake handles, and nothing happened – except to bring us closer to the B-26. Then I shut off the main switch, threw the emergency evacuation switch, and watched our B-17 hit the tail of the B-26. Fortunately, no one was hurt in either 'plane. But our B-17 had engine and fuselage damage as well as a broken Plexiglas nose.

Later, after arriving in Italy, they discovered that there was a 'dead spot' in the hydraulic motor serving the brakes, but for the moment they were in Brazil, feeling a little embarrassed, and with time on their hands. Tatler continues:

> The only facility at Belem to handle our damaged B-17 was Pan American, and they were contracted to carry out repairs. Their work force was composed of natives who were paid 50 cents a day – and once hired could not be fired. Each day my crew and I would inspect the agonizingly slow progress of repair and beg the foreman, who was an American, to get the mechanics to work faster.

When we came by on the tenth day to inspect the 'plane, we were surprised to find foot-high letters on it, painted by the Pan American foreman and his crew, spelling out the words *Tail Crazy*. We had planned to wait until Italy to christen our B-17, but we ended up completing our missions with the name chosen by the work crew.

Tatler's flight engineer, Sergeant Thomas O'Connor, had naturally been working with the Pan American people, and he was surprised and not very pleased. 'They painted it at night when I was asleep,' he remembers. 'I was shocked, but tried not to show it, thinking it would be rude when they went to all the trouble. They were grinning like a couple of chimpanzees. I knew it would never get painted over.'

Back in the USA, 21-year-old Anne Haggarty was a Junior at State Teachers College in Salem, Massachusetts, and a lot of her classmates had met Bill Tatler while he was home on leave. When they found out that he had flown off to war, they would ask her if he had named his aircraft after her. Anne Tatler recalls:

Of course I said "No", but secretly was hoping that just such a thing would happen! Bill finally sent a snapshot of his crew in front of their B-17, and I couldn't believe my eyes when I saw the name on the 'plane. Talk about shock and horror! I was pretty naive back in 1944, but I remembered having heard a few jokes with the word "tail" in them, followed by raucous laughter. So I knew that the name of Bill's 'plane was something not to be shared with my friends at college.

It was only after Bill's return from overseas and our engagement and marriage that I learned how *Tail Crazy* was named.

After a test flight over the Amazon river, *Tail Crazy* continued on its journey to war. Natal was reached on 4 February, and then came the long flight of more than eleven hours to Dakar and on to Tindouf, Casablanca, Algiers, Tunis and, finally, Foggia. Bill Tatler relates:

We arrived at Foggia Main just as the sun was setting. After landing and following a Jeep to end up in front of the Operations building, I was instructed to report to the Operations Officer and leave my crew in the 'plane.

I was told that I was assigned to the 49th Squadron of the 2nd Bomb Group, and that the airfield was Amendola, and that it was the third airfield on the right south from Foggia. They were in a hurry to get me going before it got dark.

I cranked up *Tail Crazy* and took off, flying at about one thousand feet, and counted three airfields. There were no other 'planes in the air so I called Amendola and asked if they could see a B-17 flying by. They said they could, and that I was to land south on the runway. By the time I landed it was dark. At the end of the runway I was told to turn left. I then came to a fork in the taxi strip and called the tower for directions on which way to go. Getting instructions from the tower, I proceeded to go left, right, or straight.

At one point I called the tower and told them that there were a bunch of vehicles going by quite fast in front of me, and what should I do? The tower said to hold it right there, that I was on the access road to the airfield, and that I was looking at the main highway from Foggia to Manfredonia. A truck was finally sent and I had to be pulled backwards to the taxiway, and then to the assigned parking space. We were then transported to the 2nd Bomb Group camp, which was several miles from the airfield.

Sergeant Thomas O'Connor continues the story:

It was pitch dark by the time we got to the group's area at Amendola. All I can remember is the black. No stars, no moon, just black. I was twenty-three years old and I was scared and bewildered. But that was nothing compared to what was to come later. Once we dumped our gear in a tent pitched in an olive grove – I learned next day that it had just been cleared of the belongings of a crew lost that day – we went to the group mess hall, an impressive concrete building. The mess personnel had to feed us, but it was late and they were not happy about it.

The Tatler crew had arrived at a fateful time.

The first time that *Tail Crazy* appears in 2nd Bomb Group operational records is 14 February 1944, but it aborted the mission. The pilot that day was Lieutenant George Verbruggen. Ten days later it was again scheduled, but failed to take off. The crew that day is not recorded, although naturally Bill Tatler and his crew would not have been involved so soon after their arrival. Thursday 24 February 1944 was a disastrous day for the group, and particularly for the 49th Bomb Squadron. The 2nd Bomb Group trailed the Fifth Wing formation going to Steyr in Austria, and bore the brunt of determined fighter attacks lasting about an hour. In that time the group lost a total of fourteen B-17s, and all seven aircraft from the 49th Squadron went down.

Thomas O'Connor remembers walking into the mess hall. 'There were several haggard looking guys sitting at the mess tables smoking cigarettes and drinking coffee ... The mood was dark among all the survivors. In a way they were petrified and couldn't move from the mess hall. They just sat there.'

Bill Tatler remembers; 'Everyone seemed very serious, sad, and depressed – and would not say too much to me. I felt a bit unwelcome.' Later, when he learned what had happened that day, he realized that, 'Having just arrived, I must admit that

I did not feel upset or depressed at the news. It would take some combat missions of my own and the loss of friends for me to understand a little of what the 49th Squadron must have felt on February 24. But, at that time, I figured: "That's combat". There were only three or four first pilots, including myself, left in the 49th.'

Tatler recalls the 49th holding a party in a building in Foggia city. 'I suppose it was held to boost the morale of everybody. Not many people spoke to me and my copilot, John Rice – and we stuck together.'

Tail Crazy completed her first mission on 4 March 1944 with Lieutenant Robert Cleesattel, a 96th Squadron pilot, at the controls. Lieutenant Ashmead Carson took *Tail Crazy* on her second mission, to Cassino on 15 March. It was Bill Tatler's first mission, a combat training flight. He remembers it very well because he knew it was going to be a short mission, less than four hours. He says, 'I didn't think it was necessary to wear my heated flight suit. Instead, I put on lighter clothing and darn near froze to death! It showed how inexperienced I was.'

Tom O'Connor vaguely recalls:

> The 'plane flew at least five missions before we took it as a combat crew. My recollection is we sat around in briefings and flew around in other 'planes to determine if we were combat ready. My records show the first mission with Tatler was 23 March 1944 to Verona, Italy. I'm not likely to forget it because it was the first time I ever saw flak in combat and it was frightful; like a great thundercloud above the city.
>
> Hearts grew cold when we were informed early on the morning of 2 April that the target was Steyr. The mission was really our first taste of true aerial combat. My recollection is there were ball-bearing factories there and the Germans protected them.
>
> We started off with P-38s for escort. German fighters came up from Udine in northern Italy. They attacked over the Alps where we seemed to be only a few feet above the highest peaks. I had my turret turned toward the rear when the P-38s went into action. They dropped their wing tanks immediately before engaging. I was startled by the dropping tanks as they spewed gasoline on the way down. At first I thought it was airplanes going down. I reported this to the pilot. A classic dogfight erupted behind us, but I knew then the fighters would never reach the target with us. We were on our own.
>
> I turned the turret to the right and about ten o'clock and got really scared as I saw three Me 109s bearing down on us. Of course being newcomers we were tail-end charlie and presented a suitable target. The Germans were firing 20mm and I saw them burst along our left wing and then pass me by inches. I remember instinctively ducking behind the computer sight and then thinking "what am I doing down here, it's no safer than up there". Head back up I tripped the toggles to activate the twin 0.50's and saw the tracers slam into the German

formation. They broke away under and over. I never ducked again.

Rather unusually, in my observations, the Germans were flying wing to wing and producing a great deal of fire power. For some reason or other they missed our airplane except for a few small holes in the fuselage. My observations on future missions was that the enemy pilots seemed to fly in a haphazard formation, leaving it up to the individual pilot what he wanted to do.

This was my first taste of real aerial combat in which I, as a gunner, could take an active part. Of course the P-38s could not follow us to the target. They had used up their fuel and had no additional, having dropped their wing tanks. So we went on alone with sporadic fighter opposition. The flak over Steyr was unbelievable. Some of the German fighters came through their own flak; others waited for us on the other side. I know we lost some B-17s, but I don't know how many.

The 2 April mission was the fourth attempt to attack the ball-bearing plant in ten days. It was hit hard, and Steyr was finally removed from the priority target list. The mission cost eight B-17s, and the 2nd Bomb Group's *Marishka* came home with both pilots wounded and a dead navigator.

In the middle of April it was decided that all of the specially-equipped Pathfinder aircraft assigned to Fifth Bomb Wing would be based at Amendola. The 49th Bomb Squadron would become the maintenance unit for these H2X-equipped aircraft, and all of the 49th's regular crews and aircraft would be farmed out to other squadrons. The Tatler crew and *Tail Crazy* were assigned to the 429th Squadron, where their ground crew chief was M/Sergeant John Snyder.

Tail Crazy's first abort with Tatler was on the 29 April 1944 mission to Toulon. Tatler saw flames coming from the cowling of the outboard engine, but no smoke. They tried the fire extinguisher, but they could not stop the flames until the engine was feathered. Then Tatler decided to abort the mission. After landing back at Amendola it was discovered that the exhaust ring had a big crack and, had they continued, the whole aircraft could have caught fire.

Tom O'Connor recalls:

The missions that stand out were Ploesti, Steyr, Vienna and the May 29 1944 mission to Wiener-Neustadt – I asked for and received extra ammunition which I piled in two heaps on each side of the turret on the floor ... I have no particular recollection of any others with the possible exception of once we had to go through the Brenner Pass. I think it was to Udine because we carried anti-personnel and fire bombs, the only time I remember such a bomb load. The pass had anti-aircraft guns mounted on the mountains on either side of the pass and their fire intersected at our altitude. Very frightening.

The Fifth Wing bomber formations were being disrupted by German twin-engine fighters launching rockets at the B-17s from beyond machine-gun range. In an attempt to counter this, at least five B-17s were fitted with a single 20mm cannon in the tail. Captain Philip Neal, the 2nd Bomb Group Armament Officer, is credited with the original modifications. *Tail Crazy* and 42-31590 from the 49th Squadron were cannon-armed, as were the 96th Squadron's 42-97438 and *Miss Windy City* and *Li'l Abner* from the 97th and 99th Bomb Groups. Bill Tatler says:

> The mounted 20mm cannon did not have too much flexibility, being able to go up or down or sideways only one or two degrees. Consequently, during the few times that *Tail Crazy*'s cannon was used by us, Sergeant Herman Butko, my tail gunner, would relay instructions to me to move the tail a few degrees in the direction he wished. I don't believe that we did any damage to enemy aircraft with our cannon. But the enemy 'planes did stop following behind the group as they had done, and perhaps the sight of those incendiary shells from *Tail Crazy* had an effect.

The idea of basing all of Fifth Bomb Wing's Pathfinder aircraft at one base proved unworkable, and in early June the specially-equipped aircraft were spread throughout its six B-17 groups. The Tatler crew and *Tail Crazy* both returned to the 49th Squadron. *Tail Crazy* flew her first mission with her old squadron on 16 June, to Vienna, with Lieutenant Richard Korb as pilot.

Thomas O'Connor completed his combat tour on the 30 June 1944 mission to Blechhammer, flying with Lieutenant H. L. Timian in *Tail Crazy*. O'Connor makes the point that to him it was:

> ... just another B-17 ... I don't remember any particular attachment to it. The airplane came through the war with only a few big holes while I flew with it. They were big enough that I was sure we would be non-operational, but during the night they patched them up and next day was same as the day before.
>
> The hand of God was with us on the day the 'plane smashed into the rear of the B-26. The delay caused us to miss the big February offensive when so many 'planes were lost by both the 8th and 15th Air Forces.

Tatler's original copilot, Lieutenant John Rice, became the regular pilot of *Tail Crazy* during the latter part of June and into July, flying a total of eight missions in the aircraft. O'Connor remembers Rice as 'an excellent pilot ... he and I played endless games of chess, none of which I ever won'. Rice had a mostly new crew, although bombardier Lieutenant Thomas Gregory and waist gunner Staff Sergeant Wallace Wampler were from the original crew which had brought the aeroplane to Italy. John Rice recalls:

As far as the 20mm tail gun, its effect was more psychological to friend and foe alike. The CO decided that the "great fire power" of the 20mm would be most effective at the rear of the squadron, which did not set good with my crew who by this time had built up seniority and didn't want to fly "tail-end charlie". As far as memories, time has dimmed them and we didn't have any particularly harrowing experiences. Some targets – Ploesti, Steyr, Vienna, Budapest, Wiener-Neustadt – made us a little more apprehensive. But fortunately the entire crew came through without a scratch.

Rice flew his last mission in the B-17 on 15 July against Ploesti.

Bill Tatler flew more than 30 of his 50 missions in *Tail Crazy*. A number of these, to distant and dangerous targets such as Ploesti, Steyr and Wiener-Neustadt, were 'double credit' sorties, counting as two missions towards the completion of a 50-mission combat tour. He finished up on the Memmingen mission of 18 July 1944 in 42-97920. It seems that the crew was always a little sheepish about the name that had appeared on their aeroplane that day in South America. Like O'Connor, Tatler had no 'special feelings' about the B-17, and had no feelings of greater danger if he had to fly other aircraft. In the beginning there was no guarantee that it would always get them back, but it did and, looking back, Bill Tatler feels 'pretty close' to *Tail Crazy* now.

After Bill Tatler and John Rice completed their tours *Tail Crazy* never really had another 'regular' crew. Flight Officer Duane Seaman took her on three rough missions: Linz on 25 July, Ploesti on 31 July and Friedrichshafen on 3 August, before he was lost in one of nine 2nd Bomb Group aircraft shot down during the 29 August mission to the oil refinery at Moravski in Czechoslovakia.

Tail Crazy flew her 85th and final mission on 4 November 1944, to Regensburg. Returned to the United States in December 1945, the aircraft was reduced to salvage in June 1946.

Mission to Ploesti

In April 1944 the Flying Fortresses of the 15th Air Force became involved in the aerial assault which was to be the grim highlight of their war from Italy; the campaign against the 19 square miles of rich oilfields around Ploesti, in Rumania. After the famous low-level mission of August 1943, which had cost more than 60 Liberators, the Ploesti targets had been left in peace. Oil had not been unanimously accepted as a top-priority target by the Allied strategists, and Ploesti was beyond the effective range of the heavy bombers until they moved from North Africa to the airfields around Foggia, in Italy.

The first mission of the campaign was flown on 5 April 1944, when 90 B-17s and a larger force of Liberators dropped nearly 600 tons of bombs, most of which hit and heavily damaged the Astra group of refineries. The attack was repeated twice in April, and early in May the 15th was ordered to strike the Ploesti oil installations whenever tactical considerations allowed. The target was bombed three times during that month, and early in June oil was finally established as the number one target for the heavy bombers.

Ploesti had a first-line fighter defence, and one B-17 group's historian noted that the gun batteries at Ploesti 'put up an intense, accurate flak barrage that hung like a black curtain between the Initial Point and the target'. The Germans were taking further measures to ensure a bloody, drawn-out campaign. When an attack was coming they would ignite hundreds of smoke pots which jetted streams of chemical smoke that quickly formed a thick, murky blanket over the target area. It was as effective as it was simple. Radar bombing was not yet sufficiently developed to meet the challenge.

By June 1944 the Foggia airfields were a dust bowl. Roads were blocked and traffic was slowed to a crawl to avoid creating dust clouds. At Amendola, home to both the 2nd and 97th Bomb Groups, 23 June began with a briefing for the combat crews at about 0500. The target was Ploesti.

Lieutenant Edwin Anderson and his crew from the 341st Bomb Squadron would be making their third trip to the dreaded target, and most of the crew were veterans of some twenty missions in all. They were Lieutenant Robert Newsom, navigator; Technical Sergeant John Meyer, flight engineer; Staff Sergeant Martin Hettinga, left waist gunner; Staff Sergeant Harold James, right waist gunner; Staff Sergeant Stanley Kmiec, ball turret gunner; and Sergeant Michael Sullivan, tail gunner. The regular copilot, Lieutenant George Voss, who was grounded, had been replaced by Lieutenant William Symons, from a new replacement crew. He was flying with the Anderson crew to 'get a little first-hand experience'. The regular radio operator, Technical Sergeant Don McGillivray, had been 'commandeered for some sort of hush-hush night mission, something to do with locating enemy radar sites', and was replaced by Technical Sergeant Lloyd Kane. The bombardier, Lieutenant David Kingsley, is remembered by Harold James as 'a very caring person ... a true friend. He seemed to be a person you could talk to about anything. He was also a man of very high morals. Everyone liked him and respected him.'

The Anderson crew's regular aeroplane, *Sandman*, was in for repairs. They boarded the aircraft to which they were assigned, but the magnetos did not check out, so they unloaded all their gear – parachutes, flak suits, helmets and rations – and were taken to a spare aeroplane, the 340th Squadron's *Opissonya*. As Martin Hettinga drily observed, 'Surely all this was some sort of omen'.

Opissonya was a B-17F built under licence by the Vega Division of Lockheed at Burbank. Originally it had been assigned to the 301st Bomb Group's 419th Bomb Squadron on 12 August 1943, and its first mission was flown five days later with Lieutenant Oliver Westbrook and his crew. In all it completed seventeen missions with the 301st, the last of them being the 2 November 1943 mission to Weiner-Neustadt. The 'regular' pilot was Lieutenant Irwin Miles, who flew it on seven missions. The name *Opissonya* came from the aircraft's days with the 301st, and its tail still bore traces of its original group's markings beneath the 97th Group's white triangle.

There were no problems with *Opissonya*, and the Anderson crew taxied out and took off without further incident. Ed Anderson remembers:

> We departed on time and took our assigned position, which was tail-end charlie in a seven 'plane squadron formation. During our climb the aircraft leading the second 'V' of our squadron aborted because of a supercharger fire. We moved forward to his slot.
>
> There were heavy clouds over Yugoslavia and the wing formation was disrupted. When we reached the target area the only friendly aircraft in sight were from our 97th Group, but to this point *Opissonya* was doing fine.

As they approached the cauldron of flak that boiled over Ploesti they were attacked by fighters. Anderson says, 'On the bomb run enemy fighters hit us from about two o'clock high. On their first pass they knocked out the two right hand aircraft of our squadron.' The unfortunate pair of B-17s were Lieutenant Lyle Fleener and his crew in *Hustlin' Huzzy*, and Lieutenant James Parr and his crew in 42-31351. Both aircraft crashed near Bucharest, the Rumanian capital.

Below *Opissonya* lay the target, the Dacia refinery, somewhere beneath a solid undercast. Pillars of smoke were rising through it from the fires begun by the preceding groups, and the 97th was forced to bomb by radar. Tail gunner Mike Sullivan could see no other friendly aircraft, and believes they were the last over the target.

Anderson continues:

> When we entered the heavy flak over the target the enemy fighters
> backed off. At this time there was a twin-engine enemy aircraft about
> a mile to our right at our altitude and airspeed. I was sure he was
> directing anti-aircraft fire. There was not a friendly fighter anywhere
> around to chase him away. Needless to say, the flak was right on us.

Martin Hettinga recalls:

> About the time we dropped our bombs, an anti-aircraft shell went
> through the left wing just behind the No.1 engine ... fortunately, the
> shell passed through without exploding, but it tore a jagged
> twelve-inch hole and destroyed the oil tank for that engine, making it
> impossible to feather the prop. The engine "ran away" like a scream-
> ing banshee and, expecting it to seize and tear itself from the 'plane,
> we held our breaths.

Ed Anderson explains: 'When we were hit and No.1 engine ran away we lost
at least 5,000ft of altitude before we got levelled off and slowed down. Now we were
all alone and the fighters hit us and the aircraft was badly shot up'.

The tail guns were smashed by cannon fire and Sullivan was wounded in the
head and shoulders. He crawled through to the waist area, leaving behind his
chest-pack parachute. The entire tailwheel assembly had been shot out of the fuselage, so Martin Hettinga helped him over the hole where it had been. The waist gunners guided Sullivan to the radio room, then called the bombardier, David Kingsley,
who was the first-aid officer for the crew. He began attending to Sullivan's shoulder.
The fighters were still a problem, so waist gunner Sergeant Harold James was
ordered to the tail position, but when he got there he found that one of the guns was
jammed and the sight was completely blown off. He made his way back to the waist.

Anderson says, 'We headed for home. The windmilling prop caused a large
amount of drag and vibration. We were making barely 100mph airspeed and losing
altitude. After about a half hour No.1 engine froze. The vibration stopped, our air
speed increased and we were able to maintain altitude.'

Hettinga adds:

> Since we had lost an engine, and with one prop flat to the wind
> creating drag, we could no longer keep up with the formation. We also
> discovered that our oxygen supply was low, so Andy pointed the air-
> plane southwest and down to where we would be able to breathe and
> issued orders to lighten the ship in any way we could find.
> We threw out everything loose, including a lot of extra ammuni-
> tion, and seemed to be doing okay ... We were well away from the tar-

get area and down to about 14,000ft when we flew over an enemy airfield and were immediately attacked by Me 109s. There were several
attacks, mostly from the rear.

The fighters were from a training field near the Bulgarian town of Karlovo. There
were eight Me 109s, four flown by Bulgarian pilots and four by Germans, and they
made seven separate attacks. The entire tail section of *Opissonya* had been very badly
damaged, so Anderson was not able to skid the B-17 to give his waist gunners a shot
at the fighters coming from behind. As he said, 'It didn't take long for them to find
out we had no tail guns – they came one after the other from where we couldn't
shoot back'. With her tail turret silent, *Opissonya* was doomed. It was just a matter of
time.

There were more problems. Anderson remembers, 'John Meyer the top turret gunner ducked out of his turret to tell me his guns were jammed. A 20mm cannon shell exploded in the turret and convinced me we didn't have a chance, and I
rang the bale-out bell.' *Opissonya* was finished.

In the waist Hettinga and James were manning their guns when they heard
the alarm and Anderson's voice over the intercom telling them to 'Get the hell out of
there'. Hettinga jerked the emergency release on the main fuselage door and rolled
through head-first. He believes he was the first man out, followed by Harold James
and radio operator Lloyd Kane.

When the others had jumped, Kingsley had been with Sullivan, who later
said, 'Lieutenant Kingsley attempted to locate my parachute harness. He discovered
that it had been ripped by cannon fire. He didn't hesitate a minute but took his off
and placed it on me. Carrying me in his arms the Lieutenant struggled to get me
through the door into the bomb bay and told me to be sure to pull the rip cord after I
had cleared the ship.' David Kingsley was last seen on the catwalk in the bomb bay.

In the cockpit, Anderson had got out of his seat, intending to go out through
the bomb bay. In his own words:

> The airplane stalled and fell off to the left in the start of a spin or
> spiral. I fell down and crawled to the nose hatch and got out. I remem-
> ber floating in the air by the No.1 engine and left wingtip. It seemed a
> long time until the airplane fell away and I pulled the rip cord. When
> my 'chute opened an enemy fighter circled me. I waved at him. He
> waved back, rocked his wings and flew off.

Hettinga remembered:

> After opening my 'chute, I counted the others and there were
> eight more. The airplane went into a steep dive, then pulled up into
> an equally steep climb, and repeated these oscillations several times
> before going into its final dive. It occurred to me later that Kingsley,

who had washed out of pilot training before becoming a bombardier, might well have been at the controls.

A witness on the ground, Bulgarian officer Stefan Marinopolski, watched as the crippled bomber went through her death throes. He recalls the aircraft completing two or three loops before it came down, crashing into a tree and exploding into flame. A family of three was in the shade of the tree, enjoying a picnic. Mother, father and daughter all died with David Kingsley and *Opissonya*.

The enemy fighter pilots flew directly at the Americans dangling in their parachutes, but did not open fire. Hettinga recalled that one passed so close above him that his parachute canopy was fluttering down around his head, and added that he was one terrified kid. He continued:

> My first and only parachute landing was a breeze. Although the landing area was mountainous and rocky, my 'chute canopy draped itself perfectly over a small tree, cushioning my fall completely and suspending me two or three feet above the ground. After unbuckling and stepping out of my 'chute, I threw away my heavy insulated flying boots and my bulky blue electrical suit, leaving me in khakis and olive-drab electric flying boots. We had been taught to hide our parachutes, but since I could not, my thought was to get as far as possible away from it. Knowing the enemy would be searching for us, I carefully and quietly made my way along the hillside in what seemed a westerly direction. Yugoslavia was to the west. That's where I wanted to go.

Thirst eventually forced Hettinga to approach a group of peasant farmers to ask for water, and he was taken to the police station at Sarnigor, a small village near Karlovo, although at the time he did not even know he was in Bulgaria. Anderson landed hard, hurting his feet. He tried to walk away from where he landed, but was soon taken into custody.

Harold James was captured as soon as he landed and taken to the town jail. He was scheduled to be sent to a prison camp the following morning, but early the next day he heard a rattle of small-arms fire, the jail door burst open, and four or five heavily-armed local partisans in civilian clothes stood before him. The bemused James was able to communicate with them in high-school French, and they invited him to join them. He accepted, and it was three months before he returned to the 97th Bomb Group.

The crew had been scattered over several miles, and were gradually rounded up. Sullivan and Meyer were brought to the same police station as Hettinga. The military had been notified, and some hours later a truck arrived and Stefan Marinopolski, the Bulgarian officer, took them into military custody. Hettinga tried to be friendly, later giving the Bulgarian the 15th Air Force patch from his shirt and his name and address, written on the inside of a Lucky Strike packet.

The prisoners were taken to Karlovo airfield, where they could look at the fighters which had brought them down. The gunners noted that they had inflicted a few hits on the enemy aeroplanes. The Bulgarian pilot credited with shooting down *Opissonya* was named Kristo Petrov. The American prisoners were taken to the pilots' mess and fed boiled beans and black bread, the same as the enemy pilots were eating. Hettinga remembered being surprised at such a diet for a flyer.

They were visited by a doctor who spoke some English, and as they were interrogated they finally realized that they were in Bulgaria. By then, the pilot and navigator were also at the airfield. Newsom's back had been hurt when his parachute snapped open. An officer came in with a charred billfold, and told them that it had been recovered from a body in the wreck of their aircraft. In it were the remains of a photograph of Kingsley and a bombardier's qualification card with his name on it.

Radio operator Lloyd Kane had lost his escape kit when his parachute opened, but landed safely on a hillside and hid his parachute. A few minutes later he saw soldiers climbing the hill, but he stayed put and they did not find him. He buried his 0.45 automatic. Uncertain which way to go and having no money for food, he slept in a haystack the first night and kept wondering if someone might stick a pitchfork into him.

Next morning he asked some farm workers for food and was given cold soup, bread and goat cheese. Soon a soldier picked him up and he was taken to a jail, where he was questioned, and then to a large headquarters building where they searched him and took his wedding ring, watch and pocket Bible. He joined the rest of the crew in the prison camp at Shumen, in Bulgaria.

Kmiec, the ball turret gunner, was from the Polish community in Hamtramck, Michigan, and was able to wander the countryside for several days, but he too was eventually picked up.

Anderson and the others were taken by train to Sofia, and then to the prison camp at Shumen. They were released on 8 September 1944, shortly after Bulgaria and Rumania capitulated to the swiftly advancing Russian forces.

Lieutenant David R. Kingsley was awarded the Medal of Honor, posthumously.

Miracle over Budapest

On 14 July 1944 the 15th Air Force's B-17s were sent to destroy the Shell oil refinery in Budapest, Hungary, and one more of those tales which make the B-17 legendary unfolded.

Colonel Paul Barton's 483rd Bomb Group, the sixth and final B-17 group to join the 15th Air Force, began operations on 12 April 1944 with an attack on a cement factory in Split, Yugoslavia. That mission and a handful of other early raids were flown from the 99th Bomb Group's base at Tortorella while the 483rd's own base, Sterparone, was being completed. During this phase the 483rd traded most of the new B-17Gs they had flown overseas for older 99th Group B-17Fs. This was hardly pleasing to the crews, who had to accept aircraft which, in a couple of cases, such as *Bad Penny* and *Fort Alamo II*, already had well over 100 combat missions to their credit.

One of the gleaming new aeroplanes which did manage to stay with the 483rd Bomb Group had been among the first uncamouflaged B-17Gs built by Boeing in Seattle. Delivered to the Army Air Forces in January 1944 with the serial number 42-32109, she was assigned to the 840th Bomb Squadron and given the name *Mizpah*.

The *Mizpah* crew was originally formed at Salt Lake City and, with minor changes, had become part of the new 483rd Bomb Group at MacDill on New Year's Day, 1944. The pilots were Lieutenants Ewald Swanson and Paul Berndt, the bombardier was Lieutenant Kenneth Dudley and the navigator Lieutenant Joseph Henderson. The name *Mizpah*, which had been chosen by Henderson's wife, Mary, was a Hebrew word meaning 'May the Lord watch over us while we are absent one from the other'. Other members of the crew were flight engineer Sergeant Frank Gramenzi, radio operator Sergeant George Simonelli, and gunners Arnold Kelley, Wesley Tucker, Charles Bell and Dale Hish.

The Swanson crew took *Mizpah* on the 483rd Group's first mission in April, and by the time of the Shell refinery attack they had completed the best part of 40 missions together. They were in the home stretch that summer of 1944, and had just returned from a week's rest leave on the Isle of Capri. The mission to Budapest should have been fairly routine.

Mizpah was on the bomb run when a flak shell exploded right under her nose, instantly killing Henderson and Dudley. Pilot Ewald Swanson said:

> When we were hit there was a severe jolt ... the engineer, Frank Gramenzi, left the top turret when we were hit and I recall asking him

to check the rear of the airplane as I did not know how the rest of the crew were making out. He returned in a hurry and informed me that the others had baled out. We also salvoed the bombs. The instruments were not working ... no altimeter, airspeed, intercom or windshield, also the bomb-bay doors were open and it was very breezy in the cockpit. I thought that we were in the 'plane for ten or fifteen minutes before the copilot Paul Berndt, Frank Gramenzi and I baled out. While we stayed in the 'plane I was able to keep the ship in a gentle downhill glide but we were, of course, concerned about stalling out. We were all captured immediately. I almost landed on a haystack and was hiding my 'chute under it when a Hungarian soldier walked up behind me.

Further back in the aeroplane, left waist gunner Staff Sergeant Dale Hish had been watching for German fighters, and had no idea of the full extent of the damage to the front of the aircraft. He said, 'I got over and kicked the door off, because I knew we were hit bad. Tucker came up from the ball turret and said they say leave the ship, which I never heard ... As far as I know I was first out.'

Observers in other aircraft had been stunned by the sight of *Mizpah* hanging in the air with the entire nose shot off. Sergeant Robert Toombs, waist gunner on Lieutenant Bob Orton's *Joanne*, had time to take three photographs of the doomed aircraft before it fell away. The witnesses reported only five parachutes, but in fact eight men survived to be taken prisoner. The two officers were taken to Stalag Luft III, and the six enlisted men to Stalag Luft IV. All of them survived to return home after the war.

BTO In The ETO

There were, inevitably, many Fortresses that were not really prominent in their own right, but gained fame through their connection with a notable individual or event. The 97th Bomb Group's B-17E *Yankee Doodle* carried Ira Eaker, VIIIth Bomber Command's commanding general, on the Eighth's first heavy bomber mission; the 381st Group's *Stage Door Canteen* was 'christened' by actress Vivien Leigh (of 'Gone With The Wind' fame), and so on. Perhaps *BTO In The ETO* did not command much attention at the time, but it was involved in one of the most extraordinary adventures to befall a B-17 crew.

The originator of the unusual nickname, meaning big time operator in the European Theater of Operations, is unknown, but *BTO In The ETO* was the inscription that Lieutenant Louis Hernandez and his men saw on the nose of this battle-scarred, camouflaged B-17G when they climbed down from a 6x6 truck on to a hardstanding of the 729th Bomb Squadron at Deopham Green airfield, Norfolk, early in the morning of 21 June 1944. They were recent replacements in the 452nd Bomb Group, which had suffered very heavy losses during its operations in the two preceding months. *BTO In The ETO* had survived these bad days, despite being well 'chewed up' by flak and fighters on occasions. The Hernandez boys speculated the Fortress was probably an original aircraft the Group had brought from the States when it arrived in the previous December. In fact, like them, *BTO In The ETO* was a replacement, having arrived in the UK early that year.

Most newcomers believed they were given a rough aircraft and the rough positions in the formations for the first trips. These men had flown the 'tail-end charlie' slot in the low squadron formation on their first mission, on D-Day, 6 June, and had drawn this short straw regularly ever since. Today was the seventh for the Hernandez crew, and their first in this particular B-17. But their natural apprehension as to what lay ahead was tinged with excitement that morn, for they were to be part of the first 8th Air Force shuttle mission to Russia, bombing a petroleum plant at Ruhland, south of Berlin, and continuing eastwards to land at Poltava in the Ukraine. Permission to establish the air base had been obtained from the Soviets only with difficulty, the USAAF being firmly convinced that it would add a new dimension to their strategic bombing campaign by bringing targets in eastern Europe within striking range.

In addition to shaving kit and toiletries, the airmen were told to take Class A uniforms, as this attire was more likely to gain them the respect of their Russian hosts. At 0510, in a dawning day made gloomier by extensive cloud, the last cigarette was extinguished and the crew climbed aboard *BTO In The ETO* and prepared for engine starting. Louis Hernandez and co-pilot Tom Madden made their way through the radio room and bomb bay to the cockpit, while navigator Alfred Lea and bombardier Joe Baker used the front hatch to enter the nose compartment. The rest of the crew piled in through the rear fuselage door, Technical Sergeant Tony Hutchinson, the engineer/top turret gunner, following the pilots through the bomb bay. Sergeant Jack White settled in his radio room while the ball, waist and tail gunners lounged in the rear fuselage, although they would take up bracing positions against the radio room bulkhead for take-off.

There was a stranger on board. A P-51 crew chief, Staff Sergeant Robert Gilbert, was one of several being conveyed in B-17s that day to service the Mustang escort also going all the way to Russia. Gilbert had to act as waist gunner during the flight, taking the place of a regular waist gunner who had been stood down for this mission. Gilbert was unaware that on the previous day he had lost the Mustang which he serviced as crew chief when Major James Goodson, one of the 4th Fighter Group's leading aces, was shot down.

The 452nd Bomb Group was putting up a maximum effort of 47 B-17s, split into three formations which would join with the other two groups of the 45th Combat Wing. The 8th Air Force was sending more than 1,200 heavies to targets in the Berlin area and, on approach, two combat wings totalling more than 160 B-17s would veer southeast and bomb the oil refinery targets around Ruhland before proceeding to Russia. As this would entail a 1,450-mile flight, each aircraft had an additional fuel tank installed in its bomb bay.

The formation of which *BTO In The ETO* was part began take-off at 0525, and Hernandez lifted his charge into the air some 10 minutes later, turned left and climbed steadily northwest through the scudding clouds. At 4,000ft over the Norfolk countryside Hernandez joined the 20-mile-long assembly pattern, turning *BTO In The ETO* at every left-hand turn to bring it into position in one of the three-aeroplane elements trailing the rear of the formation.

For 90 minutes the formation gained altitude and sought its place in the bomber stream. Sergeant William Cabaniss entered his ball turret, and at 10,000ft the crew were advised to go on oxygen. At 0707 Lieutenant Lea logged their departure above the English coastline at 19,000ft. A few minutes later, out over the blue-grey North Sea, bombardier Joe Baker called the gunners to test-fire their guns. There followed the intermittent brief bursts of fire and accompanying vibration as each man aimed at the sea or a clear patch of sky.

Moments later, smoke wafted up on to the flight deck. An alert over the intercom made navigator Lea turn to see burning electrical wires in the tunnel leading from the nose to the flight deck. He was about to reach for a fire extinguisher when he remembered that in this situation the toxic gas created might penetrate oxygen masks. Something had to be done quickly, as the fire threatened to engulf the Very pistol flares and had ignited an oxygen line. Engineer Tony Hutchinson arrived in the tunnel, and together he and Lea beat out the burning material with gloved hands.

They then discovered the cause of the fire. During the top-turret gun test an empty bullet case had become dislodged from its trace and fallen on the floor, rolling into the tunnel and lodging between two exposed electrical terminals used for connecting the system to a battery cart. Sufficient heat had been generated to burn an 18in hole through the fuselage skin. It was also discovered that some of the oxygen had been lost before the fire was extinguished, but it was decided that enough of this precious commodity remained to allow the flight to continue.

For the next two hours the crew experienced the usual continuous throb of engine noise that penetrated earphones, the frequent vibration of passage through rough air and other aircraft-induced turbulence, plus blinding sunlight. Flak was seen here and there, but even during the bomb run there was nothing close. Perhaps this was the 'milk run' some had prophesied. Entering Polish airspace, the entire formation performed a navigational manoeuvre called a Double Drift, so as to fly over Warsaw in a morale-boosting gesture to the citizens of the occupied city. As the bombers resumed the original course, flying eastward along the 52° north latitude line, the gunners reported a lone twin-engined aircraft flying some distance away at the same altitude and airspeed. It was obviously tracking the American force, which could not possibly return to the UK from this distance. Altitude had been gradually reduced to about 15,000ft, and there was a feeling that the worst dangers were past. The security of Russia lay ahead.

At about 52°N 23°E, some 50 miles east of Warsaw, their confidence was rudely shattered. In Alfred Lea's words, 'All of a sudden all hell broke loose!'. *BTO In The ETO* rocked under a massive concussion. The left inboard engine, No.2, was on fire, and the fuel tank directly behind it had been blown out of the bottom of the wing and hung down like a giant flap. The pilots struggled with the controls, but the bomber entered a flat spin. The alarm bell rang and the men in the waist, realizing that the ball turret had been hit, cranked it into position, undid the door and found the gunner severely wounded and semi-conscious. They got him out, clipped a parachute on him, and one of them, clutching him tight, jumped out of the rear fuselage door, pulling the ripcord just before letting go of Cabaniss when well clear of the aircraft.

In the nose Alfred Lea put on his parachute and tried to release the nose hatch door. It would not budge, presumably damaged by whatever had hit them. In desperation Lea doubled up his legs and gave the door a mighty kick, only to end up hanging half outside the stricken bomber when the door suddenly gave way. The slipstream pushed his legs up against the underside of the fuselage, and Lea was worried that if he let go he might be whipped back into the ball turret. He quickly decided to pull himself back up into the nose, then doubled up and jumped through the hatch. He was followed by the bombardier, Joe Baker, and then by the two pilots, Hernandez being the last to leave.

As they drifted earthwards they were aware of fighter aircraft in the area. *BTO In The ETO* had been the victim of a Me 109, a squadron of which had used the clouds below as cover to launch a climbing attack on the tail-end charlie of the B-17 formation, blasting its underside with 20mm cannon shells. Unknown to her crew at the time, *BTO In The ETO* was, in fact, the only bomber in the force going to Russia to be shot down. Alfred Lea watched as 'In one last screaming dive she buried herself deep in the green farmland of German occupied Poland, amidst the pall of greasy black smoke could be seen the explosions of empty fuel tanks and unspent ammunition'. The descending airmen gained some consolation from seeing that all of the crew had apparently escaped.

They all landed safely. The wounded William Cabaniss, who required urgent medical attention, was taken by German troops. Tail gunner Arnold Shumate and radioman Jack White were also captured before they had a chance to evade. The rest of the crew were more fortunate. The well forested countryside, interspersed with agricultural communities, could not be thoroughly policed by the Germans, and although an armed party had been sent out to apprehend the US airmen it had some distance to travel. Louis Hernandez had dislocated his arm in his final efforts to leave the crippled aircraft. Stunned and in great pain, he came down in a field of rye, where three Polish girls half-pulled and half-carried him to their village. There he was hidden while word was sent to a doctor in a neighbouring town. This man, of pensionable age, had to walk five miles in darkness to reach the injured pilot. The anaesthetic was several gulps of neat vodka, and the joint was restored to its socket by being yanked back while the patient was pinned down by the doctor's feet.

Alfred Lea and Joe Baker landed not far from one another in tree-bordered fields. Hiding their parachutes, the two men set off towards a village they could see in the distance. Nearby were farm workers scything hay. Lea and Baker got down and crawled into the grass, trying to make up their minds if these men would be friendly, and how to approach them. In England they had been told that people in occupied countries could be sentenced to death for helping airmen, and that great care should be taken not to expose them unnecessarily to this risk. However, one old man had apparently seen the two airmen, and came hobbling their way. When he got near they saw he was not lame, but was simply pushing a bottle of water along with his feet. He left it close to their hiding place before returning to his work. This told Lea and Baker two things; that he was friendly, and that there was danger in the vicinity. The latter was soon seen – a German patrol a field away, no doubt looking for the American airmen.

Because of the German presence Lea and Baker decided not to go to the village, but to make for a farmhouse which they thought might be connected with the grass cutters. It was necessary to cross a road to reach it, but just as they were about to do this they heard a vehicle, and hid in a culvert. There were some anxious moments when the vehicle stopped close by, but it then drove on.

The reception at the house was friendly, and it appeared that the pair's initial salutation of, 'American, American' was accepted. There was a brief doubt about this when uniformed men came into the room while Lea and Baker were having some rye bread and milk. However, it was soon obvious to the Americans that these were partisans, for the uniforms were a mixture, a few obviously being of German origin but most having a shoulder flash in the Polish national colours, red and white. Their weapons, too, were a variety of types and origins. While verbal communication proved difficult, the partisans were apparently soon convinced that the US airmen were genuine.

Word must have come that a German patrol was approaching, for the partisans suddenly indicated that they must depart, and that Lea and Baker should accompany them. They were led through fields and woods to another small village, where they were delighted to find their two pilots, the flight engineer, the waist gunner and the P-51 crew chief, all safe and uninjured. All had been befriended and hidden by Poles from the local peasant communities.

That evening a partisan arrived who could speak reasonable English. He went by a nickname which he said meant 'Dreadnought' in Polish. All the members of the force were known by false names, to hide their identities and protect their families from reprisals. The seven airmen learned from Dreadnought that they were in the hands of the 34th Infantry Regiment of the Polish partisan army, which was active in the area, attacking German lines of communication to the Russian front. The Commandant, known as Zenon, was in communication with the Polish authorities in Britain via a radio transmitter parachuted to them by the RAF. This was used to send word that the seven flyers were in safe hands, and that the other three were presumed to have been captured.

Dreadnought explained that, while his organization would do its best to get the Americans to the Russians, the Red Army's advance had brought increased German activity in the area and a transfer would be difficult to arrange. For the time being the B-17 crewmen would have to stay with the partisans. Later that night, when the evaders were trying to sleep on straw-filled sacks, another partisan officer arrived and was introduced as Zenon. Through Dreadnought's interpretation, Zenon pledged that they would be safe and that the Germans would have to kill every one of his men if they were going to capture the Americans.

There is no doubt that the Germans knew the Poles were sheltering the missing men from the downed B-17, for they continued to search for them during the next few days. However, the 34th Infantry Regiment moved their charges from village to village, or into the forest, while their informants and scouts constantly monitored the position and strength of enemy forces in the area. In fact this was no rag-tag army. It was not only well organized and led, but also well equipped and fed. The strength of the unit was between 150 and 250 men, and it had sprung from the first Resistance organization established soon after Poland was overrun in 1939.

The capabilities of the force were demonstrated nine days after the crew of *BTO In The ETO* dropped in. The Germans had evidently obtained information concerning the presence of Zenon's party, with whom the Americans were travelling, when they stopped in another village. The partisans were fired on as they fled, but they managed to gain the cover of the forest without casualties. Zenon anticipated that the enemy would return with a more substantial force, and apparently sent word to the other elements of his regiment to come to his support. He was not mistaken, for the Germans, using mostly disenchanted former Soviet soldiers who had been formed into a battalion, tried to encircle the wooded area in which the partisans were deployed. The American airmen suddenly found themselves foot soldiers, and under fire from light artillery. The fight went on for more than four hours before the enemy commander evidently decided that his ammunition was low and his casualties were high, and withdrew.

Dreadnought accompanied the Americans everywhere, acting as their interpreter. They discovered he was a film producer in peacetime, and had gained his command of English then. He was also their shepherd, advising against dangers. The Americans did not want to put their hosts in greater danger, and when the partisans presented complete aircraft manuals and proposed that they raid a nearby enemy airfield so that the Americans could steal a Junkers Ju 88 bomber and fly it to Allied territory, the suggestion was turned down. Apart from the thought that many partisan lives would be sacrificed in such a venture, it was highly probable that such a flight would be unlikely to reach friendly territory without being shot down.

The partisans regularly set ambushes for military truck convoys in remote places where there was wooded or high crop cover to afford them surprise and protection. Their forces were usually positioned on both sides of a road, so the unfortunate men in the convoy had no escape. The ambush procedure was experienced by the Americans one day early in July, when they were involved in wrecking a military train. In an effort to prevent derailments, German troops were sent down the tracks well ahead of the trains to check for damage or explosive charges. Cunningly, the Poles selected a bend to conceal their activities, and as soon as the inspecting team had passed out of view they hurriedly placed explosives under the rails and retreated into the woods before the train approached. The partisans did not have to wait and see the result of their handiwork. When the locomotive passed over the concealed charges the thunder of the derailment rang in their ears as they made themselves scarce. Under cover of darkness, the airmen marched with the partisans for nearly 45 miles through woodland to get clear of the area. Alfred walked barefoot.

The airmen were given support duties by their hosts, chiefly driving the horse and cart combinations in which the partisans moved their ammunition and equipment around the countryside, sometimes covering as much as 30 miles in a day. They also acted as 'extra eyes' for the snipers. As the weeks passed and the Russian advance continued, the front line became decidedly fluid in the countryside, presenting the partisans with the problem of telling friend from foe. Because of this precarious position Zenon decided to take his men into the Pripet marshlands, where armour could not operate, and which both the German and Soviet armies would probably avoid. Unfortunately, in the course of this movement the 34th Infantry Regiment came into contact with a sizeable German force which evidently took them to be Soviet troops. Again the partisans had to take cover in the woods, and for several days they were engaged with enemy troops. It then appeared that the Wehrmacht had departed west, so Zenon made another attempt to reach the Russian lines, only to run into more retreating German troops and again have to retreat.

Contact with the Red Army was finally established on 27 July. Next day the seven airmen were taken to Marshal Zukhov's field headquarters, where Zenon insisted on a signed receipt for his wards from a Soviet colonel. Transported to an airfield, the crew of *BTO In The ETO* eventually reached the US base at Poltava, where they learned that most of the B–17s from their group had been destroyed on the ground by Luftwaffe bombing on the night following the first shuttle mission.

In early August the seven were returned by air to Deopham Green, where they were treated as celebrities. They were, in fact, the largest number from one 8th Air Force crew to evade capture in an occupied country, and the only crew to fight with Polish partisans.

A Matter of Luck

The 100th Bomb Group, which on several occasions suffered horrendous losses, earned the sobriquet 'The Bloody Hundredth' from an unknown source in the 8th Air Force. The name caught on with the men of other bomb groups, who probably found some comfort in the belief that there was a unit sustaining greater hurt than their own. Rumours about the 100th's situation were rife, but most were false. It continued to be viewed as the 'hard luck' group, even though its overall combat experience was no worse than that of most other groups who had started operations in the summer of 1943.

Also like most other units that had started with B-17Fs, very few of its original aircraft survived a year's service, the average life of a Fortress during this period being 215 days. Thus the 100th Group, aware of its tag, was somewhat surprised to find that one of the few B-17Fs to survive the great air battles of autumn and winter 1943-44 carried the ominous nickname *Hard Luck!*.

The replacement crew of 1st Lieutenant Donald N. Mitchell landed at the 100th's Thorpe Abbotts base in Norfolk on Friday 13 August 1943 in a B-17F with a serial number ending in 13. Consideration of these facts prompted the Mitchell crew to decide on the name *Hard Luck!* for their charge, although those on the base who were of a more superstitious nature felt that this was inviting trouble, and were not enamoured with taking this Fortress on combat missions when the Mitchell crew was stood down.

Hard Luck! and its crew did not go to Regensburg and Africa with the main 100th Group force on 17 August, but flew their first mission on 3 September 1943, to Paris. Thereafter, *Hard Luck!* participated in a steady stream of missions and, belying its name, was not scheduled for the Münster mission of 10 October, when the Group formation was all but eliminated. The Mitchell crew were apparently a little apprehensive about flying their 13th mission, particularly when *Hard Luck!* was found parked on hardstanding 13 instead of the usual No.32. In the event it turned out to be an 'easy trip', neither flak nor enemy fighters being encountered.

Promotion came quickly in those days, and Mitchell advanced to captain and squadron leader, being given one of the new B-17Gs in October. *Hard Luck!* was then assigned to a new crew, captained by 2nd Lieutenant Loren Van Steenis.

The B-17G was noticeable for its 'chin' turret, but late in 1943 electronic controls for the engine turbo-superchargers were introduced which most pilots thought far more beneficial to survival. The B-17F and early G models had hydraulically actuated turbo controls which were prone to freeze up at the '50 below'

156

temperatures encountered five miles above northwest Europe in winter. Frequent exercising of the controls was required to prevent this; a laborious task that was not always possible. 'Lost' superchargers meant a drop in engine power and an inability to keep up with the formation, and stragglers were easy prey for Luftwaffe fighters.

Hard Luck! was a B-17F, yet not once in the first 25 missions did it lose a supercharger. This was most unusual during the 1943-44 winter period, and says much for good piloting techniques. The high standard of maintenance on the aircraft undoubtedly contributed to the record, for the 24-year-old crew chief, Technical Sergeant Glenn 'Zip' Myers, and his team – assistant crew chief Staff Sergeant Peter Skolosky, Sergeant Amos Hill and Corporal Leonard Muszynski – prided themselves on the fact that, with a total of 367 hours flight time and 25 missions, all four original engines were still in fine condition. Good fortune had smiled on *Hard Luck!* and its combat crews for, although it had occasionally been struck by bullets and shell splinters, no man had been wounded and the damage was minimal. During the first 25 missions 115.41 US tons of bombs had been dropped.

Hard Luck! continued to lead a comparatively charmed life. It was one of the survivors of the 8th Air Force's first major attack on Berlin, on 6 March 1944, when fifteen of the 100th Bomb Group's Fortresses failed to return; half the group's force on the raid. The Van Steenis crew flew seventeen missions of their tour in this bomber.

By the spring of 1944 the men of the 100th considered *Hard Luck!* their most distinguished B-17 through its record, the antithesis of its name. By this time, Lieutenant John Giles and his men had taken over as the regular crew. By May the bomber had 48 missions and 574 combat hours to its credit, and still sported the original Wright Cyclones. These were Studebaker-made engines, generally held to be less dependable than those from the parent company. There still had been no supercharger failures, although two had been changed.

'Zip' Myers and his men guarded their record jealously, and did not hesitate to make it known that they did not want inexperienced crews taking their bomber to war. It is recorded in Group records that one new pilot complained, 'Hell, you gotta show them your blood test before they'll even let you touch the fuselage'. Myers had a little verse which he would often recite to pilots arriving on his hardstand for a mission, 'The cough and the sneeze both spread disease. And so does flak – do bring her back.'

Despite their reliability, after two more missions each engine had reached 630 hours flying time in total, and an overhaul was due. *Hard Luck!* was out of action for a few days while changes were made. One of the original engines was found to be in such good condition that it was reinstalled after required modifications. Back in service, *Hard Luck!* continued to add to its impressive total of combat missions, and by August it was one of only two B-17Fs at Thorpe Abbotts still flown on operations. The other was *Royal Flush*, famous as the sole surviving 100th Bomb Group Fortress to return to base after the disastrous Münster mission of 10 October 1943. *Royal Flush* had some ten missions more to its credit than *Hard Luck!*, but nowhere near such a good maintenance record. At this time most B-17s with hydraulic turbo-supercharger controls had been withdrawn from operations, and only special pleas to engineering officers retained the celebrated few.

From a slim 35 per cent chance of completing a combat tour in August 1943, an 8th Air Force bomber crew's likelihood of reaching that happy conclusion now stood at nearly 70 per cent. Likewise, the individual bombers they flew generally endured for much longer. The hostile airspace of enemy-held territory was marginally safer. The men at Thorpe Abbotts expected *Hard Luck!* to come back; the aircraft was something of a minor legend. But on 14 August 1944, a year and a day after it had arrived at the Norfolk base, its luck ran out and it did not return from its 62nd mission.

The target was Ludwigshaven oil refineries, which, like all of Hitler's oil installations, were ringed with anti-aircraft artillery. The flak barrage was intense on the run-up to the Initial Point. One burst wrecked one of *Hard Luck!*'s engines and probably destroyed a second. The aircraft was seen to salvo its bomb load and gradually drop out of formation. It was last observed losing height with one engine smoking. Although it was unknown at the time, 2nd Lieutenant Donald Cielewich and his eight-man crew all baled out and were taken prisoner. *Hard Luck!* crashed into woodland in the vicinity of the target area.

'Zip' Myers was a sad, sad man that day. There was a hope that the crew had been able to nurse old *Hard Luck!* back to a landing in liberated territory on the continent, but it was not to be. In 61 missions his charge had flown more than 850 hours and hauled 249,810lb of bombs, and its gunners had claimed four enemy aircraft shot down. They gave 'Zip' a brand new 'silver' Fortress, but it could not compare with his first love.

Four days later, fate and an 88mm shell removed the 100th's last combat-worthy B-17F from the scene. *Royal Flush* went down over France on her 75th mission. Luck was a matter of chance, and chance was simply beating the average odds. Those odds were high.

Snake Hips

The ability of the Fortress to remain airborne and controllable after sustaining extensive battle damage was one of its endearing qualities. Numerous photographs depict shattered areas of fuselage, wings and tails on B-17s that were flown hundreds of miles to safe landings. A combination of the aircraft's rugged construction and inherent stability made a major contribution to such instances of survival, though it required the determination and resourcefulness of aircrews to bring these bombers home.

A contender for the title of most seriously damaged B-17 brought back to a safe landing is the 92nd Bomb Group's *Snake Hips*. This camouflaged B-17G arrived at the Group's Podington, Bedfordshire, base on 11 February 1944, and was placed in the 327th Bomb Squadron. Officially it was 42-31713, identification letters UX:T, but to the men 'on the line' it was *Snake Hips*, characterized by a seductive girl painted alongside this nickname. *Snake Hips'* combat debut occurred on 20 February, when Captain Charles Kelly took it to Leipzig during the intensive period of strikes against the German aircraft industry known as Big Week.

Snake Hips was not assigned to a particular captain, and a score of different crews flew the aircraft during its operational life. Despite exposure to flak and fighter attack, *Snake Hips* did not come to much harm during its early missions, apart from a small fire in the bomb bay when returning from Oranienburg on 18 April. It was occasionally a squadron lead aircraft, and on 29 April and 7 May, with Lieutenant John Walsh at the controls, *Snake Hips* led the Group to Berlin. Until 13 July, when it flew its 47th mission, *Snake Hips* had not suffered an abort, but on this day 2nd Lieutenant Robert J. Stewart was forced to turn back because of equipment failure. Stewart's crew flew her for eleven missions of their tour.

Nearly 60 mission-completed symbols extended along the nose when *Snake Hips* left Podington for Merseburg early on 24 August 1944. The Merseburg area held some of Germany's most important synthetic oil plants, and these vital installations were well defended by several hundred radar directed anti-aircraft guns, chiefly 88mm and 105mm. The flak barrages of Merseburg became legendary in the 8th Air Force through the toll they took of its bombers. On this day, *Snake Hips* was captained by 2nd Lieutenant John Bosko, making his seventh combat mission, while the rest of his crew were making their sixth and third in the bomber. At briefing that morning there had been moans when the target was revealed. As a relative newcomer, Bosko was unaware of Merseburg's reputation, and had to ask another pilot the reason for this verbal protest.

Soon after they had passed the Initial Point at 29,000ft, accurate flak bracketed the 92nd Group's formation. Togglier (acting bombardier) Staff Sergeant Jerome Charbonneau had just opened the bomb-bay doors as the formation bore down on the target when an 88mm shell detonated inside the bomb bay. Miraculously none of the ten 500lb bombs exploded in the aircraft. Three were blasted out of a four-foot hole in the right side of the bay, two rolling a considerable way along the length of the wing before falling off. Five more were dislodged from their shackles and dropped down on top of two that remained jammed in their shackles. Shell splinters and blast ripped out the root of the right wing at the trailing spar and wrecked the radio room, although the operator, Sergeant Bishop Ingraham, fortunately escaped serious injury. However, one thumbnail-sized piece of shrapnel entered the ball turret from the top and ricocheted round the inside, striking the gunner, Sergeant Gordon Wescott, several times and mortally wounding him.

Co-pilot 2nd Lieutenant Curt Koehnert had the controls, as it had been agreed he could fly the bomber on the target run. With the detonation, John Bosko's mind was momentarily a blank and then turned to surprise at the dirt floating around, for the flight deck had appeared so clean. There was black smoke, too. Looking back, Bosko saw engineer Sergeant Peter LaFleur sliding out of the top turret and suspected he was wounded:

> I thought "Oh boy, here we go" then realized he wasn't hit as he grabbed his 'chute and started for the front exit. I hollered down to the guys in the nose to stop Pete and turn him around. I'd yet to make a decision on baling out. A flame shot up against the windshield; we had a cockpit fire. A piece of flak had gone through the small hydraulic tank on the back of the co-pilot's seat and a spark from the electric booster motor had ignited the escaping fluid. Pete got rid of his 'chute and battled the flames. We were also losing oxygen and we could all smell gasoline over our masks, which said we had an open tank somewhere. When I looked back I could see gasoline swishing round in the bomb bay. I thought Holy Smoke, how come we haven't blown up by now? My transition instructor at Roswell, New Mexico, told me that in an emergency give yourself ten seconds. If nothing happens you might not be as bad off as you thought you were, and that flashed through my mind. Well, we'd had our ten seconds and the thing didn't blow. I hollered to Pete not to throw any of the burning material into the bomb bay or we were dead ducks. He exhausted the extinguisher and then used his body to smother the remaining flames. As a result, his jacket caught fire and I beat it out with my hands.

All of this time *Snake Hips* had been losing altitude at an average 2,000ft a minute, although maintaining its course. Bosko and Koehnert found that there was no lateral response to the controls, indicating jammed or severed lines to the ailerons. They were then a few thousand feet below the formation, which was about to unload its bombs, and they were unable to use the flight controls to turn away. Bosko tried to increase engine power on one side to pull them clear, only to find that the super-chargers were not functioning properly. Unknown to him, electronic control ampli-fiers in the radio room had been damaged and were keeping the waste gates wide open, so that there was insufficient exhaust gas pressure to speed the turbine wheels. There was a built-in safety device, but this had a delay before coming into operation.

With loss of power and no lateral control, *Snake Hips* continued to descend over the target. Bosko and Koehnert looked up apprehensively in time to see bombs on their way down from the formation above. Lady Luck smiled on them, for one stick passed just ahead of the nose, another narrowly missed the trailing edge of the left wing, and one stick dropped close by the tail. The bombs were armed when they passed, as the little arming vane propellers from the fuses were also seen to tumble past *Snake Hips*. There was some relief among the crew that they had not been knocked down or blown up by the bombs of their own group, but the situation was still critical, and unless more control could be gained it might be necessary to bale out.

As Sergeant Wescott in the ball turret had failed to respond to intercom calls, waist gunner Charles Garrison and Bishop Ingraham opened the turret door and extracted him. Although Wescott's fatal wound was hidden by his flight clothing, it was evident that there was nothing they could do for him. The men in the rear fuse-lage could also see that they were cut off from the forward part of the aircraft by the mutilated bomb bay.

All the time the aircraft was rapidly losing height as Bosko and Koehnert sought lower altitude, where both aircrew and engines would find sufficient air. As the B-17 passed 14,000ft all four Wrights came in with a roar as the turbo-super-charger waste gates closed and full power was restored. At last the throttles could be jockeyed to skid the aircraft in the general direction of home, even if progress was accomplished with a see-sawing from side-to-side. Levelling out at 12,000ft, Bosko began to take stock of his situation:

> From our briefing that morning I knew there were no major turns getting back. It was more or less a straight shot to a point south of the Zuider Zee. The navigator had been hit in the arm by a piece of shrap-nel but he did pilotage working from the map to the ground. Our Fluxgate compass was knocked out, we had two engine manifold gauges out of four and two tachometers working. Looking round, we saw the landing gear was down. I asked the co-pilot to check the gear and he confirmed it was down. So I told Pete to see if he could crank it up manually. He took the crank and went towards the bomb bay, only to be brushed aside as he made to enter. Then I realized why we hadn't blown up. The air rushing in that huge hole on the right side had a cir-cular pattern and this cross-current had kept flames and gasoline fumes

apart. Pete finally backed into the bomb bay and got the crank in, but it would not budge. He pushed so hard it bent the crank. We realized then that we had to stay with the gear down and that if any enemy fighter happened along the pilot might take this as a sign of surrender. No fighter appeared and, although we were flying across Germany at 12,000ft and an easy target for flak, not a shot was fired at us.

Our attention was taken up fully with handling the controls. It took two of us to hold the nose down. We couldn't use the trimtab as the control cable was severed and when the trim wheel was turned the cable kept on coming out in the cockpit. The engineer had to wind it up and jam it out of our way. There was a lot of buffeting coming off the elevator and the rudder pedals were chattering and banging left and right; so violently I told Curt to keep his feet off the pedals or he was going to get a broken leg. The cause; the large hole in the fuselage was creating a burble and the disturbed air was hitting the rudder. Curt found that by turning his control wheel all the way over he could get a little aileron response, only it took time to return and then we had to counter it the other way so our flight was a continuous wander one way and then the other. I just hoped we were going to have enough fuel to make it.

The next thing was to deal with the remaining bombs. I called up Charbonneau, a stand-in for our bombardier who had received an arm wound on the previous mission. Fortunately, Charbonneau had a good knowledge of ordnance, having one time been in charge of our squadron's armament section. When he came up to the flight deck I told him we had to get rid of the bombs. He took a look at them and reported that the explosion had severed all the arming wires, some vanes were turning and one bomb was fully armed and highly danger-ous. There were both tail and nose fuzes and he could not get to the back of the bay because the walkway was severed. He called up the waist gunner and radioman and told them to stop the fuze arming vanes turning and instructed how to carefully unscrew the fuzes, giv-ing the number of turns required. He told them there have to be no "oops!"; it has to be right first time; if there's an "oops!" we'll be blown to smithereens. Charbonneau watched them take turns in this task. With the slipstream tearing in that hole it was difficult and prob-ably took 40-45 minutes to get all the fuzes out and thrown clear of the airplane. Charbonneau dealt with the armed bomb and worked on the others he could reach. When they were all defuzed Charbonneau took off his 'chute and went back into the bay. He was a big kid, about 6ft 2in and 190lb, and by brute strength he raised one end of the top bomb in the pile and, using another bomb as a fulcrum, gradually eased and slid it backwards until it toppled out. This way he gradually worked all five loose bombs out with one hand while grasping the stainless steel circumferential bomb-bay stiffeners to prevent himself falling out of the bay. When I looked back I could see these stiffeners giving. Stainless steel is strong but it can snap. He could have ended up with a handful of steel and a 12,000ft fall.

Then there were the two remaining bombs on the shackles; they would not budge. Charbonneau said he wasn't going to get them free unless he had a screwdriver. Somebody in the nose said, "There's a screwdriver back here". They brought it up; it was a large one, about 20in long. It was ideal and Charbonneau went back and forced the shackles holding the two bombs. I felt the 'plane lurch slightly as each fell away.

Since the pilots were endeavouring to maintain altitude and level flight, the bomber had progressed with a slight nose-up attitude, and after the bombs had been disposed of this tended to increase. In view of the lack of control, the pilots decided to leave well alone and let the aircraft continue in this fashion. On reaching the Dutch coast Bosko asked the crew if they wanted to bale out or risk crossing the North Sea, where there would be little hope of making a successful ditching if the situation deteriorated. All voted to go on. But as *Snake Hips* was nursed out of enemy airspace and across the sea, another critical situation arose. Number 2 engine failed owing to fuel exhaustion and the propeller would not feather properly. It was fuel from No.2's tank that had been leaking into the bomb bay. The fuel supply to a second engine was near exhaustion by the time the English coast was crossed. Their luck held, for, despite haze on crossing the shore line, an airfield was seen.

But there were some anxious moments to come, as John Bosko relates:

Somebody spotted this field to our left, about three miles away. It had about an eight thousand foot runway and I thought that's for us. I told the crew I didn't know whether I could get this thing on the ground or not, so put on your 'chutes and when we pass over the field bale out. It was Woodbridge, an emergency field built for shot-up 'planes to land on and I determined to try and get ours down. Curt stayed with me and the rest of the crew jumped. Because of the haze I realized I had to get some checkpoints because I had to go out about three miles downwind before starting to skid around for the approach. There weren't going to be any go-arounds. It was get in first time or you don't get in. So we started to skid her into the turn losing quite a bit of altitude, still with the nose up. I couldn't see the runway because of the haze, I picked up my checkpoints and there was the runway. We couldn't have done it better if we had been able to see what we were doing; we were headed right down the centre. I looked at Curt and he looked at me: "Here we are, Lucky Joes again". We decided to just let the 'plane sink on to the runway, not to touch a thing until we hit and then pull off the power.

No problems until we were down to about 75ft above the ground, the runway slightly in front of us, when suddenly the nose started coming down. This must have been due to changes in air pressure as we neared the ground. The nose kept going down and now I was pulling back on the controls. We went from about a 15° pitch to a 35 or 40° pitch drop involuntarily. We were coming down at such a steep angle I thought the nose turret and the props would make contact first. It was a nervous situation. Next thing there's a little up and down motion. I looked at Carl and said, "Are we on?". I couldn't believe it, that thing went on so smooth. I brought the tail down and we rolled the length of the runway. No brakes. When I taxied in I wasn't going very fast and there's this RAF guy waving me to a parking place. I realized heck, he doesn't know I don't have any brakes. So I just reached up and shut the fuel to all engines. The props were still turning and he was standing out there by No.1 engine. He thought I was going to stop and I think the prop was about two feet from him before he realized I wasn't and hit the deck just before it went over him. When I got out on the ground he said, "I betcha you didn't have any brakes". I said, "You got it, I thought I was going to give you a haircut".

All of the crew that baled out landed safely, although LaFleur had to pull out his canopy as he fell and it only just opened in time, catching in the branches of a tree.

The people at Woodbridge were used to seeing battle damage, but this Fortress drew many sightseers. *Snake Hips* was declared Category E next day. Or, in the words of those whom it had brought safely home, 'They junked her'. John Bosko kept a souvenir; that long screwdriver.

Seattle's Five Thousandth

In the giant United States aircraft manufacturing plants of the Second World War there arose a practice among the thousands of young female workers of secretly autographing assemblies. Although this was forbidden, it was far from eliminated as many girls could not resist hiding their name and address with the prospect of receiving a letter from a lovelorn serviceman. Besides, it helped combat the monotony of the work.

Early in 1944 the Boeing Company's major plant at Seattle, Washington, was approaching the completion of its 5,000th B-17 since the United States became involved in hostilities, and the company's public relations (PR) staff saw an opportunity for a promotion. An airframe to be assembled was identified as the 5,000th built since Pearl Harbor, to be posted as such as it moved down the production line. The publicity story released says that Boeing workers spontaneously started to cover the assemblies with their names, addresses and slogans, and that, as the company was unable to prevent this, it finally invited all 35,000 workers to autograph the aircraft.

It is more probable that Boeing PR promoted the autographing from the outset, as guidelines were issued and components intended for the 5,000th aircraft were identified at an early stage. Signatures were not to be applied to the Plexiglas, rubber and specified parts such as the propeller assemblies and flight control surfaces. While the PR write-up stated that all 35,000 employees had been involved, the actual number of individual inscriptions fell far short of that figure. Even so, the extent of these graffiti gave the aircraft an unusual mottled appearance from a distance. The colour range was wide, with a preponderance of black and red. The autographing activity was recorded by camera, as was the final roll-out on 13 May.

The selection of B-17G 43-37716 as the 5,000th aircraft from Seattle was to a degree arbitrary, in that the selection depended upon which Fortress was judged the first since Pearl Harbor. Boeing PR were out to extract maximum publicity. Before factory test flights were undertaken, a bold black *5 Grand*, outlined in gold, was applied on each side of the nose, obliterating some of the autographs in the process. The PR effort followed *5 Grand* to the Cheyenne, Wyoming, modification centre where, among other changes to meet battle requirements, a new tail turret position was substituted for the old type still being fitted on the production line.

Apparently there were some USAAF officers who would have preferred to see the graffiti removed, not least because of a supposed loss of performance caused by the drag and weight of the paint. However, the publicity feature still held precedent, even to the extent of the selection of a Seattle pilot and co-pilot at Lincoln, Nebraska, to take the bomber to a combat zone. On 10 July 1944 Lieutenant Edward Unger's crew set out across the Atlantic in *5 Grand*, only to discover on arrival in England, as did many replacement crews at that time, that aircraft and men were to be parted. The crew were sent for theatre indoctrination courses while *5 Grand* received up-to-the-day theatre modifications at Burtonwood.

Later in July, *5 Grand* was delivered to the 96th Bomb Group at Snetterton Heath, Norfolk, where it was assigned to the 338th Bomb Squadron. Its maintenance was in the capable hands of 27-year-old Master Sergeant James Bates and his ground crew. Their immediate problem was to try to go about their work while a near-constant stream of men on the base came to have a look at the strange newcomer. Some took down names and addresses in the hope of obtaining a pen pal. Many girls who had painted on their names had only added telephone numbers, which were of little use to men separated by several thousand miles of ocean. This did not deter one squadron operations officer, who was seen making notes 'for after the war'. Sergeant Bates was justifiably proud of his charge. 'I'm tickled to death to get the Fort. I think we will have her do fifty and return,' was his prophetic comment, which did not seem to have a chance of fulfilment in view of what happened next.

On a local test flight, not long after it had arrived, the aircraft developed electrical trouble and the undercarriage would not lower. After failing to get the main wheels to budge, the pilot, Lieutenant Jack Bimemiller, decided to have the crew release the ball turret and then to crash-land at Honington, the major repair depot for B-17s of the 3rd Bomb Division. Whenever possible, aircraft with undercarriage failure were ordered to be crash-landed there, as better repair facilities were available and it also avoided obstructing a combat airfield. Bellied-in, *5 Grand* sustained damage to its bomb-bay doors and the underside of the fuselage, in addition to bent propellers. At this stage of the war, even if an aircraft was repairable, the more demanding cases were nevertheless declared salvage. In this case, with Boeing engineers on the airfield, every effort was made to return the virgin bomber to flying condition. Meanwhile, the PR people issued a fanciful statement that *5 Grand* had sustained battle damage on its first combat mission, forcing a belly landing.

The true first mission came on 25 August 1944, when Lieutenant Neylen's crew took the aircraft to Politz but were forced to turn back before reaching the target. From then on the bomber was a fairly regular member of the 96th Bomb Group combat formations. Second Lieutenant Bryce H. Jones's crew used *5 Grand* on several of its early missions, and then 1st Lieutenant Roy E. Brockman and his men were assigned the bomber during the autumn. Their most troubled combat trip was on 25 September, when a flak barrage at Ludwigshaven damaged 24 of the 39 aircraft of the 96th Bomb Group. *5 Grand* sustained perforations in the right elevator, and when this was replaced the Brockman crew embellished it with their names and those of the ground crew. This crew finished their tour in December without injury, although tail gunner Staff Sergeant John R. Wearing had a near miss when flak fragments struck the ammunition box just to the rear of his position.

Several different crews flew missions in *5 Grand* during the final months of the war. From February 1945 it was normally in the hands of 1st Lieutenant Edward O. Yelton and his men, who believe they flew eighteen missions in it, including the last one of their tour on 15 April. Then for three consecutive days the bomber was in the hands of 2nd Lieutenant Jack W. Hooper's crew. Their last trip in the aircraft, a mission to Karlsbad on the 19th, was *5 Grand*'s 78th and final combat sortie.

During hostilities *5 Grand* suffered several hits from flak fragments but no critical damage. One unidentified crew member is said to have been slightly injured by a shell splinter which penetrated the nose Plexiglas. Also unsubstantiated is the claim that *5 Grand* set an 8th Air Force record by flying twelve missions in thirteen days.

Early in May 1945, *5 Grand* flew two sorties to Holland, dropping food to starving civilians. Pilot 2nd Lieutenant Reese Martin and crew took the aircraft on one of these 'Chowhound' missions on 5 May. Martin recalls:

The B-17s were fitted with plywood floors in the bomb bays for this purpose. Hinged on the outer rack by a shackle that was not "cocked" and on the centre rack to an active shackle. When the active shackles were released the platforms would swing down and out of the way. The platforms were retrieved by a bungie cord at the front in order to bring them back up so that the bomb-bay doors could be closed. The food was furnished by the US and British on different days. The US rations were "ten in one" (K rations) packed in cardboard boxes so they stored very well in the bomb bay. The British rations, on the other hand, were supplied in burlap or other cloth bags and each contained specific items such as tinned food, hams, flour, sugar, etc. On this particular mission we were carrying British supplied food. As we approached the drop zone and it was time to open the bomb-bay doors, the light indicating "open" did not come on, so I sent our flight engineer, Technical Sergeant Tom Harrison, to the bomb bay to investigate. Shortly he returned and we thought that a ghost had arrived! He was totally white, not by facial expression, but from head to toe. What had happened was that during "form up" in England the 96th Group had crossed behind another formation and we got jolted about by prop wash, which in turn had shifted the sacks and one had contacted the jackscrew that operated the left bomb-bay door. When the door attempted to open, a sack of flour got caught in the drive screw and jammed the actuator. Harrison was able to cut it loose with his pocket knife so the bomb-bay doors would open, but in so doing released all the loose flour in the sack into the turbulent bomb-bay, thereby covering him with a nice white coating. As a result of this delay we dropped a bit late and some of the food went into a canal and also hit a greenhouse, according to our tail gunner, Ken Gaylord. Harrison took quite a bit of razing about being a ghost after that.

In May 1945 the 96th Bomb Group was named as one of the B-17 groups to remain in Europe as part of the occupational air forces. Its older aircraft were then transferred to other groups, homeward bound. On 8 June *5 Grand* was delivered to the 388th Bomb Group at Knettishall, where there was some criticism of its condition. In 24 hours three engines were changed and several other repairs made, and safety equipment for a transatlantic flight was installed. At 1324 next day, *5 Grand* became the first B-17 from Knettishall to be returned to the United States. Captain Noah Thompson was the pilot of the eleven-man crew.

Following an uneventful transatlantic flight, *5 Grand* was quickly used for a publicity bond-raising tour, and on 29 June it arrived at Boeing Field, Seattle, where it had first taken to the air. At this time there was a move by some prominent people in Seattle to acquire the aircraft as a memorial for the city. Although a resolution to this effect was passed by the City Council in December, there appears to have been a certain amount of procrastination, the main stumbling block being the need for a building large enough to accommodate the 103ft wingspan of the bomber. The Seattle Historical Society were interested in obtaining the bomber, but had insufficient room in their facilities. Various ideas were put forward, including public subscription towards a suitable shelter or pedestal stand, but enthusiasm waned. By this time *5 Grand* was reposing in the scrub at Kingman, Arizona, along with several hundred other unwanted B-17s. While some of Seattle's worthies continued to press for the preservation of this symbol of Boeing workers' efforts, they were apparently unable to keep interest alive and raise the necessary funds. It was soon too late, and *5 Grand* went under the breaker's guillotine.

Cologne Flak Trap

By October 1944 daylight raids by forces of more than 1,000 heavy bombers were commonplace as the 8th Air Force continued the massive campaign against synthetic oil plants and communications.

On 14 October the Gereon marshalling yards at Cologne were the primary target for a force of more than 600 B-17s. Germany's major cities had always been well defended by anti-aircraft artillery, but there had been corridors through the flak. By that October these were practically closed. Although only two of these B-17s would fail to return, more than a third of the effective force would suffer flak damage to varying degrees.

Colonel George Shockley led 37 aircraft from the 381st Bomb Group, part of the 1st Combat Bomb Wing of the First Air Division, based at Ridgewell in Essex, England. Each squadron was led by a Pathfinder equipped with H2X radar.

One of the twelve aircraft in the Low Squadron that day was *Pella Tulip*, which had been assigned to the 381st's 532nd Bomb Squadron on 1 May 1944. Named for the town of Pella, Iowa, and its predominantly Dutch community, the aircraft had flown its first mission on 31 May to Florennes, and had completed a total of about 30 missions by 14 October.

There was thick undercast all the way to the target, and the marshalling yards were hidden by cloud, so the bombing was by radar. The B-17s of the 381st were at 26,500ft, where the temperature was -38°C.

Pella Tulip was hit two minutes before bombs away. Lieutenant Charles Reseigh, the pilot, recalled seeing two large flak bursts directly in front of the aircraft and thinking that flak sometimes came in groups of three. A shell burst through the B-17 and exploded almost directly above Reseigh, tearing away part of the windshield and the top of the pilot's compartment. He was hit in the arms, legs, face and neck. *Pella Tulip* plunged out of formation, her pilot too badly wounded to pull her out of the dive.

The copilot, Lieutenant David Rautio, managed to salvo the bombs before he, too, lost consciousness. In the ball turret Sergeant Herbert Penner watched the bombs tumble down. He remembers, 'My guns were pointed down since we were in flak and bandits weren't expected. Immediately after the bombs salvoed I saw other 'planes in our group, which means the wings were vertical – or further – to the ground.'

Rautio, whose goggles and flak helmet had been torn away, was soon revived by the icy blast through his shattered windshield. Although wounded in the forehead and right arm, he was able to regain control. *Pella Tulip* was in deep trouble. Most of the engine and flight instruments were knocked out, the left elevator controls were severed and the landing gear had released. Everything in the cockpit was spattered with blood from the pilot's head, arm and leg wounds. The direct hit had torn a hole in the fuselage at Rautio's side and blown out or opaqued all the glass around him. There were deep gashes in the fuselage below the cockpit, and the top turret shell and the astrodome over the navigator's compartment were shattered. Both the navigator, Flight Officer Maryan Winicki, and flight engineer Sergeant John Nushy had lucky escapes. At the exact moment the flak shell exploded, Winicki was stooping to pick up a flak helmet and Nushy was bending down to check a flaw in his oxygen equipment. Their luck would hold, although Nushy suffered severe conjunctivitis from flying fragments of Plexiglas.

A fire was blazing in hydraulic fluid from a broken line under the top turret, but Nushy was able to extinguish it. The B-17's oxygen supply had been cut, and Rautio's main concern was to get low enough to avoid anoxia problems. He slid *Pella Tulip* down more than 14,000ft.

When the aircraft levelled off, Penner came up out of the ball turret and went forward; 'I was pulling wires from the command set out of Reseigh's arm in preparation for applying a compress, when Chuck Reseigh looked up and asked, "Herb, am I going to make it?". I pulled somebody forward to take over because I didn't want him to see the tears in my eyes.'

The bombardier, Lieutenant Paul Smith, seeing that the copilot had control, began the long job of hand-cranking the landing gear back up, taking turns with Penner and one of the waist gunners. Then he and Nushy placed the wounded pilot in the escape corridor under the flight deck, where they gave him first aid and covered him with flight jackets to try to protect him from the chilling slipstream whistling through the fuselage. Reseigh remembers, 'The crew had placed a chest pack 'chute on me and had attached a static line to the D-ring in case they had to push me overboard. The wind and cold were very severe and I was in shock. Crawled up to the cockpit and was amazed at the damage.'

Although he could see nothing through the crazed windshield, Nushy climbed into the pilot's seat, operating the throttles and occasionally taking over the controls from Rautio. He also massaged the copilot's face and neck to try to prevent frostbite.

The flaps, jammed halfway down, were robbing them of air speed and creating serious drag. The propeller governors on the two right engines had been damaged and the outboard engine began losing oil and finally seized up. For the rest of the long flight the propeller alternatively loosened and jammed, and each time it broke free its windmilling seemed to vibrate every rivet in *Pella Tulip*. The right inboard engine began overheating, and eventually quit. The real condition of the straining left engines was unknown to Rautio and Nushy because none of the cockpit instruments were registering.

The navigator's instruments had also been destroyed, but Winicki had been able to salvage a flak map and an undamaged magnetic compass. With these, plus

170

visual observations, he was able to steer *Pella Tulip* away from danger and towards home. Lacking intercom, he passed instructions to Rautio by hand signals made through the almost glassless astrodome. Two P-51s had spotted the stricken B-17 and came alongside, also helping out with hand directions as they crossed the English Channel.

Frostbitten, nearly blinded by the icy wind blast and numb with fatigue, Rautio finally flew *Pella Tulip* across the English coast and circled the 493rd Bomb Group's field at Debach. Everyone except Rautio and Nushy was in the radio room, preparing for a crash landing. While radio operator Sergeant Leonard Kaplan asked for landing instructions using a key set, his only working equipment, three of the crew rigged parachutes to the radio room hatch and waist windows to help bring the B-17 to a stop.

Rautio brought the B-17 in on two engines, without brakes, fighting to keep clear of aircraft parked near the runway. *Pella Tulip* veered as she touched the tarmac and the gunners popped the three parachutes. The one rigged to the radio compartment gun mount ripped the gun and its mount right out of the aircraft, according to Reseigh and Penner. The crippled B-17 slewed off the strip and roared across an empty hardstand. Only a few feet short of a parked B-17 the wheels hit soft ground and it shuddered to a stop, sunk over the hubs in mud.

Reseigh fainted when he stood up to leave the aircraft, and recovered on the way to hospital. Rautio's face was slightly frostbitten, and shards of Plexiglas had cut his face, but he and Nushy were able to walk to the waiting ambulance. The rest of the crew were uninjured.

Pella Tulip was condemned to salvage at Debach the following day.

Points of Distinction

There were many B-17s that were neither truly famous nor infamous, yet, having been involved in an incident that gave them a point of distinction, were held in some esteem or notoriety, as the case may have been, by the men of their operating unit. Such distinction came in many ways.

Major Boardman C. Reed, CO of the 562nd Bomb Squadron at Knettishall, England, gave one Fortress special interest:

> When not flying, pilots often sit around hangar flying or talking about it. Someone asked what was the minimum crew necessary to fly a '17. Officially it was three; pilot, co-pilot and flight engineer, but most agreed that just two could do it. None believed one man could do it alone. On an August day in 1943 I climbed into a B-17F, flipped the battery switches, got in through the co-pilot's seat (because only there could the parking brakes be released) and fired up the engines. The crew chief had a funny look as I taxied out in a completely empty airplane. After run-up I released the brakes and quickly slid over into the left pilot's seat. Take-off was normal enough, and I flew around for half-an-hour enjoying the sensation of flying a four engine B-17 all alone. Luckily nothing went wrong and everything worked properly. Preparing to land, I had to unbuckle my seat belt to reach across, half standing, for the landing gear switch. Another long reach for the flap switch, but still going too fast, used my elbow on the throttles to slow down. Back in the seat, with the left hand on the wheel, right on the throttles, I made a normal and conventional three-point landing.

The B-17 was called *Second Chance*. But 'the ship that was flown single-handed' was not around for long. On 26 November 1943 it was lost over Germany in a collision with a Fortress from another group.

Hot Nuts, 42-39888, was one of the first 384th Bomb Group B-17Gs to pass the 100-mission mark, and soon after was classified War Weary, being transferred out at the end of January 1945 for non-combat duties. But *Hot Nuts* had another point of distinction at Grafton Underwood as the B-17 that stood on its nose. Henry Heckman, turret maintenance mechanic, recalled what happened:

Crew chief John Huggatt was up in the cockpit preflighting with one of the ground crew sitting alongside him. John was jockeying the throttle backwards and forwards and the assistant crew chief was on the ground out front and trying to get his attention to the tail rising off the ground. Suddenly the tail raised really high and the nose turret and the four props slammed into the concrete. And before the tail had come down and hit the ground the guy in the co-pilot's seat had gone through the bomb bay and out the back hatch!

Another 100-mission veteran, *Fortress McHenry*, which usually stood on dispersal point No.3 near the northwest corner of Bury St Edmunds airfield, was sometimes referred to as 'The Bond Ship', and sometimes as 'The Plane That Bombed Home Town'.

As a means of encouraging US citizens to save and finance the war effort, government bonds could be purchased, offering an attractive investment for redemption postwar. As an added inducement, bond-raising drives were often linked to some precise cause or specified piece of combat equipment, aircraft being a favourite. Thus it was that the influential *Baltimore News Post* encouraged its readers to purchase bonds that would 'buy' a Flying Fortress, a matter of $250,000, coupled with a competition to find a suitable name for the acquisition. It was desired that the name should have an obvious connection with the city of Baltimore, and the one finally considered appropriate was *Fortress McHenry*, the siege of which during the War of Independence inspired Francis Scot Key to write a patriotic song which became the national anthem of the USA.

A B-17G from Boeing's Seattle factory, serial No.42-102583, was selected, and a suitably inscribed plate was attached to the inner side of the nose hatch. The bomber reached the UK early in April 1944, and after modifications was sent to the 94th Bomb Group as a replacement. Made aware of the Baltimore interest in the fortunes of 'their Fortress', the Group CO, Colonel Fred Castle, looked for a crew captain from that city who could be assigned to the aircraft. While no candidate from Baltimore, Maryland, was available, 1st Lieutenant Ralph H. Brant from LaVale, Cumberland, Maryland, and his crew were deemed appropriate. They were to fly most of their missions in this B-17. The first was to Abbeville on 27 April, and thereafter *Fortress McHenry* was regularly one of the bombers despatched whenever its squadron, the 332nd, was scheduled for a combat mission.

Although *Fortress McHenry* soon collected several battle damage holes and had to have a new fin fitted after one fraught mission, her crews were carried safely. Louis Azrael, war correspondent for the *Baltimore News Post*, visited the 94th Bomb Group in late June specifically to produce copy on this aircraft. Impressed by the stars and stripes painted on its nose, he quoted pilot Brant as saying, 'It's a great ship and we'll keep that flag flying'. In fact, fate smiled kindly on *Fortress McHenry* and, after the Brant crew finished their tour, two others flew most of their missions in it. Crew chief George Lindsay and his team were often hard pressed to keep the veteran serviceable as its operational hours mounted and a few turn-backs through malfunctions occurred.

On the morning of 30 December 1944 *Fortress McHenry* was one of a force of 39 B-17s despatched from Bury St Edmunds to attack Mannheim. Immediately after the aircraft had lifted off the main runway at 0850 and climbing out over the town of Bury, an engine caught fire. The pilot declared an emergency, and was told by the control tower chief to jettison the bombs when clear of the town. The load of twenty 250lb HE bombs was released soon after, landing on open ground at the end of Hospital Road, Bury St Edmunds, where seventeen exploded and three remained safe. Fortunately there were no casualties or damage other than broken windows. Meanwhile, the fire had gone out, and *Fortress McHenry* was able to make an emergency landing back at base.

By March 1945 *Fortress McHenry* had flown more than 100 combat missions, but its high number of flying hours and general condition were now of concern to base engineering staff. On 6 March, having completed 102 missions, flown 1,081 hours and suffered five aborts, *Fortress McHenry* was declared War Weary. Retired from combat, it was then made available for air-sea rescue duties, although it does not appear to have been used for this purpose.

Boeing's designers produced an aircraft that was able to survive considerable abuse. Naturally there were limitations, and Fortresses are known to have come apart when exposed to manoeuvres more befitting a fighter. Even so, there were many tales of Fortresses that had been put into extreme flying attitudes and survived in one piece. At Great Ashfield airfield in England, men told of a 'Fort' that had looped. As one might suppose, the story of this event had become a little coloured in the telling, for the manoeuvre was hardly a loop in the true sense.

Satan's Mate was an olive-drab B-17 that served dutifully with the 548th Bomb Squadron throughout most of 1944. Until 19 February 1945 it was best known for the busty girl motif on its nose. By that time *Satan's Mate* had completed 78 missions, marred only by two turn-backs for mechanical reasons; a record that only a few other B-17s at Great Ashfield could better at that time. On the morning of 19 February 1st Lieutenant James Fleisher's crew were given *Satan's Mate* for a mission to bomb a marshalling yard at Rheine. The weather was poor; extremely cold with much haze. After bombing, the group formation encountered cloud strata, making it necessary at times for pilots to fly on instruments.

The formation leader started a climb in an effort to get above the cloud. Fleisher followed, pulling back on the control column to start a 23° climb. Suddenly, as if clutched by some giant hand, the nose of *Satan's Mate* was lifted violently up to about 90°, and the aircraft turned completely over on its back and plunged into a dive. There was little time for the crew to understand what was happening, and there was a flash of fear that catastrophe was about to eclipse them. Those who were not strapped to their seats crashed against the top of the fuselage and were held there by gravitational force as the Fortress headed down.

Waist gunner Sergeant Robert Cory banged his head and was struck by loose

K-ration boxes. For a few dreadful seconds he was suspended there, unable to reach his parachute. Likewise, radio operator Sergeant Trevor Kevan had been whipped off his seat and spread-eagled against the Plexiglas hatch above his position. The men in the cockpit were also held in the gravitational vice, but both had hands on the control columns and strained with all available strength to pull the bomber out of its downward plunge. Co-pilot Lieutenant Paul Cowling saw that the airspeed indicator needle was on 385mph. Their efforts were gradually rewarded, and *Satan's Mate* was brought into level flight some 4,000ft below the point of its inversion. The pull-out also released those crew members who had been held against the top of the fuselage. When Trevor Kevan picked himself up he saw there was a large hole in the hatch Plexiglas which might have been made by him. Had it been any larger he might have been forced outside.

When the men had collected themselves there were some cryptic comments over the intercom. Fleisher explained that they had obviously been caught in the slipstream of an unseen B-17 ahead. In answer to his questions, various crew members reported no injuries other than bruises and no visible damage to the aircraft. However, Fleisher found the controls somewhat mushy and the Fortress now seemed to respond slowly to changes in altitude. Reaction to power-setting increases was also slower, and the aircraft appeared tail heavy. Later the tail gunner reported a slight vibration. Apart from these points, *Satan's Mate* appeared to have taken no great hurt.

Back at Great Ashfield, the crew's account of how their aircraft had been tossed into a loop by propwash resulted in engineering officers ordering a thorough inspection. *Satan's Mate* was removed to a hangar, where the leading edges of both wings were removed and the structure checked. The elevator surfaces were examined for warping or distortion, and all bolts securing the tailplanes were inspected. Apart from a fairing on the inner wing panels and the one around the tailplane, which in a few places had pulled away from their bolts, all skin and structural surfaces had smooth contours and were free of wrinkles. Paint from the rivets had chipped on both the upper and lower camber of the tailplane, indicating that tail surfaces had been under some stress.

For a B-17 that had undergone such aerodynamic torment, *Satan's Mate* appeared reasonably unhurt. Heads were scratched, but eventually it was decided that it would be unwise for the Fortress to fly more combat missions. Intrigued, the 1st Strategic Air Depot at Honington, the major repair organization, requested that *Satan's Mate* be flown to them for further investigation. Thus, after 79 missions and nearly 914 hours' flying time, *Satan's Mate* was retired.

An obvious point of distinction came from being first, and there were many firsts in the 8th Air Force. The very first to penetrate Hitler's *Festung Europa*, 41-2578, became the grand old lady of the 8th Air Force. This B-17E was on the production line at Seattle on the day the 8th was formed in January 1942, and was taken on charge by the USAAF on 18 February that year. The bomber was delivered as original combat equipment to the 97th Bomb Group at Sarasota, Florida, in May, and was further assigned to 2nd Lieutenant Harold Beasley's crew in the 340th Bomb Squadron.

In late May '578' was flown to Bangor, Maine, preparatory to the 97th's overseas movement. At this juncture a Japanese fleet threatening the US west coast found the group flying to California to be on hand to meet any threat. The Battle of Midway resolved this emergency, and the Group returned with its Fortresses to Bangor in mid-June. A month later, '578' began its movement to the UK with Beasley and crew, flying via Labrador, Greenland and Iceland to Prestwick, Scotland.

The 340th Bomb Squadron was based at Polebrook, Northamptonshire, and here '578' was allegedly reassigned to a Lieutenant Butcher and gained the appellation *Butcher Shop*.* However, this was not painted on the aircraft's nose (as was the permitted display of such unofficial tags in the 97th Bomb Group) at the time of '578's selection to lead the first 8th Air Force heavy bomber operation on 17 August 1942. On this date, Group commander Colonel Frank Armstrong and Major Paul Tibbets flew the bomber as the lead aircraft of twelve bombing Rouen railway yards.

Butcher Shop would perform two more combat missions before being exchanged for a new B–17F model from the 92nd Bomb Group at Bovingdon in late August. Bovingdon was to be the 8th's bomber operational training unit, where crews newly arrived from the US would undergo a course on theatre procedures. The B–17Es were retired from combat to serve this purpose, and Bovingdon was to be '578's base throughout 1943, assigned to the 11th Combat Crew Replacement Center (CCRC).

By the end of 1943, 11 CCRC was replacing its B–l7Es with B–17F and G models, and on 9 January 1944 41-2578 was reassigned to the 482nd Bomb Group at the radar pathfinder station, Alconbury. Here it served as a 'hack', chiefly on communications flights, until 3 March, when it was transferred again, this time to the 457th Bomb Group at Glatton. Its main duty now was towing a target sleeve over The Wash and other ranges to enable the Group's gunners to sharpen their aim. Later in 1944 it was adorned with red, white and blue stripes round the wings as an identification aid. Soon after VE Day the 457th packed its bags and returned to the USA.

Considered too worn for a transatlantic flight, '578 was passed to the 20th Fighter Group at Kings Cliffe on 20 May 1945, to serve as a communications transport for HQ personnel. Under this management a new paint scheme was applied, and the new nickname *Big Tin Bird*. The pilot was usually Colonel Cy Wilson, recently returned from prisoner-of-war confinement. Many of *Big Tin Bird*'s flights could hardly have had official approval; they included the collection of eggs and scotch from Aberdeen and barrels of Lowenbrau beer from Munich for Kings Cliffe parties. However, for the Fortress that had opened the 8th Air Force's heavy bombing campaign with bombs on Rouen, the antithesis of that event occurred three years

---

* After mush investigation, I can find no evidence that W. Butcher ever existed in the 97th BG.

later, when Cy Wilson took *Big Tin Bird* to that town to collect champagne and wine for yet another Kings Cliffe party.

In September 1945 the 20th Fighter Group prepared to depart to the USA, and *Big Tin Bird* was delivered to Burtonwood, where the oldest Fortress in the 8th Air Force was eventually reduced to scrap.

Some Fortresses gained distinction by material differences – special or unique modifications of the original airframe. A prime example was *Dreamboat*, so called because it embodied most of the improvements to the B-17 that combatants desired. A B-17E, serial 41-9112, it was flown back to the United States in February 1943 for these modifications to be made. They mainly consisted of armament improvements, with power turrets in the nose and tail. The waist guns were eliminated, and beam defence was provided by twin 0.50-calibre guns in an enlarged position above the radio room, the radio position being resited in the nose. Two-part folding bomb-bay doors and a completely revised oxygen system were other features.

Dreamboat returned to the UK later in 1943 and was exhibited at most combat stations, which led to rumour and exaggeration about a super Flying Fortress. Even German Intelligence picked up some of these tales, and for a considerable period expected to encounter formidable aerial battleships sporting as many as 25 machine guns and cannon. In reality, *Dreamboat* was never used on a combat mission.

Perhaps the most unusual Fortress, as far as armament was concerned, was the 384th Bomb Group's *West End*, which had a battery of six fixed 0.50-calibre machine guns in the nose to discourage head-on attacks by enemy fighters. The installation was undertaken by the 443rd Sub-Depot, responsible for major engineering tasks at Grafton Underwood. *West End*, alias B-17G 42-31435, was selected after sustaining damage to its nose and chin turret in May 1944. The six 0.50 guns were located in the chin turret position, and externally this installation looked like a moveable turret, although all of the guns were fixed to fire forward, with a converging range of 600 yards. This formidable battery was fired by the pilot, using a button device fixed to the control column, and was aimed through a ring-and-bead sight fixed on the aircraft's nose. Completed and tested in mid-June 1944, the installation was found to have no adverse effect on the airframe through recoil.

Several missions were flown by *West End* in late June, but on 6 July, when Lieutenant Haggart and crew took it to France to bomb an aircraft park, the Fortress was badly damaged by flak and a crash-landing had to be made at Manston on return to England. Although 384th Armament Section hoped to retrieve the six-gun structure to install in another Fortress, it was apparently too badly damaged. In any case, 8th Air Force Operational Engineering did not approve, advising that they could see no practical need for such an installation in current circumstances.

The B-17's inherent stability led to many redundant aircraft being used as engine test beds and vehicles for experimental equipment. This resulted in some unique examples, but a prime candidate for the accolade of the most extraordinary Fortress of all is *Gremlin Gus II*. This B-17F, serial 42-30595, started normal combat operations with the 560th Bomb Squadron of the 388th Bomb Group in the summer of 1943, and survived to be retired from combat in the summer of the following year.

In June a top secret project was set up under the code name Aphrodite, involving operational experiments with radio guided weapons, chiefly redundant bomber aircraft filled with explosives. The technique, known as Double-Azon, involved a skeleton crew flying a B-17 loaded with 20,000lb of explosive, setting the radio control receiver switches upon nearing the English coast, and then baling out. A following mother aircraft then guided the 'flying bomb' by radio signals over the North Sea to a preselected target. The technology for such precise targeting was in its infancy, and the project caused minimal damage to the enemy. *Gremlin Gus II* was one of the first batch of war-weary B-17Fs assigned to the Aphrodite Project for use as a drone explosives carrier, but it was spared the fate of the others.

One of the targets under consideration was the battleship *Tirpitz*, holed up in a Norwegian fjord. To penetrate its armour, it was planned to load one of the drone B-17s with torpedoes, and as these were too long to be accommodated in the B-17's bomb bay it was decided to remove the top fuselage decking to load the missiles. *Gremlin Gus II*, selected for this purpose, had the necessary surgery carried out, but at that stage the *Tirpitz* project was dropped, presumably owing to technical difficulties. In any case, the RAF finally despatched *Tirpitz* in November 1944.

The removed upper fuselage decking also included part of the cockpit framing. When the decking was replaced, however, the cockpit framing was not, resulting in the only open-cockpit B-17 in existence. It was felt that this could aid an emergency bale-out, although there was always the risk of the parachutist hitting the fin. *Gremlin Gus II* was then used for training drone crews and testing radio control.

It is said that Major Ralph Hayes, one of the project officers, had a favourite prank. Being stripped of armour, *Gremlin Guss II* was considerably lighter than a standard B-17 and, in consequence, much faster – an estimated 30mph extra at top speed. It is alleged that Hayes would find a B-24 Liberator and position to the rear. Normally a B-17 was slower than a B-24, but not *Gremlin Gus II*. At an appropriate moment Hayes would advance all four throttles and shoot past the Liberator, and as he passed the cockpit of the B-24 he would stand up and salute. *Gremlin Gus II* certainly drew attention wherever it went, the uninitiated doing a double-take at an open-cockpit B-17.

Just Trouble

A veteran crew chief, asked about a particular B-17 in his care, declined to comment other than to say it was 'just trouble'. Such a name does not appear to have been used as a nickname for any B-17, although a few were well qualified to have this slogan emblazoned on each side of their noses. Here and there a Fortress could be found that gave its ground crew continual concern, despite their best efforts and the fact that the type had a much better record of reliability than many comparable Second World War combat aircraft.

Take the case of 42-97093, alias *I'll Get By*, which completed more missions than any other Fortress in the 390th Bomb Group at Framlingham, England. Although Master Sergeant Harold Blumberg and his men toiled tirelessly to keep this bomber in trim, it repaid them by having one of the worst records in the Group for sortie failures for mechanical reasons. By March 1945, when *I'll Get By* had flown 105 missions and 1,097 hours, it also had the unenviable record of eleven aborts through mechanical or equipment failure, and was declared War Weary. Even so, the bomber was not fully retired, and flew another six missions before the war's end.

The classification War Weary, signified by the letters 'WW' painted adjacent to the aircraft's tail number, had nothing to do with the number of times a bomber had suffered an abort, but referred to its general condition relative to its total flying hours. For example, the 384th Bomb Group's *Nevada Avenger*, 42-38013, was just worn out after a year of combat flying and was a candidate for retirement with 1,026 hours' flying time. This was not an excessive total, as several B-17s flew 300 hours more and were still combat-worthy. Despite those of superstitious mind feeling that '013' would not survive for long, *Nevada Avenger* endured to complete 99 missions by February 1945. What is more, it had suffered only one abort, on 15 October 1944, when a propeller governor 'ran away'. However, in April 1944 *Nevada Avenger* was brought in for a one-wheel landing which caused extensive damage to Nos 1 and 2 engines, propellers and nacelles.

After the aircraft had been repaired, pilots complained that it was slow and sluggish, requiring excessively high power settings and making it difficult to fly in formation. Proof of this was evident in the excessive number of engine changes, 29, more than any other B-17 had undergone at Grafton Underwood. The accident had apparently caused some distortion in the bomb bay, as there were a great number of malfunctions of bomb racks and bomb doors. *Nevada Avenger* consistently required a four- or five-man ground crew for maintenance, while the average crew was three.

In December 1944 the aircraft flew only two missions, yet 1,570 man-hours were expended on maintenance. The following month *Nevada Avenger* was sent on eight missions, totalling 69 hours' flying, for 1,100 hours of maintenance, but before any further missions could be undertaken two engines had to be changed. The wing fuel tanks and hoses had deteriorated owing to age, and, given the aircraft's inherent problems, the Engineering Officer decided that restoring *Nevada Avenger* to fully operational status would require a major overhaul which could not he undertaken by his combat station at that time.

Before it was finally withdrawn, the worn veteran completed four more missions. In February 1945 it was passed to the Strategic Air Depot at Abbots Ripton, and then went to the Base Air Depot at Burtonwood. There, surveys confirmed that this prematurely aged aerial workhorse was not worthy of further attention, and in April it was demolished.

It was not only the battle-worn veterans that gave trouble. Occasionally a factory-fresh example suffered a succession of failures or posed a mysterious problem. Boeing B-17G 42-107205, *The Ruptured Duck*, was an original combat assignment to the 398th Bomb Group, and from the outset pilots were not happy with the way the aircraft handled. The complaints became more frequent when the Group began operations, '205' taking part in the first mission, on 6 May 1944. The chief complaint was that the aircraft was extremely slow, requiring higher-than-normal power settings to maintain formation. The immediate thought was that one or more of the engines was not properly tuned, but a thorough check and test of the engines found nothing amiss. Some thought that the lack of power was imagined, but the complaints continued. Pilots said that to maintain level flight at 20,000ft it was necessary to give a three-inch drop to the elevators. The mechanics in the 602nd Bomb Squadron started calling *The Ruptured Duck* a 'worry bird'.

Following a mission to Bordeaux on 15 June, the bomber's ninth and a further endorsement of the handling problems, the Sub-Depot at Nuthampstead conducted an exhaustive test on the aircraft. An excessively heavy airframe was another possibility, but weighing showed that this was not the case. Various other tests were run, with no solution. One test flight proved that, even without a load, the aircraft could not be kept in formation if one engine was shut down. The Sub Depot was perplexed. The Group decided not to use the aircraft on any more combat missions, and in early July arranged to transfer it out to the Strategic Air Depot at Abbots Ripton. At that time it had only 170 hours' flight time, of which 54½ had been on combat missions. The 602nd Bomb Squadron Flight Chief, John Colwell, recalled, 'It was a lemon from the start and we were glad to unload it'. But the ugly duckling was to have its day.

The Strategic Air Depot performed various tests and made changes and adjustments. Although it could not give a precise reason why, *The Ruptured Duck* began to handle better, sufficient for it to he reassigned to a combat group. At the beginning of August *The Ruptured Duck* was passed to the 91st Bomb Group at Bassingbourn as a replacement. No word of its previous history appears to have been conveyed to the new operators, nor is there any record of complaints by the pilots who took this Fortress on thirteen combat missions during the following five weeks.

On its fourteenth mission, on 8 September 1944, it went to Kaiserslautern. The flak was thick and accurate. One 88mm shell detonated near the right side of the cockpit, a fragment killing the co-pilot and others causing serious wounds to the pilot, Lieutenant Elbert Weeks. Despite shock and loss of blood, Weeks maintained control with one hand and brought *The Ruptured Duck* down safely on an airfield in liberated France. The bomber was so badly damaged that it was beyond reasonable repair, and it was eventually declared salvage. Elbert Weeks was later awarded the Distinguished Service Cross, the second highest award for courageous action.

The Beat Up Legend

At the Imperial War Museum (IWM) site at Duxford airfield, near the university city of Cambridge, England, there is a beautifully restored B-17G bearing the serial number 42-31983, the name *Mary Alice* and the identification letters IY:G of the 615th Bomb Squadron. But this is a bogus *Mary Alice*, a wartime identity borrowed and bestowed to suit the aircraft's particular configuration and the required camouflage scheme. Few camouflaged Fortresses had the so-called Cheyenne tail gun emplacement of this machine, which the IWM acquired from France in the 1970s.

A late production B-17G from the Douglas, Tulsa, factory, true serial number 44-83735, it was built too late to see war service, and spent most of its flying life performing high-altitude mapping photography for the Institut Geographique National at Criel. The choice of the *Mary Alice* identity was a good one, for the real Fortress of this name was arguably the most distinguished of some 300 assigned to the 401st Bomb Group at Denethorpe, England, as well as probably having suffered more repairable battle damage than any other Fortress in the 8th Air Force.

The true 42-31983 was assigned to Lieutenant Dan Knight and his men, who took it to Berlin two days after it arrived at Denethorpe. On the second mission of their tour, three days earlier, this crew had been shot up by fighters and made it back on two engines, but their second trip to the enemy capital, over a complete undercast, was a 'milk run'. It was the crew captain's prerogative to choose a name (if any) for his charge, and Dan Knight named the B-17 in honour of his mother, using her two Christian names.

If *Mary Alice*'s combat debut had been uneventful, many of the missions it was to undertake would be the antithesis of a milk run, for this bomber soon established a reputation for attracting flak and fighter attention. Dan Knight and his crew flew most of their missions in *Mary Alice* and finished their combat tour in mid June. Other crews took over and, on 13 July 1944, 2nd Lieutenant Harry Haskett and his men set out for Munich on their fifth mission, and nearly failed to return.

Positioned as a wingman in one of the rear flights in the Group formation, soon after leaving the target *Mary Alice* was subjected to a fast and furious pass by Fw 190s coming from behind. Two bursts of 20mm fire struck home. 'At about the same time my co-pilot's oxygen mask froze up and I had the busiest five minutes of my life,' Haskett later commented. 'I knew my tail gunner had been hit and the turbo-supercharger on No.2 engine also got a blast. Another shell burst in my left wing next to the fuselage, and I felt her going into a spin. I set up AFCE (autopilot) and somehow we pulled out of it.'

It was then that Haskett caught sight of a flash of flame behind one of the engines, and thought a fuel tank had taken fire. Believing at first that the aircraft was doomed, he gave the bale-out order. Fortunately the intercom was not functioning clearly, and when other members of the crew queried his edict, Haskett was able to rescind the order, the flames having disappeared.

From the sudden loss of manual control it was obvious that *Mary Alice* had sustained severe damage to its flight surfaces, and reports from crew members in the rear told of a large part of the right stabilizer shot away, and the complete top of the fin and rudder. With some 2½ hours' flying ahead before leaving hostile airspace, the prospects of getting back to England were not good. Meanwhile, Staff Sergeant Brenden Lynch, the radio operator, and Hinsom Jones, a waist gunner, extracted tail gunner Edward Page from his wrecked emplacement. A 20mm cannon shell had exploded in front of his chest, and his rescuers could see that he was mortally wounded. They administered first aid and made Page as comfortable as they could, but he died before the Dutch coast was reached.

Haskett and co-pilot Tom Davis carefully manipulated the controls, their task made all the more difficult by the loss of power on No.2 engine, which eventually had to be shut down and its propeller feathered. The pilots' oxygen system had failed, and Haskett was obliged to work with a portable oxygen bottle between his legs until height was lost. There was some relief to the crew's anxiety when the North Sea came into view. With diminishing fuel and the weather deteriorating, with increasing cloud, a homing to the nearest airfield was requested by radio. Beccles, an RAF Air–Sea Rescue base near the Suffolk coast, came into view.

Now the pilots had the problem of landing. It was desirable to return to manual piloting, but there was a risk that manual control would not be possible if the AFCE was disconnected. Haskett and Davis decided to go against the rules and attempt a landing with the AFCE still locked in. A long, gradual approach to the operational Beccles runway was made, and at 1348 *Mary Alice* touched down after almost exactly eight hours in the air.

Royal Air Force ambulancemen removed Sergeant Page, who, it was later discovered, had been hit by 35 metal fragments from the 20mm shell. He was later the posthumous recipient of the Silver Star, the third-ranking US decoration for bravery. On inspection, the damage to *Mary Alice* yet again proved the durability of the Fortress. Apart from the blasted tail gun position and the loss of the right elevator and the top of the fin and rudder, there were holes in the left wing, the fuel tank, the bomb bay and No.2 engine supercharger.

Over the next few weeks the Mobile Repair and Reclamation (MR&R) people rebuilt the rear end of *Mary Alice*. They gave her a new fin and rudder, left stabilizer and elevator, and many patches. Most of the replacement components were shiny and new, and although *Mary Alice*'s original dress was olive drab and grey, there was too much new metal skin to touch up with paint.

In August *Mary Alice* returned to Denethorpe and was soon back in the fray. Meanwhile, the Haskett crew had become a lead crew, and their old charge was taken over by Lieutenant R. W. Callaway. The 401st Bomb Group went to Weimar on the 24th and was attacked by Luftwaffe fighters, three of its B-17s failing to return. One that did return, but to an emergency landing at another airfield, was *Mary Alice*. Once more, enemy fighters had blasted it with 20mm cannon shells. The damage included severed control cables, a perforated left elevator and right flap with over 100 holes, and holes in the fin, two fuel tanks, No.4 engine and the radio room. Once more the MR&R mechanics patched her up.

The Callaway crew flew *Mary Alice* whenever it was available and they were scheduled to fly. On 5 November they collected some more flak holes over Frankfurt, and their faithful mount was again under repair for a few days. Up to this time, despite its turbulent career, *Mary Alice* had never had to abort a mission through mechanical failure. This record was maintained until 21 November, when, after the bomber had been despatched on its 66th mission, a broken oil line forced a return to base after about four hours' flight. Repair was soon effected, and *Mary Alice* was out on a practice night flight that evening.

On 29 November the Callaway crew took Mary Alice on the last mission of their tour. Next day it was turned over to 2nd Lieutenant George Cracraft, who recalled, 'She was the ugliest thing I ever saw. They told me she was mine and I almost died. She was ugly. She had one aluminium wing and one camouflaged wing. One piece of her tail was aluminium and another camouflaged. She was put together like a jigsaw puzzle.'

A synthetic oil plant at Bohlen, target for the Group on the last day of November, was expected to be 'tough'. The Germans had formidable flak defences round all their major sources of precious petroleum products. For George Cracraft and his men this was their second mission after joining the 615th Bomb Squadron, and their first in 'the most beat-up old '17 on the base' As anticipated, a murderous barrage of anti-aircraft fire was encountered around the target, with winds at high altitude slowing the formations and making them more vulnerable.

Just after the bombs were released, three flak bursts bracketed *Mary Alice*. One exploding shell put No.2 engine out of action and severed oxygen lines in the nose with shrapnel. Other fragments slashed into the nose compartment, shattered the astrodome and smashed into the chin turret actuating equipment. Another burst below the nose sent steel splinters through the floor of the navigator's compartment, smashing into his wooden table and sending jagged wooden splinters into Carl Hoag's face and eyes. He was temporarily blinded in one eye, and vision in the other was seriously impaired.

Other shell fragments had sliced through the fuselage. One piece smashed the two middle fingers of waist gunner Sergeant Irving Gordon's right hand so severely that they eventually had to be amputated. A fragment that hit an oxygen bottle caused an explosion which knocked Staff Sergeant Robert Jacquart out of the top turret and badly bruised one of his legs.

The wounded navigator and the pilot began to show signs of anoxia, and co-pilot Lieutenant Martin Karant, seeing that the oxygen flow had stopped and the system was obviously damaged, made haste to put both men on to portable bottles. Cracraft's predicament was similar to that faced by Haskett in July:

> We were flying at 25,000ft at the time. The ship was shaking severely and I had absolutely no control. We then put her on automatic pilot and began to look after our wounded. I had feathered No.2 engine and was forced to feather damaged No.3 after using it about five minutes. We thought we were going to crash at any moment and jettisoned everything but our guns and ammunition.

Despite his injuries, navigator Hoag insisted on remaining at his post, knowing that as the bomber was alone and deep in enemy territory it was vital that he maintained the course if they were to get back to England. George Cracraft gave Hoag airspeeds and instrument readings, and Sergeant Roland Cuorin, the togglier, read the maps and verbally provided the information required by the navigator. Using mental calculations, Hoag produced a flight plan that eventually took the bomber to friendly territory.

Although they had been flying on two engines for 3hr 20min, the pilots were able to maintain 15,000ft for much of the flight until they eventually let down. The first airfield seen was Boxted, but such was the frosting on the windshield and damage to the pilots' controls that it took three attempts to set *Mary Alice* down safely. For his persistence with navigation, which undoubtedly made a major contribution to the bomber's safe return, Carl Hoag was awarded the only Distinguished Service Cross, the second highest US decoration for valour, to go to a member of the 401st Bomb Group, whose personnel earned more than 1,000 awards during seventeen months of combat.

Once more, *Mary Alice* was patched up and put back to work. After the mission to Berlin on 3 February 1945, George Cracraft recorded the following in his diary:

> Flak was terrific on the bomb run and I saw two Forts explode and several go down with 'chutes popping. It was horrible. My prayers were again answered and we came through. *Mary Alice* is out of commission with No.3 wing tank out, left wing spar buckled, No.3 engine out, nose riddled like a sieve, and the fuselage blown apart.'

The perseverance of Master Sergeant Henry McKinney, the crew chief, and his mechanics was remarkable in the face of how many times the young men who took 'his' bomber out and brought it back 'beat up'. McKinney came from the quaintly named town of Evening Shade in Arkansas and was older than the average airman at Denethorpe. In addition to the excellent ground crew, Cracraft's flight engineer, Sergeant Robert Jacquart, had been a ground instructor on Wright engines before volunteering for combat. His knowledge proved invaluable on several occasions when engines received battle damage.

By the law of averages, *Mary Alice* had taken more than its share of battle damage, but it seemed to be an exception. On 16 February 1945 George Cracraft took her to Gelsenkirchen:

> We seemed to be hit all at one go from front to rear. Flak. No.1 and No.2 were out. We had to dive to keep up with the Group and we put the nose down and sacrificed a little altitude to drop on the smoke markers. No.3 was pulling less than half power and No.4 was running just as fast as it would go, it was almost molten metal. Full throttle all the way. The tail was also shot up but there were no injuries. We were all by ourselves and afraid of attack, but there weren't too many German fighters in the area at the time. We didn't have any cloud cover. We were wide open. We were losing 5-600ft a minute. As we came lower the air got thicker and the loss of altitude was coming slower and *Mary Alice* stabilized at about 7,000ft and began to fly easier. We had about a third flaps down and the nose was up on about a 30° angle, just above stalling speed the whole time. We had three choices, to bale out and be captured, to try to get back across the Ruhr to liberated territory or to keep north away from the flak and head for the Channel coast. I chose the last.

To add to their predicament, there was a loss of servo-assistance on the flight controls and the automatic pilot was also out of action. It required the strength of both pilots and the flight engineer to move the controls, because pressures were so great. Fortunately co-pilot Eldon Magee, well-built and strong, made a major contribution to this fatiguing task. At the Dutch coast Cracraft gave the crew the choice of baling out or trying to reach England. All voted to try for home, despite the risk of a ditching in the icy North Sea. On one-and-a-half engines, as Cracraft put it, *Mary Alice* limped over the grey waves. At last the coast of Lincolnshire came in sight, and the 'crash' airfield at Carnaby was contacted by radio for an emergency landing. The RAF at nearby Lisset were thus surprised to see a Fortress suddenly appear unannounced and land straight in on one of their runways.

Later, Cracraft wrote in his diary:

> Ernie Hinson went down and Steve Lazinski blew up over the target. *Mary Alice* has flown her last. She was so shot up that it wouldn't be possible to fix her. She's going to be scrapped. The left wing looked like a truck had hit her, her fuselage was riddled like a sieve. Her tail was half gone. All engines were hit. An 88 exploded in No.1 and taking No.2 with it.

But *Mary Alice* did fly again. It was nearly a month before the MR&R boys had changed three engines and the veteran had returned to Denethorpe. In its absence the 615th Bomb Squadron had taken over all B-17s with H2X ground-scanning radars to specialize in leading. There was no use for *Mary Alice* in her old squadron, and she was transferred to the 613th Bomb Squadron to see out the last few weeks of the war. However, George Cracraft and his crew had also been transferred to the 613th, and when *Mary Alice* appeared at Denethorpe on 12 March he was quick to reclaim the bomber as his own. On 28 March Cracraft set out for Berlin in *Mary Alice*, but lost an engine over Frankfurt and had to return. *Mary Alice* was still out of commission when he and his men flew the last mission of their tour two days later.

For the remainder of hostilities *Mary Alice* was mostly a ground spare, ready for a crew to take over if their assigned aircraft for a particular mission developed mechanical or equipment failure before take-off. Second Lieutenant J. P. Kerkes and crew took it on its 98th and last mission of the war on 19 April 1945. It was *Mary Alice*'s eleventh mission with the 613th Bomb Squadron.

Despite the battering this venerable Fortress had taken, it was in sufficiently sound mechanical condition to be ferried back across the North Atlantic to the USA, where it eventually met the same fate as other returnees from the 8th Air Force down in Arizona.

The B-17 at Duxford may be a bogus *Mary Alice*, but it keeps alive the memory of what was probably the most battle-battered Fortress ever to fly combat from the UK.

Kimbolton's Record Breakers

In terms of bombing accuracy, tonnage dropped, sorties flown and a low turn-back rate, the 379th was the most successful of all 8th Air Force bomb groups. This had much to do with the leadership team established under Colonels Moe Preston and Lewis Lyle, but a contributing factor was the Group's use of the radar pathfinding device known as Gee-H. A British development, Gee-H featured an airborne transmitter that interrogated fixed beacons on the ground in England to achieve very precise navigation, sufficient to position a formation for bomb release on a target. Owing to the Earth's curvature, its use was limited to a range of 300 miles.

In the spring of 1944 Gee-H was installed in lead aircraft of the three groups of the 41st Combat Wing, of which the 379th was one. Making use of Gee-H, these groups sometimes operated against short-range targets when the rest of the 8th Air Force bomber force was grounded. From the 379th's high sortie rate, it follows that several of the Group's B-17s had high totals of missions completed, and it is known that at least fifteen reached the 100-mission mark. Two of these have a special claim to fame, although strangely they received little publicity either at group or air force level. They both served in the 524th Bomb Squadron, as L-Love and H-Harry, and they were normally parked on the same 'A' Flight dispersal point at Kimbolton.

One of the pair, B-17G 42-32024, is credited as being the first Fortress in the 8th Air Force to survive 100 missions without a turn-back for mechanical reasons. Received by the 379th as a replacement on 20 February 1944, this Seattle-built aircraft was entrusted to the care of Sergeant Dommonick L. DeSalvo's ground crew. His assistant was Corporal James Abbot. Two days after receipt, '024 L-Love' was taken to Halberstadt by 1st Lieutenant Ken Duvall and crew. In the next few days they used this bomber to fly the final three missions of their tour. When Duvall and his men departed, a freshman crew of 2nd Lieutenant Joseph L. Korstjens was given the bomber. It was truly 'theirs', for they would eventually fly all but seven of their 33 missions in it.

In the early days, discussion arose about a name for the bomber. Joe Korstjens had no particular views, so co-pilot Byron Clark came up with *Swamp Fire*. The origin was a recently-read article on how the methane gas given off by swamps could sometimes ignite and travel ahead of even a slight breeze with the speed of lightning. So *Swamp Fire* it was.

'Ours was a lucky crew and this apparently was a lucky ship. None of our crewmen sustained a scratch, but of course, after most missions, Dom and his men had to patch holes in her skin.' These words of Byron Clark were echoed by Harvey

Harris, the bombardier. The most difficult time he experienced was when urine spilled over from the frozen relief tube in the bomb bay and froze the actuating motor for the doors. Harris had to go back, take off his flak jacket and put on a parachute and then, with a rope tied round his waist for safety, he clung to the bomb bay vertical stations while jumping on the doors to force them open. After this episode everyone used empty bomb fuze containers for relief, throwing them out over Germany.

Early in July 1944 *Swamp Fire* got a new regular crew, that of recently-arrived 2nd Lieutenant Bruce E. Mills. They were not impressed with the name of this 50-mission veteran, and there was discussion about changing it to something more inspirational but, on consideration, they thought it might bring a change of fortune and decided to stick with *Swamp Fire*. Name change or not, there certainly was a change of fortune, for all sorts of 'hairy' things befell the bomber and her crew during the following weeks. On their first mission, a milk run to France, they returned with fourteen flak holes.

In his diary, Bruce Mills recorded in terse terms what happened on the crew's seventh mission, on 13 July, the third time to Munich in a row:

> Bombed on PFF [pathfinder technique] at Munich. Six x 500lb incendiaries and four x 500lb demolition [bombs]. Wake up at 0100. Briefing 0200. Took off in *Swamp Fire*, climbed above clouds, assembled. Flew No.3 slot high squadron, lead group. Judged fair. Leader again off course, flew over Stuttgart, Mannheim. Flak heavy and accurate. Got eight or ten holes. Hit oil cooler No.3 engine, wings and elevators. Carl [co-pilot] 2/Lt Shedlock hit propwash and tried to get out by going down only to get in our leader's propwash. I took over, missed ship on right side. Gave it a boost, hit right wingman's propwash, barrelled through, then gave Carl hell. Told crew everything okay! Evasive action over target by leader excellent! Missed all flak there. Lead's tail gunner reported us going down out of control over Mannheim!

Bruce Mills would later recall that *Swamp Fire* was sucked under the element leader to the right, and was then turned completely on its side to the left so that its wings were vertical. It then plunged away down through the formation to the left, losing some 3,000ft before recovery was made. Understandably, there were some unnerved crew members while all this was going on.

It was not always the Mills boys who had a few anxious moments. In August, while the crew was stood down, Lieutenant Elro Lindsay took off from Kimbolton's short runway with a heavy load. *Swamp Fire* did not gain height quickly enough on becoming airborne, and there was a thud as the ball-turret struck an obstruction. As the turret seemed to operate normally, Lindsay elected to continue with the mission. On return they found that the ball turret had taken quite a whack on the exterior.

They also learned that farmer Carlton Boyd, who owned the fields beyond the runway, had lodged a complaint that one of his chicken houses had been completely demolished.

On another occasion, tail gunner Sergeant William Beddard suddenly saw a hole appear in the left tailplane. An 88mm shell had passed straight through without exploding. At 28,000ft over Dortmund on 5 October another 88mm shell had lethal effect when it exploded below and forward of No.3 engine. One piece of shrapnel penetrated the cockpit floor, severed the hydraulic brake line, slammed against Bruce Mills's leg and tore the helmet from his head. Other fragments cut the nose oxygen lines and the control cables to No.4 engine, which had to be shut down and the propeller feathered.

Bombardier 2nd Lieutenant James Whitney reported that navigator 2nd Lieutenant John McCary had been hit. Whitney gave him morphine and dressed a wound in his leg, but it became evident that McCary's condition was deteriorating. Mills landed *Swamp Fire* at one of the first airfields seen after reaching England in order to obtain medical aid for the navigator, only to find that he had died. On close inspection it was discovered that a flak splinter had passed through the navigator's seat and entered his body, the wound being closed by his heavy flight clothing. It was a black day, and such a loss was hard to accept in the close-knit camaraderie of a bomber crew.

Through all these misfortunes *Swamp Fire* had been piling up an extraordinary maintenance record. When DeSalvo's charge had reached 60 missions without any turn-back for mechanical reasons, he was recommended and approved for a Legion of Merit award, which he received in September. The record remained unbroken, and on 1 November 1944 it looked as though *Swamp Fire* would make 8th Air Force history by becoming the first B-17 flying from England to complete 100 missions without suffering a single abort through human or mechanical failure.

This time the target was a synthetic-oil manufacturing plant at Gelsenkirchen in the Ruhr. It was also Bruce Mills's and his team's last mission before being taken off operations:

> Got up at 0630, briefing at 0730, take-off 1025 in *Swamp Fire*. Rendezvous very poor in clouds up to 20,000ft. After forming up, I flew high diamond in a fourth bastard squadron. Just as I pulled up into place, the leader slowed up and I shot on by. Then he turned to the left and I cut the high flight out as nice as you please. When I got back in formation the No.2 engine, which had been rebuilt and had 2,080 hours, blew up and so we gradually fell behind the formation. Outbound, crossing the English coast, we were ten miles behind but I cut off a corner and gained a little on them. However, No.3 engine started acting up and we had to reduce power, sacrificing altitude to help. By the time we got to the Dutch coast, we were only at 16,000ft. Through a break in the clouds we saw a transport ship in harbour and

since we had no hope of catching the formation, we decided to drop the bombs on the ship. We made a 180° turn to get into a good "over the toe" bombing run as we had no bombsight on board. The tail gunner reported that he could see 88mm guns on railroad cars. Picking out a route over the clouds, to stay hidden, and after turning around, lined up to begin our bomb run. The hole in the clouds showed up just right and Lt Whitney said "bombs away" but they didn't start trailing out at 50ft intervals so he salvoed the lot, smack dab across the ship. It looked like one 88mm gun was shooting so we turned tail for home.

James Whitney recalled: 'Luckily the return flight was uneventful except for perspiration and strained eyeballs, resulting from the search for "bandits".

Youthful exuberance at completing a tour was evident in what followed, as Bruce Mills relates:

Because of our engine problems we crossed the English coast low and had to take evasive action when we inadvertently flew through a barrage balloon area. The crew chief had asked me to buzz the field as he had never had a crew or 'plane finish their missions until now. So I flew over the skeet range, barrelled down the runway, headed for the tower, scared hell out of two guys on the roof and pulled up into a chandelle, threw the gear and flaps down and greased it on the end of the runway. I was met by half the field, including fire trucks, ambulances and whatever. Seems that our waist gunner (who normally flew with another crew but was flying with us so he could finish his tour this day) had started firing red flares all the way across England from the coast. Two red flares means wounded on board, although we didn't have any. He got court martialled (half a month's pay), but he didn't care. And I had to go and see the Group Commander. I spent about two hours in the outer office cooling my heels while the administration officer glared at me. Then the phone rang and the "admin" officer went into the Colonel's office saying, "General Preston is on the phone, Sir". The door shut but two minutes later I was told to go and pack my bags and be on my way home. I found out later that General Preston, my original Group Commander, was on the skeet range when I flew over, about five feet above the trees with one dead engine and another smoking. Often wonder what was said, that I should get off so lightly.

The target of opportunity on which *Swamp Fire* unloaded the bombs of its 100th mission was a vessel placed at three miles north of Ijmuiden.

Several different crews took the bomber out to battle during the next few weeks until, on 11 December, it flew its 112th mission when 2nd Lieutenant Frank

Clipeon and crew, newcomers to Kimbolton, flew to Mannheim. The enemy's reception rendered damage that caused *Swamp Fire* to be put down on an Allied field on the continent, never to fly in combat again. Eventually, *Swamp Fire* was repaired and returned to Kimbolton, only to be transferred to Alconbury and a squadron engaged in weather reconnaissance. It had, however, earned its claim to fame as the first 8th Air Force B-17 to fly 100 missions without ever having to abort.

The other B-17 of fame in 'A' Flight never received a mention by 8th Air Force Public Relations but, as far as can be ascertained, flew more combat missions than any other Fortress in the Eighth. B-17G-10-VE, serial number 42-40003, was built at the Burbank factory in October 1943, flown to the UK in December and was received as a replacement by the 379th Bomb Group on 20 January 1944. Its first mission was flown on 30 January to Brunswick, with 2nd Lieutenant Hershell E. Stait at the controls.

Thereafter it was assigned to 1st Lieutenant Mac Hemphill's crew, who flew the last six missions of their tour in it. They decided to name the Fortress *Topper*, after the popular movies starring Roland Young. He played a character usually dressed in a top hat and formal attire who was a passport for the redemption of ghosts which he could see. The crew chief, 29-year-old M/Sgt Walter Wolcott, who had sign-writing experience, started to paint an appropriate figure on the aircraft's nose, but only had time to complete the top hat, white collar and gloves before the B-17 was battle-damaged during the first big 8th Air Force raid on Berlin.

When repaired, the 524th Bomb Squadron's H-Harry, as it had become, was assigned to 2nd Lieutenant Stephen Hennrich's replacement crew, who had undergone their combat initiation in another Fortress a week before, taking their new charge out for the first time. Lieutenant Hennrich wanted to call H-Harry *Flak Haven*, and in view of this Wolcott saw no point in completing the Topper painting. In fact, *Flak Haven* was never painted on during the three-month period that the Hennrich crew had the aircraft and completed 27 missions of their tour in it.

During this period, Freddie Thoman, a member of the ground crew, persuaded Walter Wolcott to paint *Ol' Gappy* on each side of the nose turret. This was to tease Corporal Garrett Brashear, who was much older than the average man at Kimbolton, and worked in Tech Supply and shared the same barrack Nissen hut as Thoman. Brashear was noticeable for having lost most of his teeth, but retained two prominent 'tombstones' in the front. This led to Thoman calling him 'Old Gappy'. Most mechanics thought that the chin turret spoiled the smooth lines of the Fortress, and while it may have been welcomed for its functional purposes, it was an ugly addition. In discussing this, Thoman remarked to Wolcott that it reminded him of 'Old Gappy' Brashear, the two gun barrels sticking out like his front teeth.

As the aircraft had no other appellative adornment on its nose, the men at Kimbolton then assumed that *Ol' Gappy* was the bomber's name and, not knowing the true origin, thought that it was connected with the gaps between the top hat, collar and gloves of the unfinished motif.

Stephen Hennrich and his men finished their missions in mid-June, their last in H-Harry being a short mission to a rocket-launching site in France on the 19th. The bomber also flew another mission with another crew that day.

During Stephen Hennrich's tenure he volunteered his crew to participate in a power setting, rate of climb experiment to maximum altitude. Four cases of 0.50-calibre ammunition were used to represent a load that could be moved to adjust the centre of gravity changes that would occur in seeking high altitude. He recalled, 'The crew moved the cases forth and back from the bomb bay to the waist gun area for the best part of two days. We reached 38,850ft and the old girl just didn't have enough left to go any higher. You can imagine the crew's thoughts and private words on this monumental moving task!' This must have been an 8th Air Force altitude record for a combat B-17.

During the time that '003' H-Harry was assigned to the Hennrich crew, seven other different crews took the bomber on combat missions, two of them on more than one occasion. This usually happened when the Hennrich crew were stood down, there being more assigned crews than aircraft in a squadron. Lieutenant Baine Hawthorne's men were the next to have the bomber, and put the 50th mission on it. To some men at Kimbolton '003' H-Harry was still known as *Topper*, but a growing number now referred to it as *Ol' Gappy*.

Lieutenant James H. Chute's crew knew it by this name when they took it over and flew it on most of their missions. It was Chute who took *Ol' Gappy* to Mannheim on 11 December, its 100th trip, and he finished his tour in the aircraft on 13 January 1945 and handed over to 1st Lieutenant Paul E. Horton, who flew the final ten missions of a tour at the controls of *Ol' Gappy*.

By now the venerable B-17 was one of the few camouflage-finished examples remaining at Kimbolton, and a somewhat patched and faded example at that. Sergeant Neil MacNeil, a gunner who flew three missions in *Ol' Gappy*, reflected on this:

> When you climb into '003' it looks like a well used car, everything is patched, dents all over. When you take off you always say to yourself "can this ship make one more mission?". The pilots like her because she is easy to fly (loose) and is faster than most B-17s and takes less fuel. She is the pride of the 524th. A wonder she isn't grounded for fatigue.

Walter Wolcott nursed *Ol' Gappy* for 127 missions and was then, at the beginning of March 1945, promoted Flight Chief, overseeing all the other crew chiefs in 'A' Flight. Although Staff Sergeant Joe P. Sligoski from Detroit took over, age was beginning to tell on the bomber. When Major George Lane took *Ol' Gappy* on its 125th mission he had to turn back with mechanical trouble, and the same thing happened to 2nd Lieutenant Bernard A. Vitek on 31 March.

This no doubt accounts for 8th Air Force Public Relations' failure to mention *Ol' Gappy*'s mounting total of combat sorties. The policy was to publicize only those aircraft with unblemished records, in order to stress the importance of maintenance. Vitek's was the last crew assigned to *Ol' Gappy*, and although they had taken it out on 19 February as a casual assignment, between 28 March and 25 April it was theirs for thirteen missions. The last of these, to Pilsen, was *Ol' Gappy*'s 157th.

At VE Day, 8 May 1945, *Ol' Gappy* was the only combat-status B-17 at Kimbolton in camouflage finish, and was looked upon as a 'real old ship', although only sixteen months out of the factory. In 157 missions it had 47 different crews, only six of which were assigned. On seven missions it had been loaned to other squadrons in the Group. *Ol' Gappy* was flown back across the Atlantic that summer, and by December 1945 had joined the growing collection of unwanted bombers in the arid Arizona Desert near Kingman. *Swamp Fire* also joined those ranks, where the B-17s were denuded of engines and useful equipment. At some time during the remaining years of the decade the breakers arrived and demolished these two truly historic B-17s that had served Uncle Sam so well.

Maintenance Champion

Some 100 individual 8th Air Force B-17s are known to have reached their 100th combat mission during the last five months of hostilities. As the average number of missions that a Fortress was likely to survive at this time was half that number, such champions became celebrated. The actual figure has since been assessed as an average of 47 missions for the 1944-45 period.

However, the engineering authorities became concerned that competition among ground crews to see their charges attain such records might lead to careless maintenance, through expedience to have an aircraft ready for a combat sortie. As a result, emphasis was laid on an aircraft not having its record marred by a turn-back for mechanical reasons – an abort. This was furthered by issuing a directive to 8th Air Force Public Relations that only aircraft with high mission totals where no turn-backs were involved were to be featured.

By early 1945, largely as a result of publicity in the Service newspaper *Stars and Stripes*, there was considerable interest in bombers that continued to pile up missions without the blemish of an abort. Shortly after the last 8th Air Force heavy bomber mission was flown, on 25 April, it was announced that a B-17G named *Nine-O-Nine* of the 91st Bomb Group at Bassingbourn had the supreme accolade for mechanical reliability, with 140 combat missions without a single turnback. One other 8th Air Force B-17 involved in its bombing campaign surpassed that figure but had, at some time, suffered an abort, as had others with totals ranging from 130 to 138, the runner-up with no aborts having achieved 128 completed.

Nine-O-Nine's record was rightly attributed to the care lavished upon it by Master Sergeant Rollin L. Davis and his five-man ground crew team, who had tended the Fortress. One of the last in camouflage finish, it was received in the 323rd Bomb Squadron on 25 February 1944, with 37 hours' flight time. The aircraft soon had the squadron's identification letters, OR, painted on its fuselage in yellow, together with the individual aircraft letter R. It was the sixth R-Roger to serve the squadron; three, including the last, had been shot down.

Davis's aircraft hardstanding was No.5 in dispersal area 'D'. This had been constructed at the south end of the 2½-mile-long elm-lined avenue that ran from the A14 highway towards the stately home Wimpole Hall. The A14, the main road between Royston and Huntingdon, was originally the Roman Ermine Street. Owing to the lack of suitable area on which to construct additional aircraft dispersals around the airfield, an access taxiway was built across the A14 in 1942, and road traffic was halted to allow aircraft to cross.

Rollin Davis had been assigned as assistant crew chief on *Delta Rebel No. 2* during his early months at Bassingbourn, and was given his own team when the number of aircraft in the 323rd was increased to fourteen. Davis had no desire to provide a nickname for his new charge, and the aircraft was usually referred to by the last three digits of its serial number, 909, or its call-letter 'R'.

The aircraft was despatched on its first combat operation on 2 March 1944, to bomb targets at Frankfurt – the 91st Bomb Group's 117th mission. It seems that a number of different crews used '909' for the first few weeks, but early in April it was assigned to 2nd Lieutenant Arthur A. Klinger and his men. They flew their first mission in '909' on 7 May, to Berlin, and collected a few holes in the aircraft. The Klinger crew eventually flew nineteen of their 30-mission combat tour in the aircraft. The radio operator, Sergeant Jack Grosh from Columbus, Ohio, designed a motif comprising a Christopher Columbus character astride a bomb and thumbing his nose at the enemy. This was painted on the nose of the B-17 by Corporal Tony Starcer, together with the legend *Nine-O-Nine*. Starcer, a superb artist assigned to the 441st Sub-Depot at Bassingbourn, was eventually responsible for some 130 individual aircraft motifs on the station's B-17s.

Jack Grosh kept a diary which reveals that *Nine-O-Nine* frequently returned with battle damage. Neither did her crewmen escape unscathed. The entries for the crew's second and third combat missions in this bomber reveal the hazards of the bombers' war in the spring of 1944:

> Stralsund No.11 – eleventh mission (for the crew), May 14th, 1944. The primary target was seven miles northwest of Stettin (an airfield) and oil works. All of the targets were closed in so we went up and bombed Stralsund. We carried a bomb load of 38 - 100lb. The mission lasted nine and a half hours. The flak in the target area was heavy but we did not get hit here. We got one large hole in our right wing from flak right over Stralsund. We saw about 60 Me 109s but they did not attack our wing. They were after the group on our right. Saw three B-17s go down as they attacked them. We flew in ship No.909. Our bombing was not good (in the lake).
>
> Big B No.12 – May 19th. Target Big B. The eastern section of the city. Today we flew with a nine-man crew. Tex flew as togglier and Stiles flew as navigator. We carried a bomb load of 42 incendiaries. There was a large amount of enemy fighters and flak. John Reash got hit in the head with a piece of flak that came through the upper turret. It was the only hole in the ship. We flew in 909. The mission lasted nine and a half hours. Over the target we saw about 60 109s. They attacked the group on our right. We saw four B-17s go down.

Sergeant Reash cannot have been seriously injured, as he was flying on the next mission and, on 24 May, he claimed hits on an Fw 190 with his top-turret guns. Grosh's

196

diary records that *Nine-O-Nine* was hit by flak fragments on three other occasions before the crew completed the last mission of their tour, an attack on a bridge at Saumur, in France.

The 91st Bomb Group would emerge from hostilities in May 1945 with the unenviable record of more of its aircraft Missing in Action than any other 8th Air Force group, albeit marginally so. From the summer of 1944 the loss rate per sortie flown decreased. There were still the inevitable tough missions when the Group was caught in a heavy flak barrage or set upon by Luftwaffe fighters, but *Nine-O-Nine* led an almost charmed life, often not being scheduled to fly on these 'rough' days.

As the number of small yellow bomb symbols painted on the nose of Davis's charge grew, men at Bassingbourn began to refer to the aircraft as a 'lucky ship'. After a raid on Ingolstadt marshalling yard on 15 January 1945, *Nine-O-Nine* had 100 missions to its credit with no turn-backs. The unblemished record continued until March, when 8th Air Force Public Relations took stock of the bomber's achievement in *Stars and Stripes*. At the time of its 126th mission it had dropped 562,000lb of bombs and flown 1,129 hours. Wear and tear and enemy action had led to nineteen engines, four outer wing panels, fifteen main fuel tanks and fifteen Tokyo tanks being changed. Flak damage had perforated the fuselage in a dozen places, and the patches were very evident.

Longevity was no insurance against continued endurance, for other B-17s with more than 100 missions fell in combat. The 91st loss *Wee Willie*, a veteran of 128, and *Skunk Face III*, with 106, on 8 April, the Group's twelfth from last combat operation.

Nine-O-Nine flew its 140th mission with the Group's 340th and final operation, to Pilsen on 25 April 1945, with 2nd Lieutenant Sydney O. Barnsley's crew, although for most of its late missions the bomber had been assigned to 1st Lieutenant Russell A. Blanchet. Early in June *Nine-O-Nine* was readied to return to the USA, and it departed Bassingbourn on the 10th, with ten crew members and ten passengers. Among the latter was the squadron's CO, Major William Reid, and Rollin Davis, who had recently been awarded the Bronze Star for his work. With Captain Robert M. Hoffman at the controls, the bomber was landed at Dow Field, Bangor, Maine, on 12 June. It was then flown on to Bradley Field, Windsor Locks, Connecticut, where the crew and passengers departed for the personnel transfer camp at Boston. *Nine-O-Nine* languished a while and was eventually ferried to the storage area in the Arizona Desert at Kingman, where it was officially accepted on 7 December 1945. Some time during the next three years this stalwart of the 8th Air Force was reduced to scrap.

In 1986 Robert Collings, an electronics millionaire with an interest in old military aircraft, had a B-17G he had purchased restored to military configuration. Wishing to have the aircraft finished in the decor of a famous combat veteran, he selected *Nine-O-Nine* as the most worthy candidate. Thus adorned, his *Nine-O-Nine* became a familiar performer at US air shows during the closing decades of the 20th century.

The Globe Trotter

Following the liberation of France in the summer of 1944, the French military re-established itself on home soil, relying heavily upon its American and British Allies for equipment and supplies. General Pierre Koenig, commanding the French forces raised in North Africa and engaged on the Western Front, was in need of air transport for movement between various headquarters.

Hearing of this, General Eisenhower, the Supreme Allied Commander, asked his staff to find a suitable aircraft for presentation to General Koenig for his personal service. No type was specified, and on consideration of what was on offer the French chose a B-17 retired from operations which, stripped of war equipment, was currently being used for communication duties.

This was in October 1944, but it was not until 17 December that a B-17 was formally transferred to the French by the US government. The aircraft was a B-17F, serial number 42-30177, retired from operational service and denuded of most of its war equipment, including power turrets and armour plate, so that it was more suitable for communication duties. Six seats had been installed in the rear fuselage for passenger use.

The Fortress was available for collection at Bovingdon, England, and a party of French Air Force officers were sent to collect it. As none had experience of operating B-17s, the USAAF provided a pilot, Lieutenant Hopla, and a mechanic, Master Sergeant Howard Garver, who were to remain on detachment with the French until the new owners were fully conversant with the aircraft. The French crew consisted of Lieutenant E. Jean for navigation, Lieutenant Marcel Lagatu for the radios and Lieutenant Clement Millet as crew chief. Formalities and bad weather delayed departure from England, and it was not until 21 January 1945 that the Fortress arrived at Le Bourget.

The French were soon aware that their acquisition had once seen service in hostile airspace, as the fuselage skin and empennage bore a number of patches covering shell-splinter damage. The olive drab and grey camouflage paint was well stained and faded, indicative of several months' exposure to the elements.

It was decided that something had to be done to make the spartan interior more suitable for the carriage of General Koenig. The radio equipment and operator's position were resited on the flight deck behind the pilots, and the original radio room was converted into an aerial study for the General. A top Parisian interior decorator, Paul Arzens, was engaged to advise on the fittings and furnishings. A plush divan was installed each side of the former radio room, and this cabin was padded with insulation covered with the same patterned material as the divans. Foldaway tables were also installed. The rear compartment for the General's staff had accommodation for another twelve persons, consisting of two side divans and four forward-facing chairs.

The decision was made to name the aircraft *Bir-Hakeim*, after the Libyan village where French forces under General Koenig had held out against Rommel's army. This name was painted on the lower side of the nose in bold white capitals.

General Koenig's personal pilot, Lieutenant Francis M. Lynch, was assigned to captain *Bir-Hakeim*. Highly experienced, he had served in the French Air Force prewar and had flown Blenheims with the RAF in North Africa.

Bir-Hakeim began its duties as a VIP transport on 23 February, with a flight to Marrakesh via Algiers. Similar trips were undertaken in March and July. There were also several flights to the UK and Germany from home base, which was now Villacoublay. In late August the crew were informed that they were to fly Vice-Admiral Thierry D'Argenlieu to appointments in the Far East and United States, a round-the-world flight. Lieutenant Jean was replaced by Captain Georges Goechman as navigator, but the rest of the crew remained the same. *Bir-Hakeim* and crew collected their VIP passenger at Orly, Paris, and on 6 September departed on the first stage of their round-the-world trip, an 11-hour flight to Egypt, at 1 o'clock local time. Next day they flew to Abadan, and on the 8th set off for Ceylon, with a refuelling stop at Karachi.

There was a three-day stay in Ceylon while the Admiral conducted business in Kandy. On the 12th *Bir-Hakeim* set off for Calcutta, where it remained until the 17th. With additional VIP passengers aboard, the next destination was Washington, DC, via Rangoon, Manilla, Guam, Kwajalein and Johnston Islands to Honolulu, which was reached on 21 September. The following leg of the flight required a bomb-bay fuel tank, the Hawaiian Islands being 2,000 miles from the USA. The aircraft departed on 24 September, making a flight of 13 hours 15 minutes before touching down at San Francisco. From California *Bir-Hakeim* flew to Denver and then Chicago before finally arriving at Washington. The detour to Chicago was made to spring an unexpected surprise on Howard Garver, the American flight engineer, whose wife was secretly brought to the airport and allowed to join the party and fly on with them to Washington. This surprise for Garver had been arranged with General Koenig's approval.

Unbeknown to the crew, B-17 42-30177 had flown in this patch of sky before, in May 1943, a few weeks before it was taken to the European war zone.

The aircraft then flew to Mitchell Field, New York, where a thorough maintenance check was carried out before the transatlantic crossing. On 30 September *Bir-Hakeim* was flown to Gander, Newfoundland, and next day set out on the longest leg of her epic journey, a 13 hour 45 minute direct flight to Orly, Paris, where it arrived at 1130 on 2 October. Twenty-two countries had been visited in approximately 137 hours' flying time, covering some 28,000 miles in 26 days at an average speed of 200mph. The Fortress had cruised at between 5,000ft and 10,000ft.

The flight was the only known planned trans-global flight made by a Boeing B-17, and this was a worn veteran that had in excess of 500 hours' flying time before being transferred to the French.

Bir-Hakeim returned to serving General Koenig, taking him to European and North African locations on more than twenty occasions during the following year. It is said that Generals Eisenhower and De Lattre de Tassigny were among the passengers carried during this period.

In October 1946, to facilitate General Koenig's command of French forces in Germany, *Bir-Hakeim* was based at Baden-Oss, where it remained until 1950. It frequently flew along the troubled air corridor to Berlin, being shot at by Soviet fighters on one occasion. In 1948 General Noiret took over command from General Koenig, and also inherited *Bir-Hakeim*.

Although the aircraft had been repainted since its acquisition by the French, in October 1949, during major overhaul, all paint was removed and *Bir-Hakeim* appeared in bare aluminium skin. However, it was now *Bir-Hackeim*, a more common spelling of this Arab place-name. In 1950 the Fortress operated from Wahn, near Bonn, as the French High Commissioner's personal transport. Later that year Lieutenant Lynch, who had been its captain for five years, moved to other duties. Over the next four years there were at least three changes of first pilot, the last, Captain Henri Perrin, taking over in January 1954.

Of all of *Bir-Hackeim*'s flights, the most hazardous and difficult for the pilots occurred on 17 March 1955. After take-off from Solingen, atrocious icing conditions were encountered. A thick layer of ice built up on the windscreen, and only limited visibility was possible through the side windows. The propellers began throwing ice, and this was heard hitting the fuselage. Ice also built up on the leading edges of the wings, and Captain Perrin feared that the control surfaces might become frozen and impossible to move. The destination was Paris-Orly, and when a request to reduce altitude was radioed to the ground controllers it was refused because other aircraft with the same problems were in the area, and there had been several near-misses.

By now the Fortress was becoming increasingly sluggish, and eyes were fixed on the ice on the wing leading edges, which was estimated to be nearly six inches thick. This then began to break away in large chunks, and the crew were concerned for the safety of people or property below. Fortunately they happened to be flying over a forest at the time. Eventually, as there appeared to be no let-up in the bad weather, the crew were advised to land at Villacoublay. Later, when the aircraft was inspected, many dents were found in the fuselage skin where dislodged blocks of ice had struck it. Captain Perrin was convinced that the inherent stability of the B-17 had saved them, and that few other aircraft would have survived such a battering.

However, next day, in similarly atrocious conditions, *Bir-Hackeim* and the crew were not so fortunate when coming into Wahn. Landing in a snow storm on the short, ice-covered runway, *Bir-Hackeim* did not stop when the pilot applied the brakes. The Fortress continued its roll beyond the end of the runway for about 50 yards, until a main wheel went into a shallow ditch. The rear of the fuselage rose, and the nose and propellers smashed into the frozen ground. Fortunately, none of the crew was seriously hurt, the navigator in the nose sustaining only a few cuts and bruises. The nose damage was extensive, and as a makeshift repair, the three foremost fuselage formers were removed and a short domed nosepiece constructed by riveting curved strips to a central disc.

In this blunted form the old lady was flown out to Creil on 13 May 1956, having been sold for a token 1 franc to the Institut Geographique National (IGN). Over the next two years, major overhaul and refurbishment was carried out when the IGN engineers had time. However, *Bir-Hackeim* never took to the air again, and after it had languished in a hangar for several years a decision was taken to remove valuable components and scrap the airframe. Although this famous aircraft met an unworthy end, perhaps some of its components survive in the former IGN Fortresses that have survived in museums or with private operators.

But *Bir-Hackeim* had two lives, its first being unknown to the French operators. Accepted by the USAAF from Boeing's Seattle factory on 26 April 1943, 42-30177 was assigned to the 562nd Bomb Squadron of the 388th Bomb Group as combat equipment. Lieutenant Charles Bliss and crew took it on its first transatlantic crossing on 22 June, and for the next nine months home was Knettishall air base, Suffolk.

Bliss bestowed the name *Charlene* on the Fortress before the 388th Bomb Group flew its first combat mission, to Amsterdam on 17 July to bomb an aircraft factory. This was also *Charlene*'s and the Bliss crew's first taste of war, and they were positioned at the rear of the formation as 'tail-end charlie'. In subsequent raids the Luftwaffe made determined efforts to terminate *Charlene*'s intrusions of continental airspace. On 26 July, having been peppered by flak, No.4 engine had to be feathered. The bomber then came under fighter attack, and when a missile entered the cockpit Lieutenant Bliss received a small wound from flying splinters. Number 3 engine then began to fail and had to be shut down, and the prospect of having to ditch in the North Sea arose. Loose equipment was thrown overboard, and the pilots managed to maintain a safe altitude, eventually landing at Saltby in Leicestershire. The missile that entered the cockpit was later found to have been a 0.50-calibre round, the handiwork of some careless gunner. Engine repairs took some days, but on *Charlene*'s next mission another wayward gunner put a 0.50-calibre hole through its fin.

On 6 September *Charlene* and the Bliss crew set out for Stuttgart, but clouds foiled the mission and the Group formation became separated and was then fallen upon by Luftwaffe fighters. Eleven of the 21 B-17s failed to return. *Charlene* was again tail-end charlie, but although the aircraft was damaged and the navigator wounded, it was one of the survivors that limped home.

In October the Bliss crew was broken up and *Charlene* became a spare used by a number of crews, also being loaned to the 96th Bomb Group at nearby Snetterton. More damage was sustained during the autumn and winter months and, by the spring, only fifteen mission symbols were to be seen on the aircraft's nose. B-17Fs with their hydraulically-actuated turbo-superchargers were no longer popular, and 42-30177 was transferred out of the 388th to serve on radar calibration duties. During the summer of 1944 *Charlene* flew a series of such missions, and when this work was finished the veteran was passed to Air Service Command for use as a communications transport. In December 1944 42-30177 had a change of life, and a new identity that would make it the most distinguished of its type in a peaceful role.

Queen of the Skies

Shoo Shoo Shoo Baby is unique. Although more than 50 years have passed since it left Boeing's Seattle production line on 17 January 1944, it survives to this day.

Accepted by the Army Air Forces on 24 January 1944, the B-17G was modified and flown to England, arriving at the huge Burtonwood Air Depot near Liverpool early in March to receive the final touches to prepare it for war. Assigned to the 91st Bomb Group as a replacement aircraft, 42-32076 was collected by a crew led by Lieutenant Paul McDuffee and taken to Bassingbourn, Cambridgeshire, to fill a place in the 401st Bomb Squadron. The ground crew chief, Sergeant Hank Cordes, had it named *Shoo Shoo Baby* after his favourite song. The name was neatly lettered on the nose, but later the aircraft was embellished with a Varga girl by artist Corporal Tony Starcer, and the name was expanded to *Shoo Shoo Shoo Baby*.

'*Shoo Shoo*' flew its first mission on 24 March, with McDuffee and his copilot, Lieutenant John Lafontin, at the controls. The 91st had been briefed for Schweinfurt, and the new B-17G, one of the first to leave the factory without camouflage paint, was the subject of some discussion. It would certainly stand out, and perhaps draw too much attention from the Luftwaffe.

The take-off was hazardous, the B-17s rolling down the runway in complete darkness; there was little wind and a chance that aircraft might hit prop wash while lifting from the ground. Assembly was completed without incident and the mission began as briefed, but heavy cloud and thick contrails at the Initial Point forced the 91st to attack the secondary target, Frankfurt. There was intense and accurate flak above the city, and *Shoo Shoo Shoo Baby* received some minor damage, but safely completed mission one.

Paul McDuffee, who flew the aircraft on all its early missions, recalled it as 'a gallant aircraft', one with 'no abortions, no nothing, but just damned good service ... the way that Cordes kept that damned airplane was something to marvel at!'. He continued, 'Things were so good with that kite that it was a pleasure to get out of the sack and get in it again ... that's one worry I never had with Hank Cordes crewed aircraft, I knew that I always had a good horse under me and the crew'

On 26 March they went to Marquis-Mimoyecques, a V-weapon site in the Pas de Calais. It was a short mission, perhaps 2½hr in all, and only 40 minutes over enemy territory. Visibility was good, and the flak was light though very accurate. That was the first of three missions in three days for McDuffee, his crew, and their new B-17. On 27 March they bombed the airfield at St Jean D'Angely, 65 miles north of Bordeaux. On Tuesday 28 March the target was an aircraft factory in central France. After three missions in as many days the crew was tired and perhaps a little nervy, and they had earned a break. *Shoo Shoo Shoo Baby* next took to the air on 8 April for a mission to Oldenburg.

The first extraordinary incident involving this B-17 occurred on 9 April, during its sixth mission. The 91st was briefed to bomb the Kurt Kannenberg aircraft factory at Gdynia in Poland, but again deteriorating weather upset the plan. Cloud made assembly with the 381st Bomb Group extremely difficult, and ultimately the wing leader ordered the bombers to return to base after they had been in the air about four hours. In *Shoo Shoo Shoo Baby* Paul McDuffee and his crew had sweated out the long climb to altitude only to find themselves the lone B-17 among a group of B-24s when they finally broke free of the gloom. Unable to find the rest of the 91st Group, McDuffee tacked on to another B-17 formation and followed them, little knowing that he had joined the 401st Group, which was on its way to Marienburg, not Gdynia.

A second 91st Group aircraft, *Winged Victory*, flown by Lieutenant Fred Gardner, had also joined this force, but with the 384th Group, as neither of the two straying B-17s received the recall signal. The pair completed the long flight to Marienburg, dropped their bombs, and between them gained a mission credit for the 91st Group that day. McDuffee recalled that all four engines quit simultaneously on the taxi strip as they returned, the fuel tanks almost dry after the long ride to the unbriefed target.

Two days later the McDuffee crew flew *Shoo Shoo Shoo Baby* to Stettin, and a week later there was a mission to the Heinkel factory at Oranienburg, which had ominous overtones. The B-17 was part of a force of nearly 500 Fortresses attacking targets in the Berlin area. Navigator Lieutenant Larry Sylvester recorded the events that took place:

> Coming off the target our formation headed north and as we crossed the coastline to the Baltic Sea I had completed my duty of calculating our remaining fuel, which was a total of 780 gallons. I informed Mac of the remaining fuel supply with the suggestion it was insufficient to return to England and, since Sweden was off to our right, we should land there. Mac replied that since he had only five or so missions to complete his tour, he felt we could leave the formation when we were over the North Sea, reduce to minimum power and effectively "glide" back to England. We did just that and approached the English coast at about 1,500ft altitude. As we sighted the coast, Mac asked me for a heading to the nearest airbase and a few minutes later we found ourselves in line with a runway of a Lancaster base. Without flying a landing pattern but flying right in on the strip, Mac executed a beautiful landing. Before we reached the end of our roll, two engines ran out of gas. We then refuelled and returned to Bassingbourn. It was calculated that we had landed with a total of 35 or 40 gallons of fuel remaining.

McDuffee took *Shoo Shoo Shoo Baby* to bomb the V-weapon site at Croisette-Beauvoir on 20 April, and then, two days later, it was piloted by Lieutenant John Black when B-17s took off late in the afternoon to bomb Hamm, in the Ruhr Valley. The accuracy was good, although smoke obscured much of the target as cascades of incendiaries littered the marshalling yards. The flak was only moderate, but the men in *Shoo Shoo Shoo Baby* watched anxiously as the lead aeroplane, *Just Nothing*, took a direct hit. Part of its wing was blown off and it tumbled down, but ten parachutes were counted before it exploded at about 15,000ft. The rest of the B-17s returned to Bassingbourn in darkness, coming in at around 2300 that night.

Lieutenant Roy Griesbach was *Shoo Shoo Shoo Baby*'s pilot for the mission to Brunswick on 26 April, then on the 28th Lieutenant Philip Goynes and his crew flew it to crater Avord airfield, 110 miles south of Paris. They bombed visually from 15,000ft, and although about 40 enemy fighters made one quick pass at the group, no damage was sustained. Flak claimed one B-17, and *Shoo Shoo Shoo Baby* was one of the ten aircraft slightly damaged.

Roy Griesbach was back at the controls on 29 April for *Shoo Shoo Shoo Baby*'s first visit to Berlin. There were heavy clouds along the way, but the weather cleared at the target. Over the suburbs of Berlin flak began to rise up and the sky seemed to darken from the hundreds of shell bursts. *Shoo Shoo Shoo Baby* was leading the 401st Squadron, and bombardier Lieutenant John Piland did not release the bombs until he saw the Pathfinder lead drop. The rest of the 91st had dropped early, outside the city. The B-17s were battling a strong headwind that made it seem a long way getting out of the reaches of the Berlin defences. *Shoo Shoo Shoo Baby* was subjected to intense anti-aircraft fire for more than an hour, but suffered only minor damage.

Cocooned below in his ball turret, Sergeant Ralph Rigaud could see the flashes from the batteries five miles below. It seemed as though they were lined up along the length of every street in the city. Lieutenant Dick Simonson, the navigator, felt a sharp sting and reached down to pull a piece of flak loose from his right buttock, dropping it quickly when the heat of the metal registered on his chilled fingers. It was only a superficial wound, and Simonson remembers being 'too tired – or embarrassed – to go to the dispensary to have it looked at' after the mission.

On 1 May Lieutenant Thomas Gunn commanded *Shoo Shoo Shoo Baby* when the target was the marshalling yards at Troyes, just east of Paris, then McDuffee came back to take her on her second Berlin mission on 7 May. McDuffee also flew her to the marshalling yards at Kons Karthaus, just within the German border east of Luxembourg, on 11 May. There was no flak or fighters, making it a genuine 'milk run'.

Lieutenant Bob Guenther had his first flight as *Shoo Shoo Shoo Baby*'s pilot on 13 May. They were briefed for an oil target near Stettin, but heavy cloud forced the effort to be diverted to targets of opportunity along the Baltic coast, and *Shoo Shoo Shoo Baby* loosed her bombs on Stralsund. Paul McDuffee flew two more missions in the aircraft; the Berlin attack on 19 May, and a raid on the port area of Kiel three days later. Legend has it that McDuffee celebrated the end of his combat tour with a late-afternoon buzzing of Bassingbourn, roaring over the runway only 20ft off the ground, and that Hank Cordes later found leaves and a strand of fence wire twisted around the bomber's tailwheel.

Shoo Shoo Shoo Baby aborted the mission of 23 May, turning back at the English coast because of supercharger problems on the No.3 engine, but next day Lieutenant Bob Langford took it to Berlin.

The aircraft was on the line on 25 May, with Lieutenant Sam Newton and his copilot, Lieutenant Bert Stiles, in the cockpit. Oxygen failure forced them to turn back, but they were credited with a sortie as they had crossed the enemy coast. On 27 May Lieutenant Ray Cable took it to Ludwigshafen, but next day there were more problems in the oxygen system and the aircraft failed to attack the target, although it was again credited with a sortie.

On 29 May *Shoo Shoo Shoo Baby* was part of the force sent to Posen in Poland, another distant target. As Lieutenant John Lowdermilk recalled:

> The navigator always got to the 'plane late, as the rest of the crew were ready to go, and I remember that as I walked up to the 'plane Bob Guenther asked me if I knew the way to Sweden because we might run out of gas. I stated that I did and that I had a course charted. This was all in jest, but I have often wondered what would have happened had this been overheard by the ground crew ...
>
> The plotted course was toward Berlin, then dog-legged around Berlin to Posen where the bombs were to be dropped, north to the Baltic Sea, out across Denmark, and finally down the English Channel to home.

Engineer and top turret gunner Sergeant James Shoesmith remembers that the trouble began almost immediately:

> Number three engine's supercharger waste gate locked closed, so the engine started running away immediately after take-off. Lieutenant Bob Guenther called back that we had a runaway turbo, so I scrambled back to the radio room and lifted up the floor section and swapped the control boxes so we could control the number three supercharger.
>
> We formed up with the group over England and went on toward France and diverted toward Berlin for Posen. The oil pressure started to drop on number three engine just after we entered Germany. We had quite a bit of flak and I found out later that we had a hole about three inches in diameter in the number one cylinder in that engine.
>
> Guenther tried to feather the engine, but it wouldn't, so we decided to run until it froze up or whatever. We prayed it would freeze up

but that damned thing wouldn't do that, it just windmilled the rest of the trip.

About this time we started to fall back out of formation and all our buddies opened up a path so that we could slide back. We dropped back about two miles and we were actually sitting ducks. Then we started to lose altitude, so the pilot ordered a bomb to be dropped so we could stay with the group. Lieutenant Petersen dropped one 500 pound bomb and we did gain a little bit of altitude.

Struggling to keep in touch with the formation, and with one engine gone, *Shoo Shoo Shoo Baby* was in trouble. They reached the target after the rest of the group had bombed, and were perhaps two miles behind them. Flak hit the left inboard engine over the target and a fire broke out, but as soon as the bombs were away Guenther dived and blew the fire out and feathered the engine.

In his top turret, Sergeant Shoesmith was:

... watching the group fade away in the distance toward England, and watching for the inevitable fighters to finish us off ... about this time we did sight four Me 210s as I recall. They lined up in trail formation about two o'clock position maybe five or six miles out and headed for us. I heard the pilot call out "Mayday, Mayday" and I picked this time to line up the gunsight reticules on the lead aircraft and count the seconds. Well, the first aircraft started to fire its cannon – I could see its nose light up with gunfire – and I fired the twin fifties at him with some of the other crewmen firing from their positions. We started to recite the Lord's Prayer to ourselves ... I imagine the others were doing it. I was thinking this will be the end. Then four P-51s appeared out of nowhere and the first one hit the lead 210 and down they all go and we never did see them again, they just disappeared into the clouds.

Up in the nose of the aircraft Lowdermilk was plotting a course to a little town called Istad, in the southernmost part of Sweden, because by now it was obvious that they would not make it back to England. Guenther advised the crew that they were losing altitude so fast that they would not even make Sweden unless the aircraft was lightened, so they began stripping her. John Lowdermilk continued:

As we approached the coastline Bob Guenther was interested in knowing whether or not it was Sweden. I confidently stated that it was, but after the flak started coming up as we got over land, I wasn't so sure. All of it was low and I believe the Swedes were just telling us "don't try anything". Just before we reached land we completely lost the third engine, and we were losing altitude fast.

Shoesmith remembers:

> A Swedish fighter pulled up beside us about fifty yards off our left wing tip and gave us the signal and we followed him down to Bulltofta airdrome. After we'd landed on a grass field I jumped out with a fire extinguisher and used it on number three engine which was really smoking ...'

The crew was removed from the aeroplane by armed Swedish soldiers. Pilot Bob Guenther takes up the story:

> We were taken into a building where we submitted name, rank and serial number. We were told that the American authorities would be informed of our presence. Within the next few days we were transported to a resort camp at Loka Brunn. Treatment there was good and we had two men to a room and maid service. There was a detachment of Swedish soldiers in the camp, but things were very informal. During late October 1944 we were taken to Stockholm, and on 29 October a white B-24 with a civilian crew took us out at night under cloud cover across Norway and into Northern Scotland.

The engineer, Sergeant Shoesmith, was the only one to see *Shoo Shoo Shoo Baby* again. Like the others, he bought civilian clothing and settled down for a few days, but when a request was made for crewmen to work on the numerous American aircraft in Sweden, he volunteered. The first crippled B-17 had sought refuge in July 1943 and, by the time *Shoo Shoo Shoo Baby* arrived, more than 30 Fortresses had made it in various states of disrepair. Shoesmith worked on various aircraft at Bulltofta until March 1945.

These aircraft and their crews presented some problems. The Swedish government cultivated American goodwill, and the American crews were only nominally interned. There were several ways to treat the airworthy aircraft in their hands. They could simply return them at the war's end, although America would have little need for a few extra B-17s, while Sweden was short of aircraft. Alternatively, they could buy the aircraft and incorporate them in the Royal Swedish Air Force, but there would be cost and maintenance problems. Thirdly, they could convert the bombers for civil use and employ them as commercial transports even before the war ended. Ultimately, they followed all three courses to some degree.

In December 1944 the 'Felix' programme was born, named after the American Air Attaché in Sweden, Colonel Felix Hardison. This was an arrangement under which the United States sold ten B-17s to the civilian airline Aerotransport for use as passenger aircraft. The price, a token $1 each, was a gesture made in return for the repatriation of flight crews and the generally helpful attitude of the Swedish authorities.

Seven of the ten aircraft, modified by SAAB, had their noses lengthened, radio compartments changed, and bomb bays modified to carry cargo, and 14-seat passenger compartments with flush windows were built in the fuselage. One of these B-17 airliners, which carried a crew of five, was *Shoo Shoo Shoo Baby*.

Ultimately five of the aircraft flew for Sweden, while the other two went to Danish Air Lines. After *Shoo Shoo Shoo Baby* had been completely modified it was test-flown with the Swedish civil registration SE-BAP. When, on 12 November 1945, it changed over to the Danish registration OY-DFA, it was re-christened *Stig Viking*.

Shoo Shoo Shoo Baby's new career began badly. Its first commercial flight was from Copenhagen to Blackbushe, England, in November 1945. Forced to belly-land, it was stranded in England for six months until repairs were completed in May 1946, enabling it to be flown back to Copenhagen. Then, in December, its tail section was damaged in a landing at Khartoum. Uneconomical as an airliner, the Fortress played a stopgap role as a passenger transport, and OY-DFA made its last commercial flight on 24 October 1947, after flying on many of Danish Air Lines' routes.

Late in March 1948 the aircraft was purchased by the Danish Defence Force, and was handed over to the Army Flying Corps on 1 April. Army pilots were trained on the aircraft until December 1949, when it was transferred to the Danish Navy. Finally, the Royal Danish Air Force acquired her on 24 October 1952. The Danish military used the B-17 mainly for aerial photography in Greenland, and its nose was again modified to provide a position for a photographer and three cameras. On 1 October 1953 it was retired again, having added more than 1,300hr to its flying time.

Shoo Shoo Shoo Baby was sold to the Institut Geographique National in February 1955 through the agency of the Babb Company in New York. The French organization registered the aircraft as F-BGSH and employed it in mapping missions from 1956 to July 1961, when it was retired yet again and placed in storage at Creil, France.

In 1969 Royal Frey, then curator of the Air Force Museum at Wright-Patterson Air Force Base, Ohio, recognized the desirability of having 'authentic' display aircraft such as the Liberator *Strawberry Bitch* and Bernie Fisher's A-1E Skyraider. When Frey learned of the existence of the veteran 91st Bomb Group B-17 in France he set the wheels in motion.

On Monday 24 January 1972 a team of six USAF technicians from Wiesbaden arrived at Creil to begin dismantling the old B-17G. In bitterly cold and rainy weather they started their work, and ten days later the aircraft had been reduced to manageable sections which were transported back to Wiesbaden, eighteen hours away by road. Finally the parts were loaded aboard a C-5A at Rhein-Main and flown to the Air Force Museum, arriving late in the afternoon of 14 June.

Shoo Shoo Shoo Baby sat in storage again until July 1978, when it was transferred to Dover Air Force Base, Delaware. The restoration of the aircraft to original wartime flying condition was begun as an Air Force Reserve project, conceived by

Technical Sergeant Mike Leister. Operating as the 512th Antique Aircraft Restoration Group, a dedicated band of skilled people began the monumental undertaking. They unpacked, repaired, stripped, rebuilt, and found forgotten B-17 parts in all corners of the country and the world. Gradually, *Shoo Shoo Shoo Baby* was brought back to life.

It was a daunting task. The fuselage was in four parts, the wings were cut into several pieces, the nacelles were cut off, and the engines were unserviceable. Less than 5 per cent of the original interior fittings remained. But restoration proceeded against the odds.

In the nose compartment the first step was to remove all of the non-wartime fittings that had been added over the years; then the airframe was stripped back to the bare metal for corrosion treatment. Many of the circumferential stiffeners were cut or missing, and replacements were handmade by Lou Lefebvre. Primer and the original green paint of wartime was applied, new flooring was cut and fitted, and the cheek positions were installed. The astrodome position was restored and a repaired Plexiglas bubble was fitted. As much as possible of the original navigator's equipment was replaced, and brackets for the remaining items were restored in readiness. A chin turret shell was fitted using a dummy frame until the complete turret mechanism was found.

When *Shoo Shoo Shoo Baby* arrived at Dover there were no cockpit instruments, and the panels were of French origin. The bulkhead and the side panels were thickly coated with paint, and most of the interior surfaces were under a layer of glued insulation. The complete area was stripped, treated and painted.

The work of restoring the cockpit area was begun, and Mike Leister reconstructed the main instrument panel using instruments donated to the project. The control pedestal was rebuilt, and a set of original windshields was installed. Structural repairs were made to the forward wing attachment points inside the cockpit, and brake lines, actuators and instrument tubings were installed, along with some of the overhead panels. Work also began on the repair and replacement of the side panels. Several sections of damaged skin had to be replaced in the cockpit underfloor owing to corrosion; most of this work was done by hand, piece by piece, using brushes and scrapers where power tools could not be employed.

In the bomb bay, which had been converted into a cargo area, the racks had gone and soundproofing material had been glued between the stringers. The bomb doors had been shackled shut and their actuating mechanism removed. First, the whole interior was stripped and primed, and then the bomb racks, doors and an actuator were restored and fitted. Since the bomb racks strengthen the whole fuselage at the wing attachment point, original racks were installed after the necessary brackets had been made. More than 400 parts of the bomb door mechanism had to be made or found before the doors could be reassembled. After the sheet metal work was completed, the equipment found on combat B-17s was installed in the area, including an oxygen regulator, an oxygen bottle rack, catwalk ropes, and even the relief tube.

Shoo Shoo Shoo Baby's radio room had become part of the passenger area when the bomber was converted into an airliner, and none of the original equipment remained. There was also serious corrosion in the main longeron in the area, requiring considerable work on the component and the circumferential stiffeners surrounding it. Some of the skin had to be replaced, the floor level had to be raised to its original position, and the flooring itself had to be replaced.

Four passenger windows in the radio compartment area were removed. Two of them were replaced by windows of the original design, hand-made by the restoration team, and the others were skinned over. The radio room hatch, which had been faired over, was reopened for corrosion treatment. A radio room hatch frame was located, reglazed with Plexiglas, and installed. The bulkhead which led to the waist was too badly damaged to be repaired, so the restoration team fabricated and fitted a replacement. Wartime radio equipment was donated by collectors, and the radio equipment was ultimately 95 per cent complete and operative after replacement wiring was installed.

In the rear compartments the restoration team found tracks for the airline seats and the remains of the galley and toilet. Again the fuselage was covered with insulation, and the control cables had been encased for cosmetic reasons. Light filtered through ten small windows, but the original waist gun windows had been removed and the positions skinned over. The supports for the ball turret and the catwalks in the waist area were long gone, and the control cables and wiring had been cut when the aircraft was dismantled in France.

So the entire waist section was stripped, windows were removed and stiffeners and stringers were made. The skin was removed completely from the lower half of the fuselage to allow the airframe to be treated for corrosion. The original skin was then put back, although corrosion made some replacement necessary. An original ball-turret frame was found and riveted into place, and a new turret was created from parts yielded by three wrecked units. New waist catwalks were manufactured and installed. As an airliner, the B-17's main entry door had been modified, so a rebuilt original-style door was fitted.

The tailwheel assembly was removed, X-rayed, completely rebuilt and refitted. The tail gunner's position had been seriously damaged during shipment, and required considerable sheet metal work. It was rebuilt by Dana Lakeman, the original maintenance director of the restoration project. The oxygen system, ammunition boxes, kneeling pads and windows were fitted, and the section was again bolted to the aft fuselage.

Restoration work on the fin was completed and new taper pins were made. The rudder was stripped, treated and primed. The tailplanes and elevators were similarly restored, and the fuselage was bolted together. *Shoo Shoo Shoo Baby* was beginning to take shape again.

The wings provided the most work and the most heartbreak for the restoration team. An inspection of the outboard sections revealed considerable corrosion of the truss gussets, and they had to be disassembled from the inside out. New gussets were made and fitted, and Ray McCloskey and several others spent hundreds of hours sand-blasting the inside of the wings. The corrugated reinforcing skin inside the wings had accumulated oil and grease and was corroded, necessitating cleaning with a toothbrush plus corrosion treatment. Some parts were replaced, and the ailerons were restored and the trim tab mechanisms rebuilt.

Both inboard wing sections had been cut lengthwise for shipment, and the wing attachment points had been drilled out to enable the components to be removed. The engine nacelles had been cut off at the wings, damaging their main structure longerons. There seemed little hope, but a replacement set of inboard wings was obtained from a crashed B-17 fire bomber. The left inboard wing required hundreds of hours of sheet metal work, but it did contain serviceable fuel tanks. The right inboard wing was only good for parts but, by combining the best of the original sections and the best of the replacement parts, the task was successfully completed after thousands of hours of work.

The engine nacelles demanded the very best efforts of Dan Vasey and Ray McCloskey, specialists in the major structural restoration, and took almost a year to repair and install. The wing attachment fittings were remade to the original Boeing specifications, and by October 1983 both inboard wings were fitted; a significant milestone in the project.

Two new superchargers and four old ones were sufficient for the restoration team to produce four serviceable units. The four propellers were inspected and restored by Hamilton Standard for a token fee of 25 cents apiece.

The main landing gear was completely rebuilt by a team led by Vic Rossica, and in December 1983, after more than eleven years, *Shoo Shoo Shoo Baby* was resting on her own landing gear again.

As *Shoo Shoo Shoo Baby* celebrated its 40th birthday, it seemed that its life was indeed beginning again. Both wings were completely installed, the oil coolers and ducting were completed, and the firewalls stood blankly ready to receive the four engines. The rudder, elevators and ailerons were re-covered and installed, and the flaps had been repaired and painted.

However, as Ray McCloskey, by then the Project Director, commented, putting on the wings was the brute work. Restoring the systems was the intricate part.

Over the next 4½ years the team moved closer and closer to completion. The flight controls were rigged and the instrumentation was connected and calibrated. The miles of interior wiring were run. The waist gun positions were completed. Zero-time engines were mounted, and the four propellers were installed.

On 13 August 1988 *Shoo Shoo Shoo Baby* was ready for high-speed taxying tests. At the controls were William 'Doc' Hospers and Major Quentin Smith. The B-17 performed beautifully, and next day it took off on its first flight in more than 27 years. As it taxied in after landing, dwarfed by the C-5Bs of Dover's 512th Military Airlift Wing, there was a feeling of justifiable exuberance among the pilots and the restoration team. They had achieved the impossible; it had just taken a little longer.

212

Shoo Shoo Shoo Baby's last flight took place on 13 October, when Robert Hospers, sitting in for his father, and Major Smith flew it from Dover to Wright-Patterson. At the Air Force Museum its engine oil was drained and replaced by a preservative solution, and the tyres were injected with liquid rubber. Too valuable to be lost again, it is grounded, but the process is not irreversible. The aircraft is truly a Queen of the Skies, and will be around for a long, long time to come.

Love
Keeps Her Flying

A half-century on from the Second World War the best-known, still-flying Flying Fortress in Europe, and probably world-wide, is there through love. The availability of pounds sterling might be the determining factor in keeping this old bomber in the sky, but it is love that generates the essential finance.

Love touches many aspects of *Sally-B*'s history, ever since Ted White set eyes on her in 1974. Ted, from London's East End and proud of it, was a self-made man, an entrepreneur whose passion outside his business was flying. A pilot's private licence led him to become acquainted with many professionals in civil aviation, and in 1974 he formed Euroworld Limited with qualified airline pilot Don Bullock. Euroworld was basically an aircraft ferrying service, but also dealt in used aircraft whenever an attractive opportunity arose.

Don Bullock heard that there were a few ex-French-government Boeing B-17s for sale at Creil airfield, near Paris. He and Ted White flew over to have a look. The idea of having one of these most famous of America's warplanes to fly at air-shows, with other commercial spin-offs, greatly appealed to Ted. From those on offer, the one registered F-BGSR was selected, a price negotiated and preparations made to close the deal.

The Fortress had originally been built for the USAAF in the spring of 1945 as serial number 44-85784. Designated a B-17G-105-VE, it was one of the last batch of 100 airframes from Lockheed Vega's Burbank, California, factory, the last of the three plants manufacturing B-17s to cease production. The aircraft was rolled out in June 1945, and accepted by the USAAF on the 17th of that month. The war in Europe was over, and there was little need for an ageing aircraft like the B-17 in USAAF combat units. Hundreds of these bombers were returning from the 8th and 15th Air Forces for storage at selected sites across the USA.

However, the final production batches were distributed to various units to be used in support roles. Collected from the factory airfield on 2 July, B-17 44-85784 was eventually delivered to the modification centre at Nashville, Tennessee, where it was apparently stripped of combat equipment before being assigned to Wright Field, Dayton, Ohio, where it arrived on 12 November. This was the USAAF's experimental station, and during the next four years it was home for 44-85784, which was used for various duties, including tests of experimental equipment.

In 1950 Schenectady, New York, became the aircraft's base while it was on loan to the General Electric Flight Center. For more than three years it served as a test vehicle for infra-red tracking devices being developed by the company, and for much of the time its involvement in this work necessitated the fitting of wingtip pods and a nose cone housing the infra-red apparatus, in place of the normal Plexiglas moulding. For this period of its career, 44-85784 was referred to as an ETB-17G, the E prefix indicating the loan status – which in effect transferred the Air Force's responsibilities to the contractor – and the T denoting a training or non-combat role.

By the beginning of 1954, 44-85784 was no longer required by General Electric, and on 7 February it was flown to Hill Air Force Base, Utah, for the removal of special modifications and return to a more normal configuration. In July of that year it was put in storage as surplus at Olmsted Air Force Base, Middletown, Pennsylvania, and was later sold to the Institut Geographique National (IGN), being officially struck from the USAF inventory on 28 October 1954.

In 1947 the IGN had been looking for aircraft with which to carry out carto-graphic photography of Europe and of French overseas territories. The B-17 seemed ideal for this work. It had good stability at high altitude, excellent endurance, was roomy and, because it was unpressurised, cameras could be used through open aper-tures to obtain better images. The aircraft were also cheap. In fact it appears that the French government did not pay anything for the first four acquired from the USAF that December. Another ten, from various sources, were added over the next eight years, one of the last being B-17G 44-85784, which was given the French civil regis-tration F-BGSR. For nearly 20 years the aircraft served on the IGN's geophysical and associated operations, fitted with a variety of equipment. Over this period a num-ber of modifications were made to the aircraft, mostly concerning instrumentation.

Originally the B-17s were only intended to be used until an indigenous pur-pose-built aircraft was available. Gallic pride was to be upheld by the Hurel-Dubois HD.34, the first of which was delivered in 1958, with seven more to follow, but the IGN operators still found reason to continue using several B-17s because of their superior endurance. It is tempting to believe that aesthetic appeal played some part, for the HD.34 was an ugly duckling when compared with the gracious Boeing.

Following its purchase by Ted White, and until a British Certificate of Airworthiness could be obtained, the former F-BGSR was registered in the USA in January 1975 as N17TE. On 15 March Don Bullock set off from Beauvais for Duxford airfield, Cambridgeshire, where the Imperial War Museum, in their wis-dom, could see that this aircraft would attract visitors to this then emergent 'living' aviation museum. Ted White had been giving thought to a typical American nick-name for his Fortress. He wanted to name it for the love of his companion, Danish-born Ellinor Sallingboe, known to all as Elly. When Elly was taken to see Ted's new acquisition it was adorned with a painting of a reposing nude and the bold inscription *Sally-B*.

An immediate task was to restore some of the Fortress's belligerent configu-ration, and a suitable paint scheme went some way towards this, *Sally-B* appearing at that summer's Biggin Hill Air Fair wearing the colours of the 457th Bomb Group, which had flown from Glatton air base during the Second World War. The British civil registration G-BEDF was obtained a year later, but although there was no lack of public interest in the only B-17 flying in the UK, and *Sally-B* performed at many air shows, the cost of keeping it airborne was such that little could be spent on finding and installing turrets to give it a more warlike appearance. Elly Sallingboe, who had worked as a stewardess for major airlines, joined Euroworld Limited, her main preoccupation being to meet *Sally-B*'s operating costs.

Don Bullock acquired an A-26 Invader and went his own way, sadly meeting his death in this aeroplane at the 1980 Biggin Hill Air Fair. In 1979, after seeking financial advice, Ted White and Elly formed B-17 Limited to separate *Sally-B*'s operation from the other businesses.

From the outset, much of the engineering work on the aircraft was carried out by volunteer labour. The aircrew were also professionals who gave their time freely. After Don Bullock withdrew, Keith Sissons, a highly qualified pilot with much experience of flying heavy, multi-engine aircraft, became chief pilot. Apart from this practical help, B-17 Limited was aware of an enormous amount of goodwill towards *Sally-B* from members of the public. Thus a Supporters Club was started, with its own journal and various opportunities to help 'keep *Sally-B* flying'.

A bonanza was London Weekend Television's contract for the use of *Sally-B* in its thirteen-part series 'We'll Meet Again', starring Susannah York and Gavin O'Herlihy. Based on the theme of the relationship between wartime Yanks and the local English population, the production was considered somewhat banal by some critics, but the requirements allowed accurately configured, albeit artificial, gun turrets and other much-needed additions to be made and installed. For the series, *Sally-B* became *Ginger Rogers* in a mythical bomber unit. Most of the location filming was done at West Malling.

Their time at West Malling led Ted and Elly to develop another idea to attract financial support for *Sally-B*; its own airshow. Thus the first Great Warbirds Display was set for September the following year, an air display that would bring to West Malling all of the veteran warplane operators who could be encouraged to appear. Tragically, before the event, Ted White was killed flying another of his loves, a Harvard, which crashed in Malta. The major responsibility for the Great Warbirds Air Display then fell upon Elly Sallingboe. Despite the death of the man in her life, or perhaps because of it, Elly persevered and the display was a great success, becoming an annual event.

Up to this time the B-17 had remained in bare-metal finish, as it had appeared when it left the factory in 1945. Although occasional hangarage was provided for major maintenance at Duxford, it was apparent that the often damp UK weather would have a detrimental effect on the airframe and shorten its life. So, in the winter of 1983-84, *Sally-B* was hangared and given a coat of olive drab and neutral grey, reappearing the following spring in the colours of the 447th Bomb Group which flew from Rattlesden in the Hitler war.

In 1989 Warner Brothers required B-17s for their epic movie 'Memphis Belle', to be filmed in the UK. *Sally-B* was reworked to B-17F configuration for this movie, and was seen masquerading under a number of fictitious identities at Duxford and Binbrook, where the location filming was carried out. It remained in Memphis Belle colours in the early 1990s, apart from regaining the *Sally-B* inscription on the nose and the yellow and black checkerboard round No.3 engine cowling in tribute to Ted White, whose Harvard had this marking.

From 1975 to 1994 *Sally-B* flew 672 hours and made 905 flights to add to the 5,318 hours and 987 flights made up to the time of its arrival in the UK. During that period it had been kept flying by the valiant fund-raising efforts of the Supporters Club members and the skill and labour of many volunteers; on the ground the maintenance team headed by chief engineer Peter Brown and crew chief John Littleton, and in the air by chief pilot Keith Sissons. A company motivated by the love of a beautiful aircraft, the legendary Flying Fortress.

INDEXES

2. INDEX OF PERSONS